MOTIVATION FOR ACHIEVEMENT

Possibilities for Teaching and Learning

Third Edition

M. Kay Alderman

Routledge
Taylor & Francis Group

NEW YORK AND LONDON

First published 1999 by Lawrence Erlbaum Associates, Inc.
Second edition published 2003

This edition published 2008
by Routledge
711 Third Avenue, New York, NY 10017

Simultaneously published in the UK
by Routledge
2 Park Square, Milton Park, Abingdon, Oxon OX14 4RN

Routledge is an imprint of the Taylor & Francis Group, an informa business

© 2008 Taylor & Francis

Typeset in 11/13pt New Century Schoolbook and Friz Quadrata by
Book Now Ltd, London

Library of Congress Cataloging in Publication Data
Alderman, M. Kay.
Motivation for achievement : possibilities for teaching and learning / M. Kay
Alderman. – 3rd ed.
    p. cm.
1. Motivation in education. 2. Academic achievement. I. Title.
LB1065.A477 2008
370.15′4–dc22   2007031107

ISBN10: 0–8058–6048–7 (pbk)
ISBN10: 1–4106–1427–1 (ebk)

ISBN13: 978–0–8058–6048–1 (pbk)
ISBN13: 978–1–4106–1427–8 (ebk)

MOTIVATION FOR ACHIEVEMENT

Contents

Preface

The research and knowledge base in the field of motivation continues to increase. This means that more resources are available to educators that provide knowledge and strategies to enhance motivation for learning. The increase in the knowledge base is accompanied by motivational challenges and problems presented by societal conditions such as standards for educational reform, poverty, and increasing diversity of the school population.

The purpose of this edition is the same as the first and second editions: to present content from the current knowledge base in motivation that offers hope and possibilities for educators—teachers, parents, coaches, and administrators—to enhance motivation for achievement. The knowledge base from research and theory was chosen to help teachers understand motivation of students and themselves and to provide the basis for strategies to foster motivation for all levels of student performance—from those deemed academically at-risk to those designated as honor students. The content is based on two roles teachers have for supporting and cultivating motivation in the classroom: (a) establishing the classroom structure and instruction that provides the environment for optimal motivation, engagement, and learning; and (b) helping students develop the tools that will enable them to be self-regulated learners and develop their potential.

NEW TO THIS EDITION

The organization of the chapters is the same as the previous editions. The literature and research were updated in all chapters. Topics and content were added to each chapter as warranted by the current literature. The topics in Chapters 1 and 9 were reorganized. Reorganization in other chapters occurs as warranted to provide more coherence and to account for new findings.

The strand of educational reform, standards for achievement, and high-stakes testing, as they relate to motivation, continues to be integrated into each chapter. This reform emphasis presents problems and possibilities for motivation. It is introduced in Chapter 1 and addressed in other chapters when appropriate.

Since the previous edition, achievement goal theory has continued to receive much research attention, especially regarding performance goals and the distinction between performance approach and performance avoidance goals. This was updated in Chapter 3. There are additional classroom applications for self-regulated learning in Chapter 5.

FEATURES OF THE TEXT

The text contains features to aid the understanding of concepts and the application to practice. Much of the material has been field tested in my classes over a number of years. These include the following:

- Strategy Boxes: These present guidelines and strategies for using the various concepts.
- Exhibit Boxes: There are two types: (a) forms that teachers might use for students (e.g., a form for goal setting); and (b) examples of teacher beliefs and practices and samples of student work.
- Reflections: These questions stimulate your thinking about motivational issues inherent in the topics, your experiences, and your beliefs.
- Tables and Figures: These serve as aids to understanding concepts.

OVERVIEW OF THE CHAPTERS

Chapter 1 was reorganized to begin with a definition of motivation and the perspective for this text. This is followed by a consideration of motivation challenges and problems facing educators, then possibilities for addressing these problems and challenges are described. The challenges of reform and standards are introduced in this chapter. Central to problems and possibilities is the issue of motivational equality and inequality.

Part II is composed of four chapters that focus on the social-cognitive processes that influence motivation. Chapter 2 presents the cognitive theory of attribution, the reasons we believe account for our own successes and failures, and those of other people. Attributional theory helps us understand poor performance while offering possibilities for change. It deals with questions such as these: How do one's beliefs about prior success and failure affect future expectations and actions? How can teachers help students who have given up? The attributional explanation for motivation continues to be one that teachers, parents, coaches, and counselors find especially useful. As one student who had learned about attribution in another class cautioned his classmates, "You will never look at yourself the same way again after learning about attribution."

Chapter 3 explores the role of beliefs about competence and ability as a motivational factor. Perception of ability is explained from several viewpoints. The first view is self-efficacy, which is the perceived competence about performing a specific task. The strength of our self-efficacy helps determine which tasks we undertake and which ones we persist in. A second view of ability is self-worth, a theory that explains a motive to avoid failure and protect self-worth from a perception of low ability. This perspective can help answer the question: Why don't students try? A third perspective is that of achievement goal orientation. Students may approach tasks with a goal of improving their ability, proving their ability, or avoiding the perception of low ability. The concluding topic is achievement anxiety, which is especially relevant in view of current emphasis on high-stakes testing.

Goal setting is the subject of Chapter 4. Goals are crucial for achievement, but they are usually given more prominence in athletics and work environments than in academic learning. This chapter deals with the following questions: What are the characteristics of goals that make them effective? How can goal setting be used in educational settings to improve student motivation and learning?

The development and enhancement of student motivational capabilities is the subject of Chapter 5. This chapter describes the components of self-regulation that equip students with the tools for self-direction. These include a vision of the future, volitional control, learning and metacognitive strategies, self-instruction, and time and resource management. It also addresses responses to failure.

Part III is composed of four chapters that focus on factors that influence student motivation, which teachers can affect. Chapter 6 presents two related aspects of teacher motivation that are essential to optimum student motivation: teacher expectations and teacher efficacy. These concepts deal with the following questions: How do teacher expectations affect student motivation and learning? How are these expectations conveyed to students? How do teachers' beliefs about their own effectiveness affect student motivation and learning?

Chapter 7 is concerned with the effect of the social context on student motivation engagement. A positive social environment fosters in students a sense of belonging and membership. This is an especially important topic in view of the diverse population of students and the problems of inequality. Social context addresses the questions: What promotes a climate for a sense of membership? What is the role of peers and cultural diversity in establishing a positive classroom climate? How much choice and control should there be for optimum classroom environment? What is the role of cooperative learning in establishing a social support system? What is the role of the teacher in building a supportive and inclusive classroom context?

Chapter 8 focuses on three instructional practices that affect student engagement and motivation: tasks, extrinsic and intrinsic motivation, and evaluation. Task motivation is concerned with tasks and teacher practices that are more likely to engage students. This includes the types of task that foster students' engagement and the teacher's role, the role of interest, and task value beliefs. The current perspective on the relation between intrinsic motivation and extrinsic rewards is presented in the next section. This includes the effect of extrinsic incentives on intrinsic motivation, guidelines for using incentives effectively, and practices to enhance intrinsic motivation with its limitations. Evaluation, the final practice discussed in Chapter 8, influences student effort and engagement. It includes types of assessment and motivational implications, factors such as effort in determining grades, issues in high-stakes testing and motivation, and a description of an evaluation program to enhance motivation.

Chapter 9, the concluding chapter, focuses on implementation of motivation in the classroom. It begins with discussion of concerns when beginning motivation applications. Next, programs that offer possibilities for improving motivation and achievement are described. This is followed by a problem-solving approach for devising a plan and concludes with ideas where motivation might be used.

ACKNOWLEDGMENTS

I thank the individuals who contributed their help and support. I am most appreciative of my colleagues Catharine Knight, Susan Colville-Hall, Julia Beyeler, and Rebecca Barrett. The conversations about the understanding and application of motivation knowledge for practice were most valuable. Thanks to Sharon Hall for feedback on specific areas. I am also most appreciative for the continuing support of my department members.

I am grateful for the assistance of Senior Editor Naomi Silverman for her continuous support, encouragement, and insightful suggestions. I am most appreciative to the revision survey reviewers, Kay Camperell of Utah State University and several anonymous respondents, for their thoughtful and helpful feedback.

To my brother Dan I thank you for your continuing support via e-mail and phone and otherwise.

This edition is dedicated to teachers who have the courage to make a difference and to those who have the will to start the journey that makes a difference.

—M. Kay Alderman

PART I

SETTING THE STAGE FOR MOTIVATIONAL POSSIBILITIES

CHAPTER 1

Motivation: Perspectives, Problems, and Possibilities

Education is, at least, the endeavor to get people to do things they could not previously do, to understand things they did not previously understand, and perhaps, to become the people they did not expect to become.
—Sockett (1988, p. 195)

Sockett's statement expresses a basic premise about the role of motivation: It leads to possibilities for fostering the development of students' potential or "life chances," that is opportunities to become people they did not expect to become (McInerney & Van Etten, 2001, p. x). This premise goes beyond motivation for the lesson and the test. A central theme of this book is that teachers have a primary responsibility in education to help students cultivate personal qualities of motivation that can give them resources for developing aspiration, independent learning, achieving goals, and fostering resiliency in the face of setbacks. Teachers and schools can establish the climate for the development of optimal motivation. Perhaps this responsibility is even more important in the context of the motivational problems and challenges faced in the home and in schools in the early twenty-first century.

This chapter begins with the identification of motivational perspectives and presents an introduction to the motivation perspective for this book. Next the motivational problems and challenges faced by educators are identified. This is followed by possibilities for addressing the problems and the role schools and teachers can take to foster optimum motivation. The last

3

part of the chapter presents an overview of the remaining chapters.

MOTIVATION PERSPECTIVES FOR CLASSROOM LEARNING

The criterion for the selection of theory and research included in this text is to identify concepts that provide teachers with the most powerful tools for activation and persistence of their students' motivation. *Tool* in this sense means something that is used to perform an operation or that is necessary in the practice of a skill or vocation. As such, motivational tools may take two forms: (a) conceptual understanding (e.g., understand why a student may not try); or (b) the use of tactics (e.g., an appropriate incentive). As you read this text, you can begin building a motivational toolbox (included at chapter ends) that will provide you with strategies to establish a classroom climate that supports optimal motivation and addresses the motivational problems. A form for this is provided in each chapter.

The goal of this text is to make the knowledge applicable and actionable (Argyris & Schon, 1974). *Applicable knowledge* describes relevant motivation concepts, whereas *actionable knowledge* shows how to implement motivation strategies in everyday practice. This means that learning a theory and learning a skill should not be viewed as distinct activities. Instead, knowledge must be integrated with action. Take the example of the concept of learned helplessness, a teacher learns to (a) explain this concept, (b) recognize indications of helplessness by students, and (c) select and devise strategies to help the student begin making adaptive responses to failure. The remainder of this section defines motivation and presents the perspective that reflects the content and organization of this text.

Defining Motivation

Conversation is replete with terms that imply motivation, both from motivational theories and from our everyday language. "Sam *tries* so hard," "Sarah is just not *persistent* in her *efforts*," and "There is no *incentive* for doing a good job at my work" are illustrations of three such motivational terms. But, what is motivation, what kind? Through the years, motivation has frequently been described as having three psychological functions (Ford, 1992): (a) *energizing* or *activating behavior*, what gets students engaged in or turned off toward learning (e.g., Mr. Crawford's math students look forward to the new problem to solve each week); (b) *directing behavior*, why one course of action is chosen over another (e.g., Maria does her homework before going on the chat room); and (c) *regulating persistence of behavior*, why students persist toward goals (e.g., although Eddie does not have a scholarship, he continues to run cross-country to be a part of the team). Various motivation perspectives can explain these three functions differently.

The motivation knowledge base that addresses these functions has greatly expanded from grand formal theories (e.g., achievement motivation and social learning) to a broad spectrum of motivational topics (Weiner, 1990). More recently Elliot and Dweck (2005) proposed a theory of achievement motivation with competence as the core. Two current perspectives are need theories and social-cognitive models (Pintrich, 2003). Need theories assume that, as human beings, we are born with basic needs that give direction for motivation. Although two current need theories—self-determination theory (SDT) and self-worth theory—contribute to the understanding of motivation, both integrate social-cognitive constructs with needs. Self-determination is based on the psychological needs for autonomy, relatedness, and competence (Deci & Ryan, 1985). This theory assumes that these needs are basic to human functioning and form the basis for intrinsic motivation. Although intrinsic and extrinsic motivation were previously viewed as either/or, they are now considered as a continuum in the context of self-determination theory (Ryan & Deci, 2000) (see Chapter 8). Self-worth theory will be introduced later in this chapter, and then fully explained in Chapter 3.

The focus of this text is predominantly drawn from the social-cognitive theory. Social-cognitive perspectives have been a major focus of recent motivation research especially as it relates to school achievement, the role of teachers, and the beliefs of students as learners (Pintrich, 2003).

Social-Cognitive Approach to Motivation

A unifying theme of social-cognitive theory is a focus on beliefs and cognitive and emotional variables, and environmental factors that influence striving for achievement (Bandura, 1997; Graham & Weiner, 1996; Stipek, 1996; Weiner, 1990).[1] These cognitive and emotional variables are composed of self-focused thoughts such as beliefs about one's efforts, competence, and goals. These approaches include:

- causal attributions—the reasons we give for our success and failure;
- self-efficacy—beliefs about our competence to perform a task;
- learned helplessness—a feeling and belief about the hopelessness in a situation;
- thoughts about goals—the extent to which we view a goal as a learning experience or as a reflection of ability;
- self-worth—a concern with maintaining or protecting the perception that we are competent or smart; and
- intrinsic motivation—a propensity to engage in activities for our challenge and satisfaction.

The emphasis on the role of cognitions and self in motivation is accompanied by a recognition of the importance of the social nature of motivation in schools (Weiner, 1990) as well as the role of the environment (Bandura, 1986). The approach that captures these areas and forms a central core of motivation for teaching and learning is known as *social-cognitive theory*. This framework increasingly provides research that can assist teachers in the complexities of establishing a climate that promotes motivation and helps students develop adaptive motivation strategies.

Social-cognitive theory assumes there is an interrelation between an individual's cognitive processes and the social environment (Bandura, 1997; Pintrich & Schrauben, 1992). This perspective of motivation interrelates the factors (a) cognition-personal, such as beliefs about ability and emotions; (b) environmental, such as incentives and evaluation criteria used by the

---

[1]For a historical review of motivation theories, see Graham and Weiner (1996) and Weiner (1990).

teacher; and (c) the behavior or performance of the person, such as increasing effort after a low grade (Bandura, 1986; Dweck & Leggett, 1988). These three factors interact through a process that Bandura (1986) termed *reciprocal interaction*, in which each component affects the other two. Each component may not be of equal strength. These components are shown in Fig. 1.1.

A student's cognitive process, such as belief about his or her ability, acts as an important mediator of motivation, which influences both expectations for future performance and action taken. This is a complex, continuous interaction, but an example can make it easier to understand. The interactions of the three factors are shown in Exhibit 1.1 in the example of Martin and Marty, who are both taking math.

The two students had similar beliefs about their ability to learn math but experienced contrasting instructional environments. Their behaviors or actions were influenced by their beliefs and environmental factors. These factors, in turn, influenced each student's subsequent beliefs about his or her ability in math and the actions he or she will take.

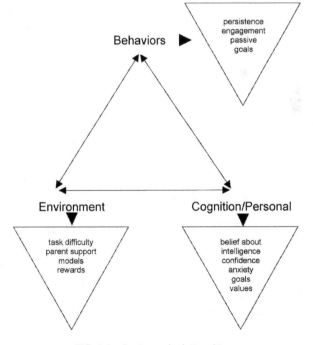

FIG. 1.1. Reciprocal relationships.

Exhibit 1.1. A Social-Cognitive Example

Cognition

Both Martin and Marty believe that either you have an ability to learn math or you do not. Furthermore, they believe that if you do not have the ability for math, there is nothing you can do about it.

Environment

Martin is in Ms. Jones' class. He is placed in the lowest math group. Ms. Jones only gives this group part of the math curriculum. Because she thinks they will not be able to "get it," she requires little homework completion.

Marty is in Mr. Crawford's remedial class. This class is structured so the students can develop their math skills. Students must get an A or a B on each test or they fail it. They must retake their failed tests until they pass with a B.

Behaviors

Martin spends less and less time on math. His confusion grows. He develops a dislike for math because the partial curriculum makes math seem very disconnected. His belief about his math ability has been confirmed. He will continue in the lowest math group until he is no longer required to take math.

Marty is surprised at the gradual improvement in her math scores. She chooses to spend more time now on her homework and is thinking about taking more math than planned. Marty is so proud of herself and she should be. Her belief about math ability begins to change.

PROBLEMS AND CHALLENGES: ACHIEVEMENT AND MOTIVATION

Various explanations have been posed for motivational problems ranging from the social values in society today to student effort. Motivational problems and challenges are described from two frameworks that are intertwined. The first perspective comes from the social-cognitive motivational research on the role of beliefs about effort and ability as they relate to school performance. The second perspective reflects motivational inequality as it affects academic achievement. Many of the problems within this framework are grounded in the problems and challenges facing society. From both frameworks, schools are part of the problem but can offer possibilities for solutions.

Effort and Ability Framework

Hidi and Harackiewicz (2000) suggested that there are two explanations for unsatisfactory academic performance of students— effort and ability. These reflect a social-cognitive perspective. What kind of motivational problems reflect an effort and ability framework? This framework refers to beliefs about the respective contributions of effort and ability to performance and achievement in school. How do the following examples characterize problems from an effort and ability framework?

- Ms. Rogers' Grade 3 students failed to master their math facts and believe they cannot learn math and thus fail to do their homework.
- Most students in Mr. Marshall's tenth-grade honors English class focus on making an A, but think they are not smart if they have to work for the grade.
- Ms. Sanders has been assigned the low track level for English. As she looks over her curriculum, she thinks: "Omit the critical thinking exercises in the text because I know this group won't be able to do that type of thinking."

In the prior problems: Ms. Rogers' students reflect lack of belief in their ability resulting in low effort; Mr. Marshall's honors students devalue the role of effort and overvalue the role of ability for their achievement; Ms. Sanders does not believe her students have the ability to do higher order thinking.

Beliefs about Ability.   What is the core of the ability problem? In 1976, Covington and Beery wrote what has become a classic description of motivation problems in the schools. The problem, from this perspective, is that "one's self worth often comes to depend on the ability to achieve competitively ... to equate accomplishment with human value" (Covington, 1998, p. 78). In our society, the tendency is to equate human value with accomplishment. Many school and classroom experiences then act to undermine an individual's sense of self-worth because students become convinced that ability is the primary element for achieving success and a lack of ability is the primary reason for failure. The notions about ability are based on comparisons to other students. In competitive situations, the fundamental motivation for many students is to protect their self-worth from the perception that they have low ability. To protect their self-worth, some students adopt strategies to avoid the perception of failure. Two failure-avoiding strategies are setting unrealistic goals (either too high or too low) and withholding effort. Both strategies provide students with reasons other than ability for not succeeding, thus protecting their self-worth. Teachers often characterize these unmotivated students as apathetic or lazy.

Beliefs about Effort.   What is the nature of effort as a motivational problem? It is both work habits and beliefs held by students about the relationship between effort and success and failure. This view of effort—characterized by Bempechat (1998) as a "lack of persistence, a preference for easy tasks over challenging tasks, or a tendency to fall apart at the first sign of difficulty" (p. 37)—is detrimental to student achievement. Darling-Hammond and Ifill-Lynch (2006) observed that a frequent refrain heard by teachers is "If I could only get them to do their work!" (p. 8). What is a classroom like when effort is lacking? The academic work problems can be seen in the following description of Ms. Foster's ninth-grade class.

Ms. Foster says a large number of students are unmotivated. She describes this unmotivated behavior as follows: Many students do not have goals; sit passively in class; turn in no homework; do not keep up with their notebooks; do not take final exams or the state-required proficiency tests seriously; and resist new approaches to learning that require the use of critical thinking skills, preferring to use worksheets as they have in the past. Cooperative learning groups are described as generally unsuccessful either because of chaos or because one person does the work.

Student disengagement or lack of investment in learning in secondary schools is another perspective related to effort (Fredricks, Blumenfeld, & Paris, 2004; Newmann, 1992). Three types of engagement are: behavior (e.g., attending in class), cognitive (e.g., using metacognition), and emotional (e.g., a feeling of belonging in school) (Fredricks et al., 2004). Behaviors indicating disengagement range from severe (e.g., skipping, disruption, failure to do assignments) to behaviors that, on the surface, do not appear to be motivation problems. This latter group of students behave well, attend classes, and complete their work, but they show little pride in their work or commitment to learning. An example of disengagement is this student's comment: "When you get home there's always something you can be doing with your friends besides homework so you just do enough to get a decent grade but you don't try to get your best grade, you do just enough to finish" (Newmann, 1992, p. 15).

REFLECTION. Does it surprise you that disengagement also includes students who seemingly are succeeding in school? How can you explain this?

Another example of effort and ability as a motivational problem comes from a comparison of Japanese and Chinese students with U.S. students regarding the role of effort and ability in mathematical success (Stevenson & Lee, 1990). These researchers found that U.S. students believed that innate ability was most important for success, whereas Japanese and Chinese students emphasized effort. Similar differences in beliefs were also found among their parents.

School and classroom practices may foster these negative effort and ability motivational patterns. One of the most prevalent is characterized as "the competitive learning game" (Covington, 1992, p. 130). This game refers to classroom practices that force students to compete against each other for grades and recognition. Such practices include grouping students by ability, limiting the range of accomplishments that receive rewards, and recognizing ability over effort. If students believe they cannot compete, they are likely to withhold effort to protect themselves from the perception that they have low ability. These topics are discussed in the chapters ahead.

Motivational Inequality as a Problem and Challenge

In 1979, Nicholls asserted that motivational inequality was prevalent in the schools. By *motivational inequality*, Nicholls meant that students who do not have optimum motivation for intellectual development are at a disadvantage compared with those who do. Students who have optimum motivation have an edge because they have adaptive attitudes and strategies, such as maintaining intrinsic interest, goal setting, and self-monitoring. There is evidence that this motivational inequality has increased rather than decreased in the years since it was first introduced (Tomlinson, 1993). Situations in which motivational inequality is dominant are captured by the following scenario constructed from Maeroff's (1988) description of the climate found in some urban schools:

> The demands and expectations are low and students say they are unmotivated and see no reason to attend school. Low achievement is accepted as the norm. Teachers do not assign homework because they have little expectation it will be completed. Students see few examples of success; their sense of future is bleak and does not include academic achievement in any way. Students have no basis for an alternative view of academic achievement because they rarely come in contact with anyone other than similarly low achieving students. Some students don't have anyone at home to say "I'm proud of you, keep up the good work."
>
> (p. 634)

This description illustrates a primary problem in school achievement—the large number of students placed at risk of failing academically. The students in this risk group predominantly come from families of poverty and are in danger of failing to fulfill their physical and mental promise (Hodgkinson, 1993; Knapp & Shields, 1990). For example, the National Center for Children in Poverty (2006) reported that 40 percent of American children live in low-income families. This does not mean, however, that the economically disadvantaged children are not motivated to learn in preschool and kindergarten (Stipek & Ryan, 1997). The authors found no differences in economically advantaged and disadvantaged preschool and kindergarten children on measures of motivation such as self-confidence and expectations for success. The difference between the two groups was on measures of cognitive competence, with economically disadvantaged children scoring lower than the advantaged group. The authors warned that, if low cognitive competence is not addressed, self-confidence and expectations could be expected to decline.

Cultural and Ethnic Diversity. Motivational inequality presents additional challenges for schools and teachers due to the increasing ethnic and cultural diversity of the school population. Nearly 46 percent of the public school population is composed of students from a minority culture, and this percentage is expected to increase in the future (National Center for Educational Statistics, 2005). The school where Ms. Foster teaches, composed of a student population of African-American, Anglo, and Hispanic cultures, is representative of the increasing diversity found in schools. The socioeconomic status (SES) ranges from a middle and upper middle professional population to a mobile, low-income population.

Why does the increasing diversity of the school population present a motivational challenge? One challenge for educators is the ethnic differences found in the level of education attainment, especially the underachievement of African-American and Hispanic students (Garibaldi, 1993; Mehan, Villanueva, Hubbard, & Lintz, 1996; Singham, 1998). A consistent and disturbing finding is that African-American students generally earn lower grades, drop out more often, and attain less education than do White students (Haycock, 2001; Mickelson, 1990). This happens despite the fact that until Grade 4 there are no differences between the performance of African-American and White students (Simmons & Grady, 1990). The difference in scores of minority and White students is referred to as an achievement gap. Hilliard (2003), however, asserts that the gap, instead of differences in the ethnic groups, "should be thought of as the gap between the current performance of African students and levels of excellence" (p. 138).

What motivational factors play a role in these performance differences? One factor is a discrepancy between African-American students and their teachers with respect to aspirations. Teachers underestimated students' aspirations and this in turn affected the type of education they provided to students (Garibaldi, 1993). Another problem is the absence of a challenging curriculum in many schools with predominantly low-income, minority populations (Haycock, 2001).

In addition, for minority students, there is sometimes negative peer pressure against behaviors associated with school success. These are referred to as "acting White" or "Anglo" behaviors (Fordham & Ogbu, 1986; Suarez-Orozco, 1989). The climate of the school is a factor in whether these negative beliefs are present or absent (Flores-Gonzales, 1999). Because this is a multifaceted problem, it is one that must be addressed by schools, teachers, parents, and the communities (Garibaldi, 1993; Ogbu & Simons, 1998).

Ability Grouping. Unfortunately, in many cases the motivational problems are compounded by school climate and teaching practices that may inhibit students from reaching their potential. One of these practices is ability grouping, the separation of students into groups based on judgments of their ability (Oakes, 1985, 2005). When ability grouping is in place, many students are not exposed to rigorous subject matter that might better prepare them for college entrance examinations and college work, and it does not prepare them for jobs (Maeroff, 1988). In addition, the lower ability level group is deprived of peer models of motivation strategies that would help them to achieve (B. B. Brown, 1993). Finally, teachers are likely to have lower expectations for this group and teach them accordingly (Oakes, 1985).

Motivational Challenges Related to Educational Reform

During the past decade, standards-based reform has been at the forefront of efforts to improve student achievement (Goertz, 2001). The emphasis is on higher academic standards, accountability, inclusion of all students, and instructional change. Support for standards is based on the belief that they can provide a focal point for raising student performance (Darling-Hammond, 1997).

What motivational challenges are inherent in the standards movement? Motivation cannot be seen in isolation from public policy about school reform (Galloway, Rogers, Armstrong, & Leo, 1998). School reform in most states has focused on raising standards through mandatory high-stakes tests that students must pass at various grade levels. The extensive use of high-stakes testing that many states require has motivational consequences for students and teachers, but the quality of student motivation has received little attention (Dembo, 2004; Meece & McColskey, 1997). Dembo asserts that students should be the focus if we expect to meet higher academic standards because their motivation is an important factor when faced with higher standards and high-stakes tests. Do the pressures on students to meet these standards and pass these tests increase their motivation to learn, or do some students give up in the face of failure? How does this affect teacher expectations? Limited research is mixed for the effects on motivation (Sloane & Kelly, 2003). Motivating students to work harder was a positive effect (Roderick & Engel, 2001), while student frustration was a negative effect (Sloane & Kelly, 2003). McCaslin (2006) argues that the problem is when the ratio between skill and challenge is out of balance. Some students are pushed too hard for the skills they have while the standards do not challenge other students.

Battistich, Watson, Solomon, Lewis, and Schaps (1999) asserted that a narrow focus on achievement in the standards reform is problematic because other outcomes of schooling, such as motivation to learn and commitment to education, receive less attention than achievement. Without commitment, more students are likely to drop out in this climate. Another motivational challenge for standards-based reform is related to the effort and ability problem. Resnick (1999) warned that the dominant view in American education that aptitude is the most important aspect in learning will undermine reform efforts. Tomlinson (1993) concluded that raising standards did not increase student effort. For standards-based reform to lead to student achievement, the traditional theories of aptitude must be broken (Resnick, 1999) and higher standards must be accompanied by higher levels of support for students (Battistich et al., 1999; Roderick & Camburn, 1999).

Finally, another part of school reform is that of inclusion—where all students are provided social and instructional opportunities in classrooms rather than in out-of-class programs (Tharp, Estrada, Dalton, & Yamauchi, 2000). Inclusion presents additional motivational challenges. Many of these students, such as students with learning disabilities (LD), have a long history of failure. A major motivational problem for these students is their belief that they cannot learn, and this is compounded by a lack of effective learning strategies (Licht, 1983). Thus, the challenge for teachers is to help students develop the motivational beliefs and learning strategies needed for success.

In response to motivation problems present in schools, a teacher observed, "They weren't like this 20 years ago." This is a refrain echoed in different ways by many teachers. Teachers are saying, "I don't know how to teach or motivate today's students." The two recurring themes in the motivation problems described from these educational reform frameworks are: (a) students do not have tools like concentration, persistence, volition, goal orientation, delay of instant gratification, and strategies for acquiring and retaining new information needed to be successful; and (b) many teachers have not acquired instructional strategies to foster and support positive motivation in these reform efforts.

REFLECTION. Have you thought about motivation problems and challenges from these frameworks? Is the lack of motivation a student problem (they just are not motivated), a school problem, a cultural problem, an instructional problem, or all of these?

MOTIVATION POSSIBILITIES AND GOALS

In view of the motivational challenges facing teachers, what are the possibilities for addressing motivation inequality and fostering positive motivation? To address the pervasive motivational inequality in schools, Nicholls (1979) described *optimum motivation* as one that provides the greatest degree of intellectual development and proposed that optimum student motivation is a justifiable educational goal. Collier (1994) also emphasized the importance of motivation in development of mental abilities: "Motivational factors determine not just the goals toward which people aspire but the way in which they seek out, process, and use information" (p. 8). Motivation is an important factor in the development of children's *resiliency*, which is the ability to bounce back successfully despite growing up in adverse circumstances (Benard, 2004; Gordon, Padilla, Ford, & Thoresen, 1994).

What is Optimum Motivation?

Optimum motivation is comprehensive, involving personal qualities of motivation and a classroom environment that supports and cultivates it. The social-cognitive model comprised of personal and environmental components addresses both. A central theme in current motivation theories and research is the focus on developing self-regulated learners. Students who have self-regulation use both motivation and learning strategies (Zimmerman, 1994). These self-regulatory processes include intrinsic values, goals, beliefs about competence, and self-evaluation (Zimmerman, 2000). Self-regulated learners also have what is known as volition, or the ability to maintain concentration in the face of obstacles (Corno, 1993). These learners want to learn, do things to make learning happen, and direct their own educational experience. Learners with these characteristics are more likely to continue to learn on their own. A similar view of optimum motivation is a will to learn (Covington, 1992, 1998; Covington & Beery, 1976). Students with a *will to learn* are characterized as believing in themselves and in their ability to think for themselves. They also develop a sense of personal competence and the belief that they are responsible for their own achievements.

- From Day 1 in seventh-grade language arts, Ms. Adler establishes this expectation: "If you fail, it's not because you are not smart, but because you didn't use the right strategy."
- "Determination + Discipline + Hard Work = The Way To

Success" is the formula for success in Jaime Escalante's classes (Mathews, 1988).

C. Ames (1992) described motivation from the perspective of a classroom structure that promotes optimum motivation. Features of a classroom that foster optimum motivation are as follows: (a) tasks that are meaningful with reasonable challenge; (b) opportunities to participate in decision making and develop responsibility; and (c) an evaluation system that recognizes progress and mastery of content. In these classrooms, student motivation to learn was described by Brophy (1983) as not only more than simply doing enough to meet requirements but purposefully engaging in academic tasks by attempting to acquire the knowledge or skill involved in them. Thus, motivation to learn is more than high test scores (Brophy, 1999).

Similarly, Newmann (1992) contended that student engagement in academic work is critical to school success. Student *engagement* in academic work is defined as "psychological investment in and effort directed toward learning, understanding, or mastering the knowledge, skills, or crafts that academic work is intended to promote" (Newmann, Wehlage, & Lamborn, 1992, p. 12). Marks (2000) concluded, "Engagement is important in school experience because of its logical relationship to achievement and to optimal human development" (p. 155).

A comprehensive classroom management program implemented in an inner city elementary school documented fewer discipline problems, increased student engagement, teacher and student expectations, achievement motivation, and academic self-concepts.

(Freiberg, Stein, & Huang, 1995)

The School's and Teacher's Roles

Do reform efforts such as standards offer possibilities for optimum motivation and learning? Yes, according to Diez (2001), "standards make it possible for the teacher, whether K-12 or higher education, to embrace the responsibility for developing learners" (p. 24). The teacher guides students to internalize standards as goals, thus creating a climate for more involvement by all learners. Resnick (1999) described such a school climate as

"effort based schools in which academic rigor and a thinking curriculum permeate the school district for every student" (p. 39).

What roles do schools and teachers play in addressing these
problems and in developing student motivation to learn? As
Darling-Hammond (1997) contended, to achieve the level of
learning proposed by standard-based reform, an understanding
of motivation is critical. A primary assertion in this text is that
motivation has to be explicitly addressed as part of instruction
and socialization rather than treated as a by-product. This
premise has been expressed in various ways. One example is
Sockett's (1988) contention that teaching qualities of personal
capability, such as effort, perseverance, concentration, self-
restraint, and punctuality, is a role of the school.

Stated in another way, the task for schools is to foster a will to
learn and the teacher's role is to "foster both confidence and high
achievement in their students" (Covington & Beery, 1976, p. 5).
The conditions for acquiring self-regulated learning and volition
can be fostered in schools (Corno, 1993; Pintrich, 1995). Thus,
teachers and schools have a specific responsibility to assist students in becoming self-regulated learners. Brophy and Kher
(1986) maintained that teachers should be able to develop
student motivation to learn by socializing students' beliefs,
attitudes, and expectations concerning academic activities and
by instructing their students in information-processing and
problem-solving strategies. Newmann (1992) saw the teacher's
role as one of engaging students in the hard work of school—the
continuous cycle of studying, producing, correcting mistakes,
and starting over again as in the following example: "I like to
work hard and I guess I'll just pound it into myself if I don't
understand. If I don't understand something, I make sure that I
work at it until I do understand, and I keep it up and I never give
up. I'm not a quitter at all" (Newmann et al., 1992, p. 14).

What types of motivational knowledge do teachers and schools
need to address these problems and foster optimum motivation?
Two standards-based organizations—Interstate New Teacher
Assessment and Support Consortium (INTASC) (1992) and the
National Board for Professional Teaching Standards (NBPTS)
(1990)—have the goal to strengthen the teaching profession,
including a motivation component for the teacher's role. According to INTASC, "The teacher recognizes factors and situations

that are likely to promote or diminish intrinsic motivation and knows how to help students become self-motivated" (p. 20). NBPTS state that teachers "understand how to motivate students to learn and how to maintain their interest [confidence] in face of temporary failure" (pp. 13–14). . . . "Teachers are concerned with their students' self-concepts, with their motivation, with the effects of learning on peer relationships, and with the development of character, aspiration, and civic virtues" (p. 19). For teachers to fulfill their motivational roles, they need competencies in process skills and to be proactive decision makers (Rohrkemper, 1985). This means that teachers must actively plan for motivation, not just react to motivation problems as they occur. With these process skills, teachers can diagnose the need for motivation strategies, determine the effectiveness of strategies, and fine-tune or revise strategies. Consider the following incident:

> A parent was in a teacher education program where she learned about the motivation strategies of goal setting and attributional feedback (which will be described in Chapters 2 and 4). Her sixth-grade son indicated a desire to improve his reading grade, and his mother said she would assist him. She had him set goals and provided him with feedback about his accomplishments. His grades began to improve. When the son was given his interim report, he saw that his grade was lower than he expected and was very discouraged. The parent talked with the teacher, who explained that he had given lower grades than students were actually making on all interim reports. The teacher reasoned that students slacked off the last weeks of school and the lower grade would motivate them to work harder. After the parent explained that this had actually undermined the strategy she had been using with her son, the student was given his correct average. On his final report card, he had five As and one B—his best of the year.

REFLECTION.   What is your reaction to the previous scenario? What does it say about the importance of teachers having a strong understanding of motivation principles and strategies?

This incident illustrates several points about understanding motivation and choosing strategies for enhancing motivation:

- The motivation knowledge base has not been widely disseminated in forms that provide teachers with the basis for effective strategy decision making. Thus, we might assume that the teacher was unaware of other potential strategies for maintaining motivation.

- The motivational dynamics of success and failure must be understood, especially students' reactions to them. For example, the teacher had a misconception about how failure may affect student motivation.
- Some strategies are more powerful than others. Powerful strategies are likely to be more complex or involve combinations of motivational variables that increase the strength of a strategy, as in the prior incident in which the parent combined goal setting and attributional feedback.
- In this example, one strategy appeared to facilitate motivation, whereas the other appeared to undermine it.

Are the possibilities for optimum motivation relevant for culturally diverse populations of students? Early motivation research was predominantly concerned with determining differences among ethnic groups—an approach that often led to misconceptions about the motivation of African-American students (Graham, 1994). Motivation for culturally diverse populations is more than comparing differences among different groups. For example, research (McInerney, Roche, McInerney, & Marsh, 1997) found that motivational profiles of Western culture and non-Western indigenous students were more similar than different. An important aspect is to identify the motivational qualities that are neutral across cultures, are valued by those cultures, and at the same time recognize individual differences (Sockett, 1988). Tharp (1989) observed that some motivational factors such as motivation for accomplishment, reward, and recognition receive relatively consistent support from parents and the community across cultures. Competence motivation is another aspect of motivation that is prevalent in all cultures (Elliot & Dweck, 2005). Different cultures may share basic motivational processes such as ability and effort but use the processes differently (J. G. Miller, 1996).

Schools that have been successful with culturally diverse or primarily minority populations are characterized by factors such as a sense of belonging and social support (L. Anderman & Freeman, 2004; Goodenow & Grady, 1993). T. Perry (2003) describes such a climate as "a culture of achievement that extends to all of its members and a strong sense of group membership where the expectation that everyone achieve is explicit and is regularly communicated in public and group meetings" (p. 107). Cultural identity is important within the sense of group membership of the classroom. Finn (1989) suggested that identity with sense of belonging comes from identification with school activities where students are successful and have a sense of competence.

Comer (2005) described a successful school where the focus extends beyond the curriculum to a focus on overall development (including motivation and competence) of children and adolescents. For example, the teachers establish a climate for a sense of belonging and also help students learn self-regulatory beliefs and thinking. Ms. Toliver is an example of a teacher who does this:

> Ms. Toliver's eighth-grade math students in P.S. 72 have been recognized for their accomplishments. She tells students at the beginning of the year, "This is a new day and we will work from here. I do not believe in failure. Mathematics may be hard to learn—it takes dedication and hard work—but I let my students know two things from the beginning: (1) I am with them to teach, and (2) I expect to be met halfway."
>
> (Toliver, 1993, p. 39)

As you work your way through this text, you will come to understand the extreme complexities of initiating and maintaining a motivating classroom. Although the motivation problems seem overwhelming and optimum motivation may seem like an elusive goal, the good news is that there is now a substantial knowledge base from motivation research and theory that will enable teachers to actively facilitate the motivation of students and establish a positive motivational classroom environment. The synthesis of research presented here provides a sturdy foundation of motivation building blocks to allow you to begin making informed decisions concerning the most effective motivation strategies. The knowledge base of motivation is so extensive that the crucial factor is making the best choice for a particular problem. If we have not learned the extensive motivational knowledge base, then our choices are limited. Chapter 9 presents a problem-solving model that will assist you in making decisions to enhance motivation for both yourself and your classroom.

REVIEW OF MAJOR POINTS

1.   Motivation is often described as having three functions: (a) energizing or activating behavior, (b) directing behavior, and (c) regulating persistence of behavior. Current motivational topics focus around self-focused thoughts. Social-cognitive theory, which assumes a reciprocal relationship among an individual's cognitive and emotional processes, environmental and social factors, and the behavior or performance of the person, is the primary basis for this text. Similarly, the interrelationship of these factors is more appropriate for working with culturally diverse populations than previous comparative approaches.

2.   Educators are faced with motivational problems and challenges. One set of challenges stems from the effort and ability problem, in which the focus on ability, to the exclusion of effort, leads some students to adopt strategies, such as not trying, to avoid the perception of failure.

3.   Another challenge is inequality in education and motivation. This includes the number of students at risk of failing academically and the increasing diversity of the school population, with the underachievement of African-American and Hispanic students. These challenges are compounded by ability grouping.

4.   Other challenges are presented by school reform movements such as standards, high-stakes testing, and inclusive school efforts.

5.   Optimum student motivation is a justifiable educational goal because the motivation knowledge base provides many possibilities for addressing problems and challenges. The school's and teacher's roles are to provide a climate that supports student motivation for a diverse population and to help students develop self-regulatory capabilities.

Motivational Toolbox

1. Important points to think about and lingering questions

2. Strategies I can use now

3. Strategies I want to develop in the future

PART II

SOCIAL-COGNITIVE PROCESSES THAT INFLUENCE MOTIVATION

This part moves from the problems and challenges to understanding the motivational processes students bring to the classroom—a first step in helping students develop self-regulation. The first three chapters in this part explain the social-cognitive processes of causal attributions for success and failure and the consequences of these beliefs, the concepts of ability and evaluation of competence, and setting goals for accomplishment. They affect students' effort, persistence, and confidence in undertaking or avoiding tasks. As educators and parents, understanding these processes can open windows into understanding student motivation. These processes might be thought of as the building blocks of self-regulation. Chapter 5 presents additional components of self-regulation: possible selves, volitional control, learning and metacognitive strategies, and time and resource management.

CHAPTER 2

Attributional Beliefs and Motivation

Children will not reach potential if . . . they are prone to beliefs about and behaviors in school that are not conductive to learning, such as a lack of persistence, a preference for easy tasks over challenging tasks, or a tendency to fall apart at the first sign of difficulty.

—Bempechat (1998, p. 37)

What explains beliefs such as these that are not conducive to learning? What beliefs are conducive to learning? The motivation theory that provides insight into beliefs that are detrimental or conducive to learning is attribution. *Attribution* is a cognitive theory that considers a person's beliefs about causes of outcomes and how those beliefs influence expectations and behavior. An understanding of attribution theory will help you:

- distinguish between beliefs that are detrimental or conducive to learning
- understand reasons for lack of persistence
- understand and address lack of effort
- identify strategies that can be used to help students succeed and gain in confidence
- understand your own causal beliefs about success and failure and how these influence student motivation.

Because attribution is concerned with causes given for outcomes, it is the theory of motivation that is most directly concerned with this question: "Why do people do what they do?" This question is particularly important to teachers and students. Consider the example of Sylvia:

> Sylvia has been failing and has no confidence in herself to do the work. As a teacher, you believe that the main thing Sylvia needs is to experience success on the task. So you ask another student to help her with the task. Sylvia is able to complete the task successfully. You now expect her to be more confident. However, when you ask Sylvia about the likelihood of completing other similar tasks, she seems doubtful that she can do it. "I only did it the last time 'cause Sharon helped me."

Why was Sylvia still doubtful? When students like Sylvia lack confidence, a common response by teachers is to help them attain success on a task, as in the example. Although Sylvia had a successful experience, she still lacks confidence. Examples of the variety of causal explanations that students may give for their performance are shown in Fig. 2.1.

Attribution theory began with the common-sense psychology of Fritz Heider. Heider (1958) was interested in the reasons people give for an outcome such as success or failure on a task. The causes that people believe are responsible for an outcome are important determinants of their future expectancies and behaviors. Heider identified two primary reasons that people use to explain their performance: *can* and *try*. Can refers to whether

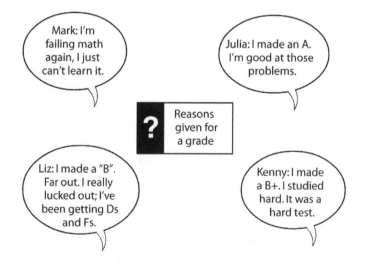

FIG. 2.1. Reasons given for a grade.

one has the ability to do a task, and try refers to how much effort a person puts forth. If we fail at a task, our expectations for future success differ depending on whether we attribute the failure to lack of effort (try) or to not having the ability (can) to succeed on the task. For example, if Cathy fails a math test and says "I'm just no good at numbers," it is unlikely that she will expect to improve in the future. Consequently, she will not try very hard in math classes. If Cathy fails and says "I didn't spend enough time studying, I thought I understood it," it is likely she will work harder on the next test.

ATTRIBUTIONAL PROPERTIES IN ACHIEVEMENT SETTINGS

What are the properties of attributional thinking? Weiner (1979, 1985, 1986, 1992) generated much research that identified properties involved in attributional thinking in achievement settings. The properties include the specific reason for success and failure, different ways we view the reason, the source of the belief, and factors that influence change in expectations.

Descriptions of Attributional Thinking: Content and Dimensions

What reasons for success and failure can teachers typically expect to find in a classroom? The research by Weiner initially identified four reasons most frequently given as the cause for success and failure in achievement settings: ability, effort, task difficulty, and luck. Subsequent research identified learning strategies as a fifth possible reason for success and failure (Clifford, 1986). These reasons are defined as follows:

- ability—how we rate our aptitude, skill, or knowledge ("I'm just not good at sports." "I understand how a bill becomes a law.");
- effort—how hard we tried, including mental and physical work, and time spent to accomplish a goal;
- task difficulty—how difficult or easy we believe the task to be;

- strategy—the type of strategy used for learning (e.g., a pre-reading strategy);
- luck—the extent to which we believe luck was a factor.

Ability and effort have typically been found to be the most frequent reasons given for success and failure in achievement contexts (Weiner, 1992). Strategies were given by students only if teachers had emphasized the importance of strategy use for a successful performance (Clifford, 1986). If strategies were not emphasized, students did not consider them as a possible reason for their performance. However, in a course where strategy use was emphasized, strategies were the most frequent reason indicated by college students for success or failure (Alderman, Klein, Seeley, & Sanders, 1993).

The reasons given for success and failure have been further classified into three dimensions or ways to look at causes (Weiner, 1979, 1992):

1. Attributions are classified according to an internal–external continuum or where the responsibility lies. This refers to whether the cause is a factor within the person (ability or aptitude, effort, mood) or a factor outside the person (luck, task difficulty).
2. The second dimension is a stable–unstable continuum. The stability classification refers to whether the perceived cause is seen as consistent or variable over time. Unstable causes for success or failure are those attributed to temporary factors that can be modified.
3. The third dimension, a controllable–uncontrollable continuum, refers to the extent we believe we have influence or control over the cause of an outcome. An uncontrollable factor is luck, whereas effort is generally believed to be controllable.

Table 2.1 presents attributional examples classified according to dimensions. The examples are from the student's perspective.

In this classification, if Cathy fails an exam and says "I did not try hard enough," we can infer that she believes that she can try harder—an internal-unstable attribution that she can control. Effort is sometimes perceived as stable, as when we characterize

TABLE 2.1
Examples of Attributions by Dimensions

	Internal		External
	Controllable	Uncontrollable	Uncontrollable
Stable	• I've really improved my keyboarding skill due to my practice over the last six months. • Since I've consistently used the PQ4R, my grades have improved.	• I'm not good at math. • I can't draw a straight line.	• Mr. Jones' tests are impossible to pass. • I'm not a good writer because I never had a teacher that made me write.
Unstable	• I didn't overlearn material for the last exam. I wasn't well organized in studying. • "Success, success." I did better than I expected. I put my best efforts into passing and came up with good results. I studied until the terms became second nature.	• I was sick all week and couldn't study for the test.	• I got a good grade because my tutor helped me. • I made an A; the test was easy.

Note. There is no external-controllability column because, from the view of the student, external factors are uncontrollable.

ourselves as "basically lazy" or if I think "my six months of hard work paid off when I was chosen to be a member of the ensemble."

It is especially important for teachers to understand the stable–unstable dimension. Research typically found that students view ability and task difficulty as relatively stable. When Sylvia fails and says "I will never be able to learn math," she is referring to her math ability as stable. This is an internal-stable attribution, and her reason for failure appears to be fixed, a self-defeating attribution for Sylvia. As teachers, we want students to think of ability as a skill or knowledge that is learnable—an unstable quality. For example, a student with poor writing skills who believes that writing is a stable ability, perhaps even innate, is not likely to revise drafts of papers or seek help, such as going to a writing lab.

Do students always have some idea of what determines their success and failure? Apparently not. Alderman et al. (1993)

found explanations such as "I don't know what happened" as reasons for a low grade and termed these as *mystery* attributions. In a study of causal factors given by elementary students, Butler and Orion (1990) found that attribution of test outcomes to unknown causes was more prevalent among students who were low achieving. In addition, students may offer more than one reason for success and failure (Dresel, Scober, & Ziegler, 2005). Teachers may need to probe further. Knowledge of how students use these attributions to account for success and failure in school settings (academic and sports) can help teachers predict students' expectancies and plan intervention strategies when needed.

Sources of Attributional Information

How do we decide what caused our success and failure? What cues do we use to explain whether an outcome was influenced by our ability, effort, or some other factor? Information comes from direct and indirect cues (Graham, 1991). Some information comes from direct cues, like failing a test when other students succeeded. Information is also obtained from more indirect cues, often conveyed unintentionally, such as when a teacher communicates pity to a student who failed a test. In addition, there may be a bias with some causes given more often (Weiner, 1992).

Direct Attributional Cues

One of the most important informational cues is the outcome of the task. Here students have a direct cue as to their performance. Another source of attributional information comes from comparing one's performance to that of others (Weiner, 1992). When most of the class fails a test, students are likely to attribute the failure to the difficulty of the task, not to their ability. However, if Sam failed and everyone else in the class made an A or B, he is likely to believe the failure was due to his low ability. If Sarah fails a test and a peer says, "I didn't study at all and I made an A," Sarah may take this as a cue that failure must be due to her ability. When a teacher sees students comparing grades on a test, information other than the test score is being communicated. An important role of the teacher is to help students interpret the possible reasons for test scores and make an adaptive attribution.

Indirect Attributional Cues

In school, feedback that students receive from teachers is a source of much information about ability. Students' attributional interpretations may be based on the attributions that teachers communicated to them overtly or covertly (Reyna, 2000). Graham (1991) identified three groups of feedback as sources of indirect cues: praise versus blame, sympathy versus anger, unsolicited help, and ability grouping.

Praise versus Blame. The praise or blame a student receives from a teacher can function as an indirect low-ability cue (Graham, 1991). The cue provided by praise or blame interacts with difficulty of the task and effort expended by a student. Praise acts as a low-ability cue when a student is praised for completing an easy task. Young children, especially, interpret the praise for the easy task as high ability (Graham & Barker, 1987). A low-ability cue is also conveyed when a student fails a task but receives no blame, like lack of effort. The student can interpret this to mean, "There's nothing I can do about the failure." Chapter 8 presents guidelines for effective and ineffective praise.

Sympathy versus Anger. Did it ever occur to you that communicating sympathy to a student could be interpreted as evidence that he or she has low ability? Graham (1984) found that, when teachers conveyed sympathy following poor student performance, the failing students took this as a cue that they had low ability. Obviously a statement like "I feel sorry for you because you made such a low score" would be a low-ability cue. What might a teacher say that unintentionally conveys a message of low ability to a student? One student remembers a class being told, "All students have to do this except Holly and Ramon." Holly took her omission as a cue that she would not be able to do the task. In contrast, mild anger for failure can provide an indirect cue that one is capable. For example, "You can do better than this. You handed this paper in with no editing" provides a cue to the student that he or she is capable of more.

Unsolicited Help.   Another low-ability cue for students is unsolicited help by the teacher (Graham & Barker, 1990). Graham and Barker found that, regardless of whether a helper was a peer or teacher, other students judged the student who received unsolicited help as lower in ability than nonhelped peers. The important factor in this example is *unsolicited.* When the teacher consistently gives help to Sylvia before she requests it, this suggests that the teacher knows that she will not be able to do it.

Ability Grouping.   One powerful cue for ability that affects large groups of students is tracking according to ability groups. Students in both high and low tracks are defined by labels such as *high ability, honors, low-achieving, slow,* and *average* (Oakes, 1985). These labels are powerful cues about one's ability. Oakes observed that students in the lower track are usually seen by others as dumb and also see themselves in this way. A label may have an adverse effect on students in the high-achieving class as well. Students in a high-track class may take this label as a cue that they have naturally high ability and then assume inflated self-concepts. This belief can interfere with students working to develop their academic skills.

It is important that teachers be aware of the subtle cues that may have unintentional effects on students' perception of ability. Students can sometimes interpret commonly accepted practices of generous praise, minimal blame, sympathy, and unsolicited help as low ability (M. D. Clark, 1997; Graham, 1991). M. D. Clark found that responses given to students with learning disabilities (LD) are often interpreted as low-ability cues. Graham further suggested that these cues raise important questions pertinent to motivation of minority students such as African Americans. For example, are minority students more likely to be targets for feedback that conveys sympathy—thus receiving a cue for low ability? Reyna (2000) took this a step further, stating that labeling and indirect cues can lead to stable beliefs about ability and have the negative effect of stereotyping students as low ability.

Attributional Bias

Attributional bias is a predisposition to make certain attributional judgments that may be in error (Weiner, 1985). Several variations of attributional bias have been identified that are relevant to achievement settings. A common misjudgment is a *hedonic bias*, the tendency to attribute success to self but not attribute failure to self (Weiner, 2000).

Previous knowledge can also lead to attributions that are erroneous (Frieze, 1980). Potential sources of errors in attributional judgments can be found in stereotypes about certain groups (e.g., minority, gender) (Reyna, 2000). These preconceptions about certain groups can serve as ready-made explanations for why a student achieves or does not achieve. There is a danger that the stable, uncontrollable attribution for low performance will lead to lower expectations.

The implication for educators is to recognize that a number of possible causes may explain any given success or failure. Thus, it is important to be aware of potential stereotypical attributional biases. Explore other possible causes by gathering more information when bias may be a factor (see Strategy 2.1).

Strategy 2.1. Collect Attributional Information

- Simply ask students why they succeeded, failed, or improved. Some teachers elicit information by having students give their reasons for how well they did after assignments or exams. See Exhibit 2.1 for an example.
- Attribution information can be obtained through the use of *learning logs*, in which students keep records and write about their goals, successes, and failures.
- Conduct an attributional task analysis of student performance. Is it because the student cannot or will not? A teacher may believe that a student is not performing well because he or she has low ability or is lazy. Instead the student may be performing low because he or she does not have the essential skills.
- Look for clues that will enable you to determine if the student has the essential skills. Does the student have prerequisite knowledge or skills? Does the task require formal reasoning whereas the student is functioning at the concrete reasoning level? Does the student have the necessary learning or memory strategies?
- If the student cannot, then teach the prerequisite skill or guide student to the appropriate source of help.

Emotional Reactions Generated by Attributions

What emotional reactions might be generated by one's attributional beliefs about the causes of success or failure? How do these emotions affect motivation? Attributional beliefs produce emotional reactions such as pride, shame, hopelessness, guilt, anger, and pity (Weiner, 1985). According to Weiner, attribution to internal factors produces more pride and shame than attribution to external factors. We experience more pride when we attribute success to ability and effort. Nicholls (1979) found that attribution to high ability following a success often triggers the emotion of pride. This is evident when a student makes a statement like, "I ran a mile; I'm so proud of myself." A caution: students may feel too much pride resulting in overconfidence and expend less effort (Lewis & Sullivan, 2005). However, one experiences a greater sense of hopelessness when failure is attributed to ability: "I'll never be able to pass the proficiency test." This type of attribution is one that teachers want students to avoid because it affects the students' future expectations. Guilt as an emotion, in the way of regret, may be expressed when a student says, "I should have done my homework."

However, attribution to external causes tends to minimize achievement-related emotional reactions. If students say they succeeded on a test because they lucked out or people say that luck was responsible for their getting a job, their feeling of pride is minimized. Students might be happy if they made a good grade on an easy test, but would they feel pride as well?

Shift in Expectancies After Success and Failure

What role does attribution play in changing our goal expectancies for success and failure? In a typical change (without accounting for attributions), expectancies tend to rise after success and drop after failure (Weiner, 1986). This tends to confirm the saying that "success breeds success and failure breeds failure." However, the decisive factor for change in expectancy is the reason given and how stable it is. How shifts in expectancies are affected by success and failure with the resulting attributions are shown in Fig. 2.2.

Prior performance	Performance level	Causal attribution	Resulting expectancy
High-achieving student	High	Internal-stable "I'm good in math"	Very high
	Low	Internal-unstable "I didn't have time to study for the test"	High
Low-achieving student	High	External-unstable "I lucked out" "My tutor helped me"	Low confidence
	High	Internal-unstable "I did all my homework this week"	Increased confidence (hope)
Low-achieving student	Low	Internal-stable "I'm stupid"	Very low confidence

FIG. 2.2. Shift in expectancies.

REFLECTION. Examine Fig. 2.2. What makes sense to you, and what does not? What causes a student to continue to have low expectations after experiencing success?

The first two lines show students who have performed at a high level. The student attributes success to his or her math ability—a stable factor—thus his or her expectancy continues to be high. If he or she has a lower performance and attributes it to insufficient effort—an unstable, controllable cause—his or her expectancy also continues to be high. What about a student who has a history of failure? Notice the third pattern in Fig. 2.2. Did it seem logical to you that a student continues to have low confidence after experiencing success? This was the case with Sylvia in this chapter's opening example. This is a pattern that has puzzled teachers. Intuitively, as in Sylvia's case, teachers know the student needs to be successful and will do something to help her attain success on a task. The critical aspect in this example is

Sylvia's attribution. If the attributional belief for success is stable, external, and uncontrollable (e.g., helped by someone), there is no reason to believe that she can be successful next time. This can explain Sylvia's continuing lack of confidence.

The fourth line shows a student who has a history of failure, experiences success, and attributes the success to her effort in the form of practice. Her expectancy for success is on the rise. The example in the fifth line in Fig. 2.2 is the most difficult to change. The student has a history of failure and attributes this failure to lack of ability. This student does not believe she can do anything to change her situation.

In summary, expectancies are more difficult to change when attribution for failure is made to a stable factor of ability than to an unstable factor of effort (Graham, 1991; Weiner, 1985). This belief pattern is known as *learned helplessness* and is discussed later in this chapter. As is seen, the crucial strategies for teacher intervention are to focus the student's attributions on (a) unstable, controllable factors of effort and strategy use, and (b) ability as knowledge or skills that can be learned. How this can be done is explained later in this chapter.

USING ATTRIBUTIONAL INFORMATION

The first step in using attributional theory is to learn to collect and interpret attributional statements made by students. Attributional information enables teachers to:

- estimate the extent to which students will expend effort to attend help sessions, practice on needed skills, and so on
- give appropriate attributional feedback (i.e., effort, strategies, skills)
- identify groups of students whose attributions may be especially self-defeating (e.g., female students in math and science, students classified with LD, high-anxiety students)
- identify helpless students in order to plan strategies for intervention.

Exhibit 2.1 suggests ways that teachers can gather information about student reasons for success and failure.

Exhibit 2.1. Student Attributional Rating Form

Score on Test _____

My test score is a: success   nonsuccess

The reasons I received this score include:

1.
2.
3.

How I prepared for this test:

1.
2.
3.

This is what I plan to do next time:

INDIVIDUAL AND SITUATIONAL DIFFERENCES IN ATTRIBUTIONS

The beliefs one has about the cause of success and failure may vary according to age, cultural influences, gender, and type of task. How attributions are related to these factors are discussed in the following sections.

Situational Differences in Attributions

Does the particular type of task or situation influence a student's attributions? Frieze and Snyder (1980) had elementary school students judge the following tasks: art project, football, academic tests, and frog catching. Students gave different attributions for different tasks. Ability was believed to be more important for an art project and for winning or losing in football. However, task difficulty was more important for frog catching. The difference in attributions was explained as follows: Frog catching is an activity that students had no standards or criteria on which to judge their performance, whereas they are familiar with standards for art and football. For academic testing, effort was perceived as the most important cause.

A more recent study examined explanations 6- and 7-year-old children gave for success and failure in mathematics, painting, reading, and getting their work done (Gipps & Tunstall, 1998). Effort was the most frequent reason given for success and failure for all types of subjects. The authors noted that effort was emphasized in these classrooms. In the area of music, attributions for performance by students have been mixed. In some cases, ability was viewed as more important; in other cases, ability and effort were judged as causes of success and failure (Leggette, 1998). Leggette found that younger students tended to place more emphasis on ability while older students placed emphasis on effort and ability.

An important implication for teachers is to determine the type of attributions for success and failure that students make in their particular subject area or on different types of tasks. If students think ability is the key factor for success in an art project and believe they cannot draw a straight line, the teacher will have to plan instruction so that ability (drawing) is perceived as a skill that can be developed.

Developmental Differences in Attributions

Are attributional patterns associated with age or developmental stage? Indeed, there is a developmental trend in how the relationship between attribution and achievement is viewed, especially involving the respective roles of ability and effort (Nicholls, 1978, 1979). Younger children see effort and ability as the same and believe increased effort leads to increased ability. Prior to age 10, children believe that if two children attain the same outcome, the one who tried harder is the smartest even if he or she got the lowest grade. The child who made the highest grade is said to have tried the hardest even if he or she did not. Young children see ability as more modifiable than do older students.

As children develop cognitively, they increasingly make distinctions between effort and ability and become more accurate about the causes of success and failure. At about age 10, children begin to believe that a child who has low ability must compensate for it by increased effort. However, Nicholls and Miller (1984) pointed out that the developmental pattern of differentiating effort and ability can have negative effects on student motivation. If low achievement is attributed to ability, effort may be viewed as useless and students may actually decrease effort to protect self-worth. Thus, younger children have a more adaptive attributional pattern than older children by believing that increased effort should lead to increased success and ability.

The differentiation of effort and ability can have particularly debilitating effects on the motivation of adolescents who tend to see ability as the most important reason for performance outcomes (Covington, 1984). Because adolescents often judge their ability in comparison to the ability of their peers, this poses a new problem for teachers. Adolescents often equate expending more effort with having less ability. In the classroom, this translates to, "If you have to study a lot, then you must not be smart." Teachers may contribute to this by inadvertently giving more recognition to a student who succeeds with no effort than to one who worked for the success. This is further explained by self-worth theory in Chapter 3.

Gender and Attributions

Do male and female students differ in their explanations for success and failure? In some cases, yes. Overall, the attributions of girls reflect a lower expectancy pattern (Meece & Courtney, 1992). Studies that examined gender differences found that girls are more likely than boys to (a) attribute failure to their lack of ability even though their achievement is higher (Nicholls, 1979), and (b) make more external attributions (luck) for their successes. Gender differences in attributions for ability are particularly prevalent in subjects like mathematics (Wolleat, Pedro, Becker, & Fennema, 1980) and science (Licht, Strader, & Swenson, 1989), which have traditionally been gender-typed. Although there may be no differences in actual performance, female students tend to have a lower expectancy pattern for their ability. Vermeer, Boekaerts, and Seegers (2000) found that gender differences were prominent in problem solving among sixth graders; girls were more likely than boys to attribute bad results to lack of ability.

Where do these different expectations begin? Yee and Eccles (1988) found that parents hold different perceptions of their sons' and daughters' math success. Parents rated talent for math as the most important reason for their sons' successes, whereas effort was the most important reason given for their daughters' successes. What is the significance of crediting boys with math talent and girls with effort? When effort was believed to be responsible for success, the child was considered by the parent to be less talented in math. In contrast, they may have less confidence in their daughters' ability to be successful in math.

However, there is reason for hope. A recent study reported that the gender gap in mathematics achievement is narrowing and girls showed promising gains in their attributions for mathematics success (Lloyd, Walsh, & Yailagh, 2005). The research compared students at fourth and seventh grade. Girls and boys equally attributed success to effort, and both rated ability as most important for success. There was a grade difference for effort; fourth graders attributed success more to effort than did the seventh graders. Girls attributed failure more to lack of effort and boys to task difficulty.

Attributions and Motivation Among Ethnic Groups

Do attributional explanations for success and failure act as an important motivational force in different ethnic groups? According to Graham (1989, 1994), because attributional theory considers the role of thought in determining behavior, it is particularly fruitful in examining motivation in different cultures and ethnic groups.

Beliefs about Effort and Ability

Are attributional belief patterns similar among different ethnic groups? A comparison of poor African-American, Hispanic, Indo-Chinese, and White fifth- and sixth-grade students found similar attribution patterns for all groups (Bempechat, Nakkula, Wu, & Ginsberg, 1996). All groups rated ability as the most important factor for success in math. In a subsequent study comparing African-American, Hispanic, Indo-Chinese, and White fifth and sixth graders, Bempechat, Graham, and Jimenez (1999) found cultural similarities as well as cultural specifics. For all ethnic groups, failure was attributed to lack of ability and success to external factors. In contrast, Indo-Chinese students had stronger beliefs that failure was due to lack of effort. Attribution for failure due to lack of ability is a problem for all students because it is believed to be uncontrollable.

Graham (1984) compared middle- and low-SES (socioeconomic status) African-American and White students on attributions for failure following a problem-solving task. The middle-class children in both ethnic groups were more likely to attribute failure to lack of effort and maintained consistently higher expectancies for success after experiencing failure. For both groups, this is indicative of an adaptive attributional pattern following failure, similar to that found in research by Diener and Dweck (1978). The findings of this research are important because they demonstrate the positive motivation pattern of African-American students—a pattern that has received little attention.

As mentioned in Chapter 1, Stevenson and Lee (1990) compared beliefs of American and Asian students concerning the role of effort and ability for success in mathematics. They asked mothers in Minnesota, Japan, and Taiwan to assign 10 points among ability, effort, task difficulty, and luck to rank their importance in academic success and school performance. All the mothers assigned the points in the same rank order: (1) effort, (2) ability, (3) task, and (4) luck. American mothers scored ability and effort as about equal. In contrast, Taiwanese and Japanese mothers assigned effort a higher value than ability. Peak (1993) noted that, in Japanese elementary schools, ability is rarely mentioned, whereas effort is consistently portrayed as the key to success. In contrast, in the United States, students who try very hard are often labeled *nerd* or *grind*. This attitude is further described in Chapter 7.

These perceptions of effort and ability take on increased importance when homework is considered in the context of effort. Japanese and Chinese students spend at least twice the amount of time and effort on homework than do American students (Stevenson & Lee, 1990). American teachers assign less and consider it less valuable. Peak (1993) pointed out that homework reflects teachers' beliefs on whether extra practice makes a difference and whether students are willing to engage in extra effort on behalf of their studies. American parents do not appear to consider good study habits as critical to academic success as do Asian parents.

Implications for Teachers

What can teachers draw from the attributional beliefs among different ethnic groups in terms of classroom practice? The important issue is to understand the motivational processes, such as attribution, operating within a particular ethnic group (Bempechat et al., 1996; Graham, 1994). When similarities are found across ethnic groups, educational interventions do not necessarily have to be targeted to children differentially based on their ethnic group membership.

Graham (1989) emphasized the importance of teacher feedback in influencing concepts of ability and expectations of minority, low-SES students. Recall the previous discussion of indirect attributional cues. It is important to be aware of feedback that may indirectly convey to students that they have low ability. Graham (1994) suggested that, in view of the number of African-American children in negative educational situations, it is especially important to be sensitive to how minorities feel, think, and act in response to nonattainment of goals.

Attribution guidelines to keep in mind for students of varying culture, ethnicity, and gender are presented in Strategy 2.2.

Strategy 2.2.   Attribution Guidelines for Culture, Ethnicity, and Gender

- Listen carefully to student expectations and attributions for performance to identify patterns of attributions that might be gender- or culture-related.
- As a teacher or prospective teacher, examine your own beliefs about competence for subjects like math and science that have been traditionally gender-typed. If you are an elementary school teacher, do you think of yourself as a math teacher? As a science teacher?
- Provide feedback that helps both male and female students make more realistic estimates of their ability.

- Become familiar with cultural values for ability and effort. What is the relative value placed on effort and ability? The suggestions recommended in Strategy 2.1 can be used to become familiar about attitudes toward effort and ability.
- Be prepared to discuss attributional beliefs and their implications with parents.
- Be especially sensitive to giving feedback that might be interpreted by students as sympathy and thus be interpreted as having low ability.

TWO ATTRIBUTIONAL CONSEQUENCES: LEARNED HELPLESSNESS AND HELP SEEKING

It was established earlier that the reasons one gives for success and failure have consequences that influence both actions and expectations. Two areas of consequence that are of extreme importance to educators are learned helplessness and help seeking.

Learned Helplessness

A student who has a history of failure and does not expect this to change will attribute failure to ability—an internal and stable factor. This pattern is characteristic of students classified as having *learned helplessness.* These individuals expect that their actions will be futile in affecting future outcomes. Consequently, they give up. Learned helplessness was first investigated in young animals that had been presented with inescapable electric shocks in one situation; when placed in a different situation, they failed to try to escape or avoid the shock (Seligman & Maier, 1967). Animals that demonstrated no connection between their activity and avoiding the shock had learned to be helpless. It was further hypothesized that humans responded the same way: they were passive in situations where they believed their actions would have no effect on what happened to them. In this original explanation, helplessness was viewed as global—affecting all domains of one's life. Later research found that people may experience helplessness in one situation and not in others (Alloy, Abramson, Peterson, & Seligman, 1984). This means that a student may feel helpless in learning math but not in learning history.

Helplessness exists in achievement situations when students do not see a connection between their actions and their performance and grades. The important aspect of learned helplessness is how it affects the motivational behavior of students in the face of failure. The attributions a student makes for failure act as a bridge between a student's willingness to try again and the student's tendency to give up.

Helpless and Mastery Orientation

In a now-classic study, Diener and Dweck (1978) identified two patterns of responses to failure following success in problem-solving tasks: a maladaptive–helpless orientation and an adaptive–mastery orientation. Children showed different response patterns to failure in their thinking, self-talk, affect, and actions. A comparison of the two response patterns is shown in Table 2.2. Keep in mind that the students in the study had the same failure experience while performing the tasks, but there were two different patterns of response to the failure outcome. The thinking, self-talk, and actions of the helpless-oriented children formed a self-defeating pattern. When failure is attributed to lack of ability, there is a decline in performance. Attribution to lack of effort does not show this decline (Dweck & Goetz, 1978).

TABLE 2.2
Helpless and Mastery Patterns in Response to Failure

Helpless	*Mastery*
• Attribution to personal inadequacies such as deficient memory, problem-solving ability, intelligence	• Attribution to effort
• Negative affect: dislike for task, anxiety, self-talk irrelevant to task, lack of positive expectation	• Remains optimistic, "I did it before, I can do it again"
• Decrease in effort	• Persistence in difficult tasks, looks for new strategies
• Avoids challenge	• Seeks challenge
• Performance declines in difficult tasks	• Maintains and improves problem-solving strategies

Source. Based on Diener and Dweck (1978) and Dweck and Leggett (1988).

Are there ability differences in learned helplessness? But-kowsky and Willows (1980) compared good, average, and poor readers. They found that poor readers had lower expectancies of success on a reading task. Poor readers overwhelmingly attributed their failures to lack of ability (68 percent compared with 13 percent for average readers and 12 percent for good readers). They took less responsibility for success, attributing success more to task ease—an external cause—than did the good and average readers. In the face of difficulty, poor readers became less persistent—a self-defeating behavior.

Helplessness was also found when children studied new material that required them to read passages with confusing concepts. In a study by Licht and Dweck (1984), half the children received material with a clear passage, and the other half received a confusing passage. There were no differences between mastery orientation and helpless orientation when the passage was clearly written. In contrast, when the passage was not clear, most of the mastery children reached the learning criterion, whereas only one-third of the helpless children did. This investigation is important because some academic subjects, like math, are characterized by constant new learning, which may be initially confusing to students. Mastery students will not be discouraged by the initial difficulty, whereas helpless students immediately lose confidence although they may be equally competent. When teaching new material, teachers can be especially alert for this pattern of helplessness in the face of initial difficulty.

Learned Helplessness and Students with Learning Disabilities

Are some students more prone to experience a sense of helplessness? One group of students particularly susceptible to the pattern of learned helplessness are those students who are identified as having LD (Licht, 1983). Children with LD experience much failure over a long period of time on a variety of school tasks. As a result, these children come to doubt their academic abilities, with the accompanying belief that nothing they can do will help them be successful. This is followed by the self-defeating response of decreasing effort. Children with LD have been found to exhibit the following characteristics of the learned helplessness pattern (Licht, 1983):

- score lower than non-LD children on measures of self-esteem and perceptions of ability;
- are more likely to attribute difficulty with tasks to lack of ability;
- are less likely to attribute failure to insufficient effort; and
- lower their expectations for future success and display greater decline in expectation following failure.

It is important for teachers to be aware of the characteristics of helplessness because learned helplessness may explain the student's apparent lack of motivation. How can a teacher identify a helpless pattern? What can a teacher do to lessen the likelihood of helplessness and help students who have this tendency? Butkowsky and Willows (1980) suggested that educators must begin to rethink failure as a necessary component of the learning process and not as a damaging experience to be avoided. Strategy 2.3 provides guidelines for assisting students who show patterns of helplessness.

Strategy 2.3. Assisting Helpless Students

- Observe student reactions to failure in order to identify helpless patterns. Clues may be in what students say and how they approach tasks: (a) Are their explanations optimistic or pessimistic? (b) Do they easily give up or try new approaches? (c) Do they fail to try at all? (d) Are they generally passive? (e) Are their attributions for failure due to stable factors?
- The past history of the student may provide clues. Students who have a history of failure may be especially prone to helpless patterns.
- Teachers can anticipate new learning, in math or other subjects, which may be confusing at first to students. Then they can help students by:
  o establishing an attribution that all students can learn math;
  o attributing the learning to effort and ability, such as "I understand conversion to metric now because I worked the extra problems and practiced the conversions every day last week";

> o teaching the students learning strategies; and
> o structuring the material so it is more readily acquired by students.
> • Attribution retraining is recommended for students who have a pattern of failure (Reid & Borkowski, 1987). This training is described in a later section of this chapter.
> • The LINKS model described in Chapter 4 integrates several motivational concepts to address helplessness.

Does the pattern of learned helplessness show up in young children? Dweck and Sorich (1999) concluded that there is clear evidence of a helplessness pattern in children younger than age 8. After experiencing failure or criticism, they show signs of helplessness like self-blame, lowered persistence, and lack of constructive strategies. Mastery-oriented children, in contrast, assumed they were still good even when their work had errors, and believed they could improve through effort. An important implication for parents and teachers, according to the authors, is to be very cautious when giving feedback to children. Extremely positive or negative feedback can be detrimental to children's beliefs about their competence.

Help Seeking

Do you ask for help when you need it or do you have the view, "I have to do it myself, no one can do it except me"? From a motivational perspective, help seeking is an adaptive cognitive strategy that indicates a striving for mastery and achievement (R. Ames, 1983; Karabenick, 1998; Newman, 1998) and a general problem-solving strategy (Nelson-Le Gall, 1985). If help seeking is an adaptive strategy, why do teachers observe that students who are most in need of help are often the most reluctant to seek it? We have learned from research that seeking help from others can have negative connotations (Newman, 1990, 1991). Help seeking may be seen as threatening if the student thinks it is a sign of low ability. In this case, there is a personal cost to seeking help: Students may feel incompetent.

Help seeking is positive when students seek assistance in order to make a change in their learning. The attributional process is an important factor in whether help seeking is seen as positive or negative and consequently whether students attend academic help sessions. R. Ames and Lau (1982) identified factors that affected the extent that college students attend help sessions:

- Low-performing students were more likely to attend help sessions if they were given specific positive information about the effects of the sessions (e.g., "students who attended improved their performance").
- Students who attributed success to effort were more likely to attend.
- Students who did not seek help used more external attributions for failure, such as "tricky test questions," and used these external reasons as excuses.

Newman's (1990, 1991) investigations of help seeking among children in Grades 3, 5, and 7 provided a fuller understanding of help seeking. For example, who seeks help, individuals with high or low self-esteem? For all grades, the higher the perceived competence of the children, the less they felt there were personal costs to help seeking (e.g., being thought of as low ability). Students with low self-esteem were especially unlikely to seek help, whereas those with high self-esteem were more likely to seek help. Similar results were obtained by Nelson-Le Gall and Jones (1990) for average-achieving African-American children.

Newman (1991) also found differences between younger and older students in views about help seeking. Seventh graders were more aware than younger children that negative fallout might result from help seeking (e.g., embarrassment). However, older children were also more likely than younger ones to believe that smart classmates rather than "dumb" ones ask questions of the teacher.

Help seeking by college students showed a pattern similar to that of children. Karabenick and Knapp (1991) found that students with low self-esteem were more threatened by seeking help. One important and perhaps surprising finding was that students who use more learning strategies are more likely to seek help when needed, whereas students who use fewer strategies are less likely to seek help when needed. This attitude presents a double bind for those needing help. Not only do they lack the necessary strategies for success, but they do not seek the needed study assistance. The authors concluded that students need to learn to judge when they need help and that help seeking should be included in learning strategy and motivation programs.

These findings on help seeking are important for teachers and counselors so that they can plan ways to get students to attend help sessions or seek help in counseling when needed. Nelson-Le Gall (1985) emphasized the need to think of help seeking as an adaptive coping strategy rather than as a self-threatening activity. Some ways to accomplish this are listed in Strategy 2.4.

Strategy 2.4. Help Seeking

- The overriding task is to have students view help seeking, when needed, as a smart move instead of a dumb one.
- Establish a classroom climate where students are encouraged to ask questions. Document attendance and improved performance as a result of the help sessions and show this to students.
- Be sure students who have improved after attending help sessions attribute the improvement to the help sessions.
- Teach students a self-talk script to practice asking teachers for help in classes where they were having problems, as one middle school teacher did. See Chapter 5 for self-talk examples.

TEACHER ATTRIBUTIONAL BELIEFS AND STUDENT PERFORMANCE

How do teachers' attributions for student performance affect student motivation? The beliefs that teachers hold about the role of ability and effort affect their responses to their students, which, in turn, affect motivation. Weiner and Kukla (1970) conducted a study in which prospective teachers were given information about the ability level, usual effort, and outcome of the students and were asked to assign rewards.

REFLECTION.   How would you reward students with the following patterns of ability, effort, and success? Evaluate them on a 10-point scale ranging from +5 (*highest reward*) to –5 (*maximum punishment*). Compare your evaluations with the results of the study and think about the reasons for your rating.

high ability	high effort	success
high ability	high effort	failure
high ability	low effort	success
high ability	low effort	failure
low ability	high effort	success
low ability	high effort	failure
low ability	low effort	success
low ability	low effort	failure

Results reveal that the students who were characterized as having high effort were rewarded more for success and punished less for failure; those characterized as having low ability–high effort and success received higher rewards; and those with high ability–low effort and failure received the most punishment. Weiner (1992, 2001) concluded that students who do not try evoke the most anger from teachers, who, in turn, respond with more punishment. Students who had low ability but tried hard and succeeded were viewed more favorably. He suggested that these findings might be explained in terms of our culture's value system, which tends to value the person who is able to overcome handicaps and succeed. In other cultures, however, this pattern may not hold. M. D. Clark and Artiles (2000) found student ability was more influential on Guatemalan teacher responses than was effort.

Other studies examined teacher attributions for students with behavior problems. Medway (1979) surveyed the reasons teachers gave for the problems of students whom they had referred for psychological services. The results indicate that teachers believed student characteristics to be more responsible for problems than what the teacher did. In addition, they attributed learning problems to the students' ability and behavior problems to students' difficulties at home. Consistent with the findings of

Weiner and Kukla (1970), teachers placed more emphasis on effort cues in their responses to students. For example, teachers who attributed student problems to lack of effort gave more negative feedback to those students in the form of warnings and criticism. A study by Tollefson, Melvin, and Thippavajjala (1990) provided additional insight to teacher beliefs about effort. The reason most frequently given by teachers for unsatisfactory work was low effort. Although teachers indicated that low-effort students could improve, they viewed effort as stable, not expecting students to be successful in the long run.

Teacher attributions have also been examined as they relate to special education students (M. D. Clark, 1997). M. D. Clark concluded that teacher attributions and response to children with LD are based in part on the beliefs they are deserving of more pity and will fail more. According to Palmer (1983), teacher attributions are influenced both by special education labels and previous performance of students. Generally, teachers attributed the failure of educable mentally retarded children to low ability and attributed the failure of children who have not been so labeled to either low effort or an external cause (Rolison & Medway, 1985). These studies suggest that the labels assigned to students may influence teachers' expectations for their performance. It is important to be aware of this possibility to avoid unrealistically low expectations. Awareness of beliefs about special education students is increasingly important as these students move into inclusive classrooms.

From these studies, it can be seen that teachers' beliefs about the causes of students' performance and behavior can affect the feedback and evaluation of these students.

REFLECTION. Explore your beliefs about the role of effort and ability by thinking through Exhibit 2.2. What reasons do you give yourself for student performance and behavior? What cues do you use? Think about how these beliefs might influence your evaluation of students, your expectations, and the feedback you provide them.

Exhibit 2.2. Effort Reflection: Exploring Teacher Beliefs on Effort and Ability

OBJECTIVE: To make explicit your present view of effort and to operationalize effort in concrete terms.

ACTIVITY

1. Compared to ability, state how important student effort is to you. Do you think of effort more as a character trait or as a habit that is learned?

2. List student behaviors that mean effort to you in your classroom.

3. List what you think students mean when they say they tried hard.

4. Compare your meaning of effort with that of students.

5. What is the reward for trying in your classroom?

6. Make a list of your effort strategies. These can be shared with your students.

ATTRIBUTION RETRAINING

Types of causal attributions typically given by students to account for success and failure have revealed that attributions can be either adaptive or debilitating to one's future perform- ance. What can be done when students display self-defeating attributions, such as thought patterns and strategies associated with learned helplessness? The most effective approach is known as *attribution retraining*. Retraining generally means an attempt to restructure a student's maladaptive explanations for failure and success to adaptive ones. The desired outcomes are to increase student persistence, positive expectations, and success. A number of different approaches have been developed: effort retraining, self-instruction, and antecedent information. Within these types, Robertson (2000) summarized findings from two approaches for training—direct and indirect. Students make attributional statements to themselves in direct training; a tutor or teacher models statements in indirect training.

Effort and Ability Attribution Retraining

The importance of effort has been a central focus of attribution training. Many of these change programs involve two stages: (a) students achieve success; and (b) following success, students are taught to attribute success to effort.

Attributions to effort are emphasized because effort is internal, controllable, and usually perceived as unstable. In a ground-breaking study, Dweck (1975) carried out training for 12 children identified as *helpless*. Prior to training, all children showed a severe decline in performance following failure. The training experiment involved two conditions: (a) success only where children attained success with no attribution modification; and (b) success where children were taught to take responsibility for failure and attribute it to effort.

The results of the study reveal that children who were taught to attribute failure to insufficient effort continued to persist even after failure on the tasks. The subjects in the success-only treatment did not show any consistent improvement in their persistence after failure. This again explains the expectation pattern shown on Fig. 2.2 (and by Sylvia), where the student continued to have low expectations after experiencing success. The student made no connection between effort and success. Andrews and Debus (1978) modified the training procedures by adding positive reinforcement in the form of verbal praise for attributions to effort. Their results support Dweck's (1975) finding that students who attribute failure to effort persist longer. The authors suggested that systematic reinforcement for effort as given in this study may be used to enhance adaptive attributions.

Other training has provided effort and ability attributions for success. The reason for doing this is that students may value being viewed as "smart" more than as hard workers (Weiner, 1986). In attribution retraining for female students gifted in physics, Ziegler and Heller (2000) provided both ability and effort feedback because these students often underestimated their ability. After 10 weeks of training, the retraining group showed increase in the use of internal attributions and demonstrated more physics knowledge than the control group. The control group, however, showed an increase in helplessness.

Self-Instruction

In another approach to retraining, Reiher and Dembo (1984) taught eighth graders self-instruction procedures to change causal attributions. Students were told to give themselves instructions such as "I really want to do my best effort here" as they performed a task. The training was effective in getting students to attribute success and failure more to internal causes of effort and ability. They also persisted longer in the tasks over time. The authors concluded that the self-instruction procedures used to change attributions are feasible for teachers to use in the classroom. This training is described in Chapter 5.

Antecedent Information

A different approach to attributional training used antecedent information to lead to more adaptive thinking. This approach, in a sense, provides students with possible attributions for success in advance of a learning activity. In one study, college students were given antecedent information, via a videotape, for succeeding in a difficult class (Van Overwalle, Segebarth, & Goldchstein, 1989). In the tape, students who had taken the course previously are seen discussing their learning difficulties, the causes of the difficulties, and how they improved their performance. Students who saw the video models improved more than the control group on both the next exam and all exams the next year. The training was more effective for students who attributed their initial failure to intelligence; it had less impact on those who attributed their failure to strategies. This is the most important factor. By hearing the video models talk about difficulties they experienced and how they improved, the experimental students came to view intelligence as unstable—an adaptive belief. Strategies for providing antecedent attributions are presented in Strategy 2.5.

Strategy 2.5. Establish Antecedent Attributions

- Communicate the expectation that study strategies and effort are the keys for learning (this minimizes unknown or mystery attributions when students say they do not know why they made a low grade). Supply students with strategic attributions when they do not have them for both success and failure.
- Establish a climate for help seeking; one aspect of being smart is knowing when to seek help. If needed, let students practice how to seek help through role-playing or a self-talk script asking teacher for help.
- Establish that all students can learn the particular subject.

Retraining for Students with LD

As noted previously, students with LD often display helplessness and maladaptive styles. Attribution retraining has been directed toward students with LD who display these maladaptive styles (Robertson, 2000; Shelton, Anastopoulos, & Linden, 1985). The most powerful intervention occurs when attribution retraining is combined with cognitive strategy instruction (e.g., memory strategies and reading comprehension strategies such as summarization: Borkowski, 1988).

Borkowski and colleagues have conducted a number of studies to address commonplace learning impairments in memory and reading comprehension of inefficient learners (learners who fail to use strategies when it would be helpful to do so). In one study, students with LD (ages 10–14) received six lessons about both reading summarization strategies and the role of effort in using strategies (Borkowski, Weyhing, & Carr, 1988). There were four groups in the experiment:

1. Reading strategies plus complex attribution (strategies and attributions in two phases; see Fig. 2.3),
2. Reading strategies plus attribution,
3. Attribution control, and
4. Reading strategies control.

FIG. 2.3. Strategies plus attribution.

Groups who received attributional training plus strategies scored significantly better on reading comprehension than the two control groups (about a 50 percent gain compared with 15 percent). The researchers concluded that training students in strategies without simultaneous training in attribution is not effective for students who have lengthy records of poor self-esteem and negative attributional beliefs about the importance of personal control. Furthermore, the authors concluded that it is important to include specific attributional training in each content area. Otherwise students are likely to use the strategies only in the content area where they were trained. Based on a retraining procedure from this study, Fulk and Mastropieri (1990) developed steps for retraining strategies (Table 2.3). Examples of strategies taught included summarizing a passage in reading or solution steps in math.

Guidelines for Attributional Feedback

The goal of attributional feedback is to focus the student on effort (operationalized), strategies, and ability or skill as the reason for success and on lack of effort or strategy use as the cause of failure. Although attributional feedback is an important aspect of retraining, Foote (1999) found that third-grade teachers rarely used it. This may be true for other grades as well.

What factors are important for giving adaptive attributional feedback? "That's great, Julie" does not give Julie specific information about her performance. The important factor is to operationalize effort by linking how the student tried to the improved performance (e.g., "Good job, you now know how to use the web browser to find a source"). There are important considerations

TABLE 2.3

Steps for Attribution/Strategy Training

Step	Strategy
1	Describe the purpose of the new strategy.
2	Describe the important role of effort in attributing outcomes to controllable causes.
3	Provide examples and nonexamples of how the strategy works.
4	Provide models of positive attributions combined with strategy use (e.g., "I got this one right because I used the strategy and tried hard").
5	Have students practice combined strategy–attribution sequence with feedback (e.g., "That's great! You worked hard to use the strategy and got the right answer").
6	Have students do independent practice of strategy with continued monitoring and corrective feedback as needed (e.g., "Remember to attribute your outcomes to your effort plus these steps").
7	Conduct formative evaluation.

Source. From Fulk, B. & Mastropieri (1991), "Training Positive Attitudes: 'I Tried Hard and Did Well.'" *Intervention in School and Clinic, 26*(2), 79–83. Reprinted by permission.

when giving feedback for failure. The type of attribution for failure is very significant in terms of the student's future expectation for success. If the student attributes her failure to "I didn't use the right strategy," she is more likely to be motivated to try again than is the student who believes she failed because "I'm not one of the smart ones." When giving attributional feedback, one must be cautious when assigning lack of effort as the cause of failure. Be sure the task was within the student's zone of proximal development (i.e., their capability of performing with assistance). For instance, "Shannon, I noticed you did not carefully edit your essay and revise. When you attend to this, your essay will be much better." The following are guidelines for attributional feedback:

- Ensure that students believe they have the ability to succeed (Robertson, 2000).
- Use direct approaches in which students give themselves attributional feedback (Robertson, 2000).
- When students indicate that they do not know why they failed, suggest a strategy that will help them accomplish the task and, in turn, attribute success to the strategy.

- Give attributional feedback that links past achievement with effort to promote task involvement, skill development, and self-efficacy. Stressing only future achievement does not have the same effect (Schunk, 1982).
- The sequence in which attributional feedback is given makes a difference. For difficult tasks, the early feedback should be to effort; as skills develop, the feedback should shift to ability (Schunk, 1984b).
- Effort feedback is more productive for underachieving students (Ho & McMurtrie, 1991). Ability feedback may promote confusion for students who believe they lack ability.

Cooperative learning has been found to facilitate more productive attributions. This may be even more effective if students are taught to give attributional feedback to each other. Strategy 2.6 gives ways to practice attributional feedback.

Strategy 2.6. Practice Attributional Feedback

- Providing students (or anyone else) with attributional feedback requires practice. Begin by writing attributional feedback statements for effort, ability, and strategy use for a successful experience, and then for failure. Examples of attributional feedback are:
  - o Effort: "Julie, that's great, you got it right because of the extra practice you did in dividing fractions."
  - o Ability: "Julie, that's great, you really understand how to divide fractions now."
  - o Strategies: "Julie, you got it right because you applied steps in order, then checked your work."

When the Outcome is Failure

- Failure will occur, and the attribution for failure is very important in terms of the student's future expectation for success. If the student attributes her failure to "I didn't use the right strategy," she is more likely to be motivated to try again than is the student who believes she failed because "I'm not one of the smart ones." One must be cautious when assigning lack of effort as the cause of failure. Be sure the task was within the student's zone of proximal development (i.e., her

---

capability of performing with assistance). When students indicate that they do not know why they failed, the teacher can suggest a strategy to be able to accomplish the task and in turn attribute success to the strategy. "Shannon, I noticed you did not carefully edit your essay and revise. When you attend to this, your essay will be much better."

DEVELOPING ADAPTIVE ATTRIBUTIONS

In summary, findings from the studies on attributional training offer possibilities for a set of tools for intervening in some of the most difficult motivational problems. Robertson (2000) questioned why we do not use these tools more often. Strategy 2.1 gave suggestions for collecting attributional information. With this information, a teacher can play a major role in devising strategies to help students develop adaptive attributions, which lead to persistence and higher achievement. This chapter concludes with Strategy 2.7, which has suggestions for helping students develop adaptive attributions.

Strategy 2.7. Developing Adaptive Attributions

Operationalize and Reward Effort

- **Make sure that you and your students have the same perceptions of effort; be in agreement about what *try* means.** Use Exhibit 2.2 to analyze beliefs about effort. At the beginning of the school year, have your students discuss the meaning of *effort* so there is a common agreement on what it means in your classroom.
- **"Take the magic out."** Give them a strategy. Emphasize effort as a strategy that can be developed. Operationalize effort as more than time spent on a task. Examples include specific memory strategies, reading comprehension strategies, practice, and seeking appropriate help.
- **Productive effort.** Help your students differentiate between productive and nonproductive effort. When a student does poorly and says "but I worked so hard," ask her to tell you what she did while working hard.

- **Link effort to outcome.** Establish an evaluation system so effort pays off for the student. An example is to tie student trials and homework to exam grades. Make effort the number of trials. Use feedback that specifies what the student did that led to success or failure. Make sure students see the relationship between homework and test scores.
- **Help students shift their criteria for success and failure from how their peers performed to their own prior performance.** Adolescents especially attribute success and failure to ability. "If you were smart, you would not have to study." Have them keep records of their test scores, and other grades so they can see their own progress.
- **Focus on strategies and effort.** Praise or reinforce mastery attributional patterns. Begin this in the early grades. Use student errors as an opportunity to teach them to handle failure, to adjust strategies, or to apply a stronger effort toward a particular concept.
- **Student responsibility.** If test results are good, get students to say what they did that contributed to the grade; if bad, discuss what they might have done differently. Be sure this relates to a criterion or standard, not a comparison to other students.

Shift Perception of Ability from Stable to Unstable

- **Help students develop attributions that ability is a skill or content that can be learned through instruction, practice, and feedback** (e.g., math, computers, writing, reading, music, and tennis are all areas that one learns).
- **Make students aware that new learning is frequently confusing at first.** In particular, helpless students need to understand this as they are likely to believe they will never understand the new concept or procedure. Show them that learning is acquired in incremental steps. Proximal goals (Chapter 4) and self-talk (Chapter 5) will be useful for this.
- **Have peers model antecedent attributions and coping strategies either through video or audio training.**
- **Collect examples of attributions such as those in Exhibit 2.1 and place them on bulletin boards and/or in student informational material.**

REVIEW OF MAJOR POINTS

1. Attribution is a cognitive theory that considers a person's beliefs about causes of outcomes and how those beliefs influence expectations and behavior. Causes of outcomes include ability, effort, task difficulty, strategies, and luck. Three dimensions are internal–external, stable–unstable, and controllable–uncontrollable.

2. Knowledge of how students use these attributions to account for success and failure in school settings (academic and sports) can help teachers predict the expectancies held by students and plan strategies for intervention when needed.

3. Attributions are influenced by direct and indirect cues. A direct cue is results on a test. Indirect cues may be conveyed by teacher communication—praise and blame, sympathy and anger, and help and neglect—and labels like *high ability, low achieving, slow*, and *average*.

4. Attributional beliefs produce emotional reactions such as pride, shame, hopelessness, guilt, anger, and pity. Attribution to high ability after success often triggers the emotion of pride; a greater sense of hopelessness may be experienced when failure is attributed to ability.

5. Attributions play a role in changing goal expectancies for success and failure. The decisive factor for change in expectancy is the reason given and its stability. Expectancies are more difficult to change when failure is attributed to ability as a stable factor.

6. Attributions for success and failure are related to the cognitive levels of children; younger children see effort and ability as the same and believe increased effort leads to increased ability. As children develop cognitively, they increasingly make distinctions between effort and ability.

7. Gender differences identified in attributions for success and failure include the following: Girls are more likely than boys to attribute failure to their lack of ability, although their achievement is higher, and make more external attributions (luck) for their successes; girls tend to underestimate their performance, whereas boys tend to overestimate performance.

8. Similar attribution patterns have been found among different ethnic groups. A comparison of poor African-American,

Hispanic, Indo-Chinese, and White fifth- and sixth-grade students found that all groups rated ability as the most important factor for success in math. The way in which children, regardless of ethnic group, conceptualize effort and ability is the important issue.

9. Learned helplessness, a consequence of attributional explanations, exists when individuals expect that their actions will be futile in affecting future outcomes. The important aspect of learned helplessness is how it affects the motivational behavior of students in the face of failure. Two patterns of responses to failure were identified: maladaptive–helpless orientation and adaptive–mastery orientation. Mastery students are not discouraged by the initial difficulty, whereas helpless students immediately lose confidence, although they may be equally competent. Students with LD are particularly susceptible to a pattern of learned helplessness because they have experienced much failure over a long period of time on a variety of school tasks.

10. The attributional process is an important factor in whether help seeking is seen as positive or negative. For all grades, the higher the perceived competence of the children, the less they felt there were personal costs to help seeking. Students with low self-esteem were especially unlikely to seek help, whereas individuals with high self-esteem were more likely to seek help. It is important for teachers to emphasize the need to think of help seeking as an adaptive coping strategy rather than as a self-threatening activity.

11. The beliefs that teachers hold about the role of ability and effort affect their responses to their students. Students who do not try evoke the most anger from teachers, whereas students who have low ability but try hard and succeed are likely to be viewed more favorably.

12. Attribution retraining generally means an attempt to restructure a student's maladaptive explanations for failure and success to adaptive ones, with the desired outcome being to increase student persistence and positive expectations. Approaches to attributional retraining include effort retraining, self-instruction, and antecedent information. The most powerful intervention occurs when attribution retraining is combined with cognitive strategy instruction.

Motivational Toolbox

1. Important points to think about and lingering questions

2. Strategies I can use now

3. Strategies I want to develop in the future

CHAPTER 3

Concepts of Ability
and Motivation

Schools must foster . . . a will to learn and to relearn; . . . students must be encouraged to believe in themselves and in the validity of their own thought processes . . . they must develop a sense of personal effectiveness . . . teachers must foster both confidence and high achievement in their students . . . confidence and competence must increase together for either to prosper.

—Covington and Beery (1976, pp. 4–5)

The central concern in this chapter is students' perceptions and evaluations of their ability and how it affects their motivation. In every aspect of life, whether people are thinking about trying out for a play or an athletic team, worrying about taking a test, applying for a job, comparing their capabilities to their peers, or deciding what courses to take, they are evaluating their ability and competence. Wigfield and Eccles (2000) distinguished ability beliefs from expectancies for success: ability beliefs focus on present ability, and expectancies focus on future outcomes. An understanding of perspectives about self-perceptions of ability will assist educators in fostering students' confidence, competence, and adaptive coping skills presently and in the future.

SELF-PERCEPTIONS OF ABILITY:
AN OVERVIEW

Self-perception of ability is a major component of many current perspectives of motivation: perceived competence, expectancy-value, self-efficacy, self-worth, goal orientation (Pajares, 1996), and intrinsic motivation (Connell & Wellborn, 1991). A central influence on perceptions of one's competence is a belief about effort and ability (Paris, Byrnes, & Paris, 2001). Student perception of low ability is a serious motivation problem for educators (Graham & Weiner, 1996) and stems from distorted views about ability and effort (Paris et al., 2001). These beliefs about ability are closely related to the expectancies students have for success on an upcoming task and the values they hold for the task (Bandura, 1986; Meece, Eccles, & Wigfield, 1990). When students believe they can succeed in a task or subject, they are more likely to undertake it and their value for it increases (Bandura, 1986; Mac Iver, Stipek, & Daniels, 1991).

What do we know about developmental trends in ability beliefs? As a general rule, children's beliefs about ability become "more differentiated and complex throughout the childhood years" (Wigfield & Eccles, 2001, p. 2). Young children tend to overestimate their likelihood of success (Stipek & Mac Iver, 1989). This overestimation may be moderated as they grow older and become more realistic. There is some evidence that self-perceptions of academic competence decline with age (Eccles, Wigfield, Harold, & Blumenfeld, 1993). These declines are assumed to be a result of both developmental changes and the classroom environment.

An important question is whether children perceive themselves as equally competent in all areas. The prevalent view today is that children as young as age 8 can differentiate abilities among the domains of cognitive or academic competence, physical competence in sports, social competence with peers, and general competence (Harter, 1982). Self-perceptions of ability are not only domain specific, but also distinct for different subject areas (Bong & R. E. Clark, 1999). For example, students might have a high self-concept of their ability in math, but a low one in language arts (Marsh, Byrne, & Shavelson, 1988).

What are sources of perception of ability? An important source is the information used by individuals to judge their performance. They may use *social comparison* criteria by comparing their performance with that of others or individual criteria (*self-referenced comparison*) comparing their present performance to a previous one. There is also a developmental pattern for comparisons of performance (Dweck, 2001). Dweck pointed out that although young children may be aware of their standing in comparison with others, it has no meaning for them. Older children use more social comparison. In the following sections you will see the differential effects of social comparison and self-referenced criteria on beliefs about ability in positive and negative ways.

The primary focus of this chapter is on social-cognitive perspectives of self-efficacy, self-worth, and achievement goal orientation. In each of these theories, beliefs about ability by teachers and students are central and impact teacher practice and student confidence and effort. To begin this focus, consider the varying beliefs that students in Ms. Foster's science class hold about their capabilities (Fig. 3.1).

The students' competence beliefs may be inferred by their statements and behaviors. All the students made self-evaluations

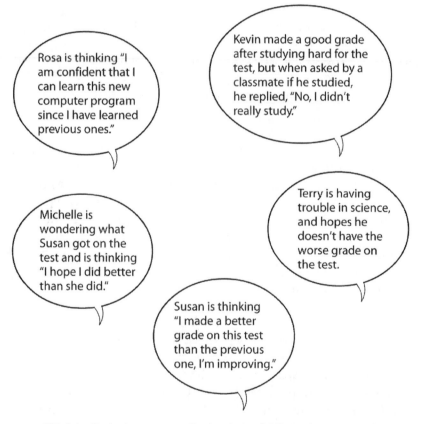

FIG. 3.1.   Student responses reflecting views of ability and competence.

about their competencies or abilities. However, there are important differences in the source of the evaluation and the confidence expressed by each student. Some beliefs will help students improve and succeed in school, whereas others are likely to limit development of their capabilities. Although Ms. Foster is aware of some beliefs, she is unaware of other subtle clues about beliefs with their motivational implications. The perspectives in this chapter will help teachers understand student beliefs about ability, the motivational implications, and practices to cultivate adaptive beliefs. Self-efficacy is the first area explored to better understand beliefs about competence.

SELF-EFFICACY BELIEFS

"Self-efficacy refers to beliefs in one's capabilities to organize and execute the courses of action required to produce given attainments" (Bandura, 1997, p. 3). It is a judgment students make about their capability to accomplish a *specific* future task; as such, it is a strong predictor of student learning regardless of the skills they might possess (Bandura, 1986). A key assumption underlying self-efficacy is that there is a difference between having the skills to perform a task and using the skills in a variety of circumstances. How does this assumption affect motivation?

According to Bandura (1986), there are two types of expectancies in thinking about possible outcomes: outcome expectancy and self-efficacy expectancy. An *outcome expectancy* is an individual's anticipation that a given action can lead to a certain positive or negative outcome ("If I use effective learning strategies, I will make at least a B in the course"). A *self-efficacy expectancy* is a person's judgment of his or her capability to perform the skills, actions, or persistence required for the given outcome ("Will I be able to use the learning strategies needed to make a B in the course?"). The most influential factor is the efficacy expectancy—how effective will *I* be? Beliefs of personal efficacy are the fundamental element of agency—actions carried out with intent. They regulate choice, behavior, effort, and persistence.

Self-efficacy judgments are important factors affecting motivation in areas ranging from academic tasks to career choice to athletic performance. It differs from self-concept and self-esteem which are more general judgments of expectations. Self-efficacy judgments are more domain, task, and context specific rather than general (Bong, 2002; Pajares & M. D. Miller, 1994). That is, self-efficacy in reading is not likely to predict self-efficacy in using the Internet.

Self-efficacy may also reflect a social judgment of confidence or collective efficacy, as well as an individual one. Bandura (1997) defined *collective efficacy* as "a group's shared belief in its conjoint capabilities to organize and execute the courses of action necessary to produce given levels of attainment" (p. 477). In a collective task, group members hold beliefs about the capability of the group as a whole to be successful, as well as beliefs about their personal capability. This may pertain to the beliefs of teachers in a school as a whole, students in a cooperative learning task, or athletic teams. More effective groups will have a strong sense of collective efficacy.

Self-Efficacy Influences in Academic Tasks

Self-efficacy judgments, whether accurate or inaccurate, help determine (a) which activities to undertake and which to avoid, and (b) how much effort we will expend and how long we will persist in the face of obstacles (Bandura, 1986). We are more likely to undertake tasks we believe we have the skills to handle, but avoid tasks we believe require greater skills than we possess. For example, students who have doubts about their math ability are likely to avoid taking math courses whenever possible. In addition, the stronger the self-efficacy, the harder individuals will try to accomplish a task. This is particularly important when facing difficulties (Bandura, 1986). Individuals with strong self-efficacy are less likely to give up than are those who are paralyzed with doubts about their capabilities.

A study conducted by Collins (cited in Bandura, 1993) illustrates how the belief one holds about ability influences strategies. Collins selected children at low, medium, and high levels of math ability and gave them hard problems to solve. In each ability group, there were children who were confident about their math ability and those who had self-doubts. Children's beliefs about their capability, not their actual ability, proved to be the factor that differentiated the problem-solving strategies used by children in each group. Confident children chose to rework more problems and were quicker to abandon ineffective strategies than were children who had doubts about ability. In fact, perceived self-efficacy was a better predictor of positive attitudes toward mathematics than was actual ability. This confirmed that self-efficacy is not just a reflection of one's ability, but the beliefs one holds about that ability.

Similarly, Bouffard-Bouchard, Parent, and Larivee (1991) found that, regardless of grade level (the sample included junior and senior high school students) or cognitive ability, self-efficacy was more apparent than cognitive competence. As Bandura (1993) pointed out, people may perform poorly either because (a) they lack the skills, or (b) they have the skills, but lack the confidence that will allow them to use them well.

The level of self-efficacy is a key aspect in self-regulatory strategies used by students. Examples of research findings are:

- Students with higher self-efficacy set higher goals and expend more effort toward the achievement of these goals (Zimmerman, Bandura, & Martinez-Pons, 1992).
- Academic self-efficacy increases in subject areas as students progress through school (Zimmerman & Martinez-Pons, 1990).
- Students with higher self-efficacy use more cognitive and metacognitive strategies and persist longer (Pintrich & De Groot, 1990).
- Students with higher self-efficacy undertook more difficult math tasks (Bandura & Schunk, 1981).
- Self-efficacy was related to junior high school students' confidence in using the Internet (Joo, Bong, & Choi, 2001).
- The level of self-efficacy that students reported during their first year of college was a powerful predictor of their expectations, overall satisfaction, and performance (Chemers, Hu, & Garcia, 2001).

Is there an optimal level of efficacy beliefs? Bandura (1986) suggested that the most useful efficacy judgments are those that are slightly above what a person can perform on a specific task.

Sources of Self-Efficacy Judgments

What sources of information influence people's beliefs about their capabilities? Beliefs about capabilities come from four sources of information: prior task accomplishments, vicarious experiences (observing others), verbal persuasion, and physiological states (Bandura, 1997). It is not the source per se but the individual's evaluation of the information. These sources are not equally influential. They are described in order of their power to influence self-efficacy (see Fig. 3.2).

Prior Task Accomplishments

Remember the students' thoughts at the beginning of the chapter? Rosa is confident that she can learn a new computer program because she was successful at learning one previously. This is an example of self-efficacy that is based on her personal experience—a successful task performance in the past. Personal experience is the most influential source of efficacy information because it is direct evidence of whether one can do whatever it takes to succeed. It follows then that successes tend to raise efficacy expectations, whereas failures tend to lower them. However, the source itself is not the direct influence on efficacy, but how the person interprets the experience (Bandura, 1997). It is especially detrimental to one's sense of confidence if failure occurs early in the learning experience unless it is attributed to an internal-unstable factor, such as lack of effort.

Vicarious Experiences

A second source of self-efficacy beliefs comes from a vicarious experience, such as observing the performance of others.

FIG. 3.2. Sources of self-efficacy beliefs.

Although a vicarious experience is not as powerful as a previous successful performance, seeing a model is especially useful when individuals have limited skills or are attempting to learn a new skill. Students observing a model successfully perform in a threatening situation are more likely to develop an expectation that they can acquire the same skill. Not only is the model demonstrating the skill, but he or she is also demonstrating coping strategies, such as persistence or trying several ways to attack the same problem (Schunk & Hanson, 1985). Live models as well as video or audio models can be used to provide vicarious learning. In this context, students are using a social comparison judgment as an adaptive source of information about their competence.

Verbal Persuasion

"You can do it." How many times have you heard those encouraging words when attacking a new problem? Verbal persuasion is most effective when people already have some degree of evidence that they are capable. Although telling a student "you can do it" is a widely used strategy, the effect on increasing efficacy expectations is likely to be weaker than feedback that comes from direct or vicarious experience. In other words, telling students they can learn to write is not as influential as the direct experience of successfully writing an essay. Note that both positive and negative messages effect a sense of efficacy. However, negative messages have an even greater influence on lowering efficacy expectations than positive messages do on increasing efficacy (Bandura, 1986).

Physiological State

People also get information about their competence from the physiological responses of their bodies. Physical symptoms such as sweating or rapid heart rate may provide clues about efficacy (Schunk, 1989). Think about the last time you stood up to make a presentation. Too much anxiety in approaching a task may lead to either avoiding the presentation or negative thinking about your possible performance. Anxiety can interfere with perceptions of self-efficacy; this, in turn, interferes with performance.

These four sources of self-efficacy may interact as Smith (2001) found in a study of sources of influence on computer efficacy. A notable finding was that self-efficacy influences differed according to gender and ethnicity. Task accomplishment experiences were most significant for White male students and vicarious experiences were the most powerful influence for female students and non-Whites. In a study of students entering middle school, Usher and Pajares (2006) found verbal persuasion was a stronger influence than mastery for females and for African Americans.

How can knowing about sources of self-efficacy help teachers? Pajares and Schunk (2002) argued, "Teachers should pay as much attention to students' self-beliefs as to actual competence, for it is the belief that may more accurately predict students' motivation and achievement" (p. 18). Knowing the types of knowledge that students use for information about their capabilities can help teachers provide appropriate feedback and devise strategies to support and enhance students' self-efficacy. Remember what students *think* they can do is a better indicator of successful achievement than their actual ability.

Development of Self-Efficacy

The origins of self-efficacy are rooted in mastery experiences provided by parents and caregivers. Parents who have a high sense of efficacy are more likely to construct environments that are favorable for children's development (Bandura, Barbaranelli, Caprara, & Pastorelli, 1996). These experiences begin with actions by the infant followed by recognition that an action (e.g., striking a mobile and seeing it move) produces an outcome (Bandura, 1997). The child's developing self-efficacy, in turn, influences the parents' self-efficacy. Throughout the school years, as children learn and develop skills, their self-efficacy tends to increase (Schunk & Pajares, 2002). Older students express a higher sense of efficacy than younger ones.

But if the child begins school without a positive sense of self-efficacy, what can teachers and schools do? How can teachers use self-efficacy knowledge to strengthen motivation and achievement?

Identification and Awareness of Efficacy Beliefs

Pajares and Miller (1994) believed that identifying, understanding, and altering students' inaccurate efficacy beliefs will provide teachers with insight about student motivation that goes beyond teachers' awareness of students' prior knowledge of a subject. Teaching strategies that flow from this awareness of student efficacy can enhance self-efficacy and increase student achievement.

Students who come to school prepared cognitively and motivationally learn quickly, and schools serve them well (Bandura, 1997). However, students enter learning situations with different beliefs about their capabilities (Schunk, 1989). Are there areas where students' judgments of capability are consistently low or underestimated? Yes, mathematics is one area where beliefs about capability are influential. Researchers consistently find that female students have lower self-efficacy in mathematics than male students (Pajares & Miller, 1994; Randhawa, Beamer, & Lundberg, 1993). Pajares and Miller pointed out that actual ability in mathematics does not correspond to what undergraduate students believe about their capability. Instead of making choices on actual ability, students' beliefs about their capability are a critical factor in making career choices, as well as asking questions such as "Will my major field require math?" and "Will my teaching field specialty be math?" and making statements like "I will be an elementary teacher because I know a lot of math won't be required."

Special education students as a group have consistently exhibited a low sense of self-efficacy. For example, Gresham, Evans, and Elliott (1988) found that, when self-efficacy comparisons were made among mildly handicapped, nonhandicapped, and gifted children, mildly handicapped children experienced lower academic achievement and social self-efficacy than nonhandicapped and gifted children. Lakaye, Margalit, Ziv, and Ziman (2006) found that seventh-grade students with learning disabilities (LD) reported lower self-efficacy perceptions than non-LD students. Gresham (1984) explained that this persistent finding of low self-efficacy among mildly handicapped children is due to the history of academic and social failures they have experienced. Hampton and Mason (2003) found that LD students had less access to the sources of self-efficacy (e.g., task accomplishment) that contributed to the lower self-efficacy perceptions.

Becoming aware of low self-efficacy leads to the next step: What can teachers do to promote self-efficacy of students?

Strengthening Self-Efficacy

What is known about strengthening self-efficacy? A range of strategies that can be used by teachers to enhance self-efficacy has been identified (Schunk, 1991). Strategies that teachers can use to influence self-efficacy include (a) goals and feedback, (b) rewards, (c) self-instruction for verbalization of strategies, (d) participant modeling, and (e) various combinations of these strategies. Keep in mind that self-efficacy, skill development, and strategy use go hand in hand—whether it be math problem solving, soccer skills, or expository writing. Students learn strategies that enable them to develop skills resulting in increased self-efficacy.

Goals, Feedback, Rewards, and Verbalization

Because task accomplishment is the most powerful source of self-efficacy information, an important approach is to use strategies that can strengthen task accomplishment. The strategies of goal setting, feedback, rewards, and self-talk or verbalization were used in various combinations to help students categorized as LD or remedial to strengthen self-efficacy.

Schunk and Cox (1986) investigated the combination of strategy verbalization and effort feedback on the performance and self-efficacy of students with LD. While solving subtraction problems, students verbalized or said the task steps aloud to themselves; they were then given feedback that their successes were due to their effort. The combination of verbalization and effort feedback led to problem-solving successes, higher self-efficacy, and subtraction skills. The authors believed that the two strategies—verbalization and effort feedback—serve different purposes. Verbalization was useful for training students to systematically use the task strategy. Giving students feedback that effort is responsible for success communicated attributional feedback that they are developing skills and that they can continue to perform well with hard work.

A teacher may sometimes overlook the importance of feedback for enhancing self-efficacy. Pajares and Johnson (1994) conducted a study in a language arts course for preservice teachers. The students received feedback from their teacher on attempting and completing writing tasks, but they did not receive feedback on their specific writing skills. The end of course assessment revealed that, although the students improved on writing skills, their self-efficacy judgments about their skills did not increase. The authors concluded that, when teachers note a growth or decline in skills (in this case, writing), it is imperative for them to give the students feedback about their specific skill development. As emphasized earlier, students will make future judgments not just on their actual skills, but also on their perception of their competence in using the skill. These perceptions of self-efficacy are more likely to increase with specific teacher feedback.

Participant Modeling

Vicarious experience is the second most powerful source of self-efficacy. The most frequent form of vicarious experience for students is seeing a model (another student or teacher) perform a skill they are attempting to learn. Which is a more effective model: a peer or teacher, or a mastery or coping, model?

Peer or Teacher Model? Schunk and Hanson (1985) had students, ages 8 to 10, observe either a peer or teacher model solving fractions on a videotape. Children who had observed a peer model had higher self-efficacy and achievement scores on the math assessment than did students who had observed the teacher model. The authors concluded that the increase may have been because the children saw themselves as more similar to the peer model. The use of peer models is especially recommended for enhancement of self-efficacy among low-achieving students who are more doubtful about attaining the level of competence demonstrated by the teacher.

Mastery or Coping Model? Which model do you think will be more effective in strengthening self-efficacy: an expert who demonstrates at a high level of expertise or one who is competent, but demonstrates the strategies they used to acquire the skill? Previous research found that observers' beliefs about competence are influenced by their perceived similarity in competence to the model (e.g., Zimmerman & Ringle, 1981). Models can reflect either mastery or coping behaviors (Schunk & Hanson, 1985; Schunk, Hanson, & Cox, 1987). A *mastery* model demonstrates a task at a high level of expertise with a high level of confidence. In contrast, a *coping* model demonstrates the task along with the difficulties students experienced and the strategies (e.g., effort) they used to overcome the difficulties. Schunk et al. (1987) compared the effectiveness of coping versus mastery peer models. The two types of models demonstrated strategies as follows:

1. Peer coping model: Made errors at first and verbalized negative statements that reflected self-efficacy (e.g., "I'm not sure I can do this"). The teacher then gave a prompt (e.g., "What do you do when denominators are the same?"). Next, the coping model made statements about how they overcame failure (e.g., "I need to pay attention to what I'm doing") and eventually performed at a mastery level.
2. Peer mastery models: Performed all problems correctly while working at average rate. Verbalized high self-efficacy and ability (e.g., "I'm good at this." "That was easy.").

The findings indicated that the subjects judged themselves as more similar to the peer coping model. Students who observed the peer coping model demonstrated higher self-efficacy for learning, and greater posttest self-efficacy and skill development, compared with those who observed a peer mastery model.

Modeling is a resource that is readily available in the classroom. This is a case of positive social comparisons with others (Schunk, 2001). The important implication for teachers is to use caution in choosing peer models. An alert, sensitive teacher can identify appropriate peer coping models in their classrooms and use them to strengthen the self-efficacy of many students.

Using Self-Efficacy in the Classroom

Pajares (1996, 2006) reminded us that there is no kit for enhancing self-efficacy. Nevertheless, the research findings provide teachers with resources to (a) promote efficacy of all students, and (b) target students where low self-efficacy is apparent. The first step in using self-efficacy is to gather information about students' judgments of their competence. Zimmerman and Martinez-Pons (1990) suggested that self-efficacy measures can be used to better understand students with little motivation, as well as to identify areas of student giftedness. Strategy 3.1 suggests ways to gather information about student competence and strategies to enhance self-efficacy.

Strategy 3.1. Developing Self-Efficacy

Use of Models

- **Choose peer models carefully.** It is important to choose a peer who can be an effective coping model to highlight the importance of persistence and strategy use. Also be alert for influential students who spontaneously present themselves as mastery models. Ask them questions about how they worked out difficulties to elicit the coping strategies they might have used.
- **Act as a coping model.** Although as a teacher, coach, or parent one might easily be a mastery model, act as a coping model instead. For example, a ninth-grade writing teacher modeled beginning expository writing by composing a draft of an essay on an unfamiliar topic. She then put her draft on a transparency to demonstrate for her students the beginning stages of process writing.
- **Share self-efficacy stories.** Write a self-efficacy story about how your self-efficacy beliefs helped you overcome a setback or failure. Have students write or tell self-efficacy stories.
- **Estimating the strength of student self-efficacy.** A scale developed specifically for the task in mind can easily assess self-efficacy strength. Gathering this information is especially important in areas where low self-efficacy is likely, such as female students and mathematics, or when teaching a difficult

topic. The following scale, with an example, is adapted from Bandura and Schunk (1981).

On a scale ranging from 1 to 100, rate how sure you are that you can write a one-page document on a word processor and print it out.

Not sure at all   Very sure
1 — 10 — 20 — 30 — 40 — 50 — 60 — 70 — 80 — 90 — 100

- **Attributional feedback.** One of the most important methods to increase self-efficacy is feedback to students that indicates that they are making progress on specific skills or strategy use. Think back to the previous chapter on attributions. Feedback about effort and strategies is more likely to increase self-efficacy. "Charles, the effort you showed by restudying the words you missed paid off. Look at your improvement."
- **Strategy use.** Teach students specific strategies for remembering, comprehending, and problem solving. Link subsequent improvement to the specific strategies used by the student.
- **Goal setting.** Encourage students to set specific goals then compare present performance to their present goal. When they see they have improved, it is likely to increase their sense of self-efficacy (Schunk, 1989). See Chapter 4 for more explicit guidelines on goal setting.
- **Rewards.** Rewards increase self-efficacy when they are tied to specific accomplishments (Schunk, 1989).
- **Teacher self-efficacy.** Teacher beliefs in their own competence to make a difference in student learning influences student self-efficacy. Teacher self-efficacy is addressed in Chapter 6 as teacher efficacy.

We have seen that self-efficacy beliefs about confidence to achieve a task are important motivationally, influencing whether students will attempt a task and the amount of effort and persistence involved in completing the task. The following two sections, self-worth theory and achievement goal orientation, explain two other perspectives of judging ability and the influence on motivation.

REFLECTION. Think about a self-efficacy story in your life—a story about how beliefs in your own capability helped you to accomplish a goal or overcome a setback. How can you use it to remind yourself of your own motivational resiliency?

SELF-WORTH THEORY: SELF-PROTECTION OF PERCEIVED ABILITY

Another perspective on perception of ability and its influence is the self-worth motive. This motive is based on the premise that a central part of all classroom achievement is the need for students to maintain a positive image of their ability (Covington, 1992). In our society one's self-worth is often equated with one's accomplishments (Covington, 1998). Students often believe that ability is the primary element for achieving success and lack of ability is the primary reason for failure. Their motive then becomes one of avoiding failure and protecting their self-worth from the perception that they have low ability. They do this by the use of self-defeating strategies that follow. This self-protective motive is more prevalent during adolescence.

Attributional explanations are important components for the self-protection of ability. When students attribute a failure to putting forth little effort, the attributions serve to protect them from the explanation that they failed because of low ability (J. Brown & Weiner, 1984). This explains why Kevin, after making a good grade, claimed he did not study, when, in fact, he did. Kevin believes that if people were aware that he had to study to receive a good grade, they might think that he lacked ability. For students who believe success is unlikely, the main priority is to avoid failure that is linked or attributed to ability through the use of failure-avoiding strategies (Covington, 1992; Covington & Beery, 1976).

Classroom Practices and Self-Worth Protection

The negative motivation patterns of failure avoidance are often fostered by school and classroom practices. Perhaps the most prevalent practice is the competitive learning game (Covington,

1992). The *competitive learning game* refers to situations that force students to compete with one another for grades and rewards. The following are classroom practices that force students to play the competitive game:

- offering insufficient rewards that force students to compete or give up;
- rewarding student ability without considering effort;
- basing grades on how each student compares to other students; and
- grouping students according to abilities.

These practices are damaging to students who believe that ability reflects their self-worth.

Failure-Avoidance Strategies

What are the failure-avoidance strategies used by students to protect themselves from the perceptions of others that they have low ability? Three broad categories are low effort, self-handicapping, and guarantee of success.

Low Effort

The most common way to avoid perceptions of low ability is to use low-effort explanations. Low effort is demonstrated in behaviors such as false effort and nonparticipation (Covington, 1992). These behaviors may seem logical to the student, but may seem irrational to a teacher or parent. However, they must be recognized as strategies—strategies to protect themselves from the appearance of low ability.

Self-worth theory helps explain why students may not try, which is one of the most frustrating problems for teachers. If a student tries hard (spends extra time studying for a test) and then fails, the danger is the belief that he or she lacks ability. This allows students to protect their self-esteem by denying that they tried hard and rationalizing that if they really did try they would succeed. Tactics they might use to maintain this illusion of trying are as follows:

- false effort such as pretending to understand by answering only easy questions;
- trying to avoid the teacher's attention by keeping their eyes or heads down; and
- avoiding any work not absolutely required (Covington, 1992).

Effort has been called the *double-edged sword* (Covington & Omelich, 1979). This means that "students must exert some effort to avoid teacher punishment and personal feelings of guilt, but not so much effort as to risk incompetency-linked humiliation should they try hard and fail anyway" (Covington, 1984, p. 10). Students are often confused by teachers' contradictory responses to effort. On the one hand, teachers value and reinforce effort. On the other hand, when teachers are asked to predict which students will learn the most, they view ability, not effort, as the most important factor. Although these strategies may protect students from negative judgments of their ability by others, it is likely to sabotage their performance in the long run.

Self-Handicapping

Another group of failure-avoiding strategies are known as self-handicapping behaviors. These are behaviors or thoughts that occur prior to or simultaneously with the activity and interfere with performance (Urdan & Midgley, 2003). These provide self-protective excuses for failure in advance. The forms of self-handicapping behaviors described are: procrastination, unattainable goals, underachieving, and academic wooden leg.

Procrastination is when students irrationally put things off without good reason for a delay (Covington, 1992). This provides students with the excuse that "Because I studied at the last minute, I can't be blamed for failure" (i.e., "at least my ability can't be blamed"). Procrastination may take the form of (a) last-minute studying, (b) staying busy with little to show for it, (c) collecting resources for a project but never starting it or delaying starting it, or (d) undertaking many activities but not allowing sufficient time for any of them.

Unattainable goals is another failure-avoiding strategy (Covington, 1992; Covington & Beery, 1976). Covington and Omelich

(1979) pointed out that setting unattainable goals allows students to "fail with honor" (p. 170). Such failure does not imply low ability. For example, if a student is taking 15 credits, holding down a 30-hour-a-week job, and aspiring to make all As, it is no reflection on ability if he or she fails—no one else could have done this.

Students classified as *underachievers* tend to avoid testing their ability by refusing to work. They take a sense of pride in their unwillingness to achieve and minimize the importance of work (Covington, 1992). Mike Rose (1989) described a powerful example of this phenomenon in the autobiographical account of his experience when he was mistakenly assigned to a vocational tracked classroom:

> Ken said, "I just wanna be average." . . . That woke me up. Average! . . . Who wants to be average? . . . Ken Harvey was gasping for air. . . . If you're a working class kid in vocational track, options in dealing with complexities of school will be constrained in certain ways. You're defined by your school as "slow"; you're placed in a curriculum that isn't designed to liberate you but to occupy you or if you are lucky train you, though the training is for work the society does not esteem. What Ken and so many others do is protect themselves from such suffocating madness by taking on with a vengeance the identity implied in the vocational track. Reject the confusion and frustration by openly defining yourself as the "Common Joe." Champion the average. . . . The tragedy is you have to twist the knife in your own grey matter to make this defense work.
>
> (pp. 28–29)

Academic wooden leg occurs when students publicly admit to minor weaknesses to protect themselves from greater imagined weaknesses (Covington, 1992). This may be seen when a student claims he or she has test-taking anxiety because appearing anxious is preferable to appearing stupid.

Guarantee of Success

Three strategies students may use to guarantee success are overstriving, cheating, and goals that are too easy. *Overstriving* as a self-protective strategy may not seem apparent and, at first glance, may be viewed as positive. An overstriver's behavior is driven by hope and fear, resulting in a tendency toward perfectionism. According to Covington and Omelich (1987), although students are successful, they are fearful of failing.

Because self-worth and ability are intertwined in the minds of some students, a competitive situation will often activate the strategy of cheating. Covington and Beery (1976) reported the following examples of this type of self-protection of ability from elementary school students who cheated:

- I know someone who studies hard for tests and cheats too. They feel really bad but it is better than being yelled at for bad grades (p. 55).
- People cheat because they are afraid of doing poorer than other kids and feeling miserable for being different and behind. Some do it to be the best in the class or to move to the next group (p. 55).

Setting goals so easy that one cannot fail is a strategy to guarantee success. This occurs when students continue to choose tasks they have already mastered or lower their expectations. An example is the student who is making Bs saying before taking an exam, "I just hope I pass."

Self-Worth, Failure-Avoiding Strategies, and Minority Students

For minority students, the focus on ability to achieve in school may bring other risks to perceptions of ability. Claude Steele (1992) first described the special risk faced by African-American students as vulnerability to racial stereotypes that leads to disidentification with school—a risk that entails double jeopardy. For African Americans, a low grade on a test might simply reflect incompetence in the subject. However, the low grade can be used by others to confirm a broader inferiority related to ethnicity or culture. Steele (1997) extended this explanation for self-worth protection to other categories of students in areas where there are stereotypic images, such as female math students. Students who are vulnerable to stereotypic judgments may resist the values and goals of school. For example, they might shift their basis for self-worth to other areas, such as peer relations. An example is the finding by Hare (1985) that the source of self-esteem for African-American boys depended more on peer relations than on school achievement.

What is it that contributes to this disidentification with schools and academic success? Steele (1992) explained that a major factor is the prevalence of images in society that lead to a devaluation of race—a devaluation based not necessarily on racism, but on images that do not give a full portrait of the African-American influence in U.S. society. This may be done in subtle ways. For example, teachers may fail to appreciate the best work or talent of a student. Steele described the case of Jerome to illustrate devaluation by teachers. As a third grader, Jerome showed exceptional talent in art. However, as Jerome moved to higher grades, teachers made little mention of his talent. As a consequence, Jerome acts as if he does not care about his unrecognized talent. By not acknowledging his artistic talent, he is less vulnerable to the possibility that it will not be valued—a form of self-protection.

Steele (1992, 1997) identified several guidelines to address failure avoidance in minority students:

- Make students feel they are valued and that their culture is valued. Include minority experience in the mainstream curriculum, not limiting it just to separate programs or special times of the year.
- Stress that there are multiple intelligences or capabilities in school.
- Challenge students without overwhelming them by taking into account their present skill levels and pacing them so the challenge is achievable.
- Communicate to students that they belong in school and profess your belief in the potential of the student.
- Know the student beneath the stereotype.

Although Steele suggested these strategies for African-American students, they are useful for all students. Identification and disidentification with school for minority students are further discussed in Chapter 7.

ACHIEVEMENT GOAL ORIENTATION

Achievement goal orientation offers another perspective on how beliefs about personal competence or ability affect motivation.

Achievement goal theory integrates cognitive beliefs and emotions that focus on the underlying purpose for achieving a goal and, as such, can be adaptive or maladaptive (Dweck, 1986, 1992). This is distinguished from goal-setting content, such as a goal to make the soccer team, which is the subject of Chapter 4. Consider the responses of three students, Chandra, Latrell, and Stephanie, who are preparing a speech to be presented in class:

> Chandra is thinking, "I've always been self-conscious about speaking in public and this presentation will give me a chance to see if I'm ready for our final evaluation." Latrell, on the other hand, is thinking, "After this presentation, everyone will see that I'm the best speaker." Stephanie is thinking, "I just hope my presentation is not the worse one in class and the teacher gives me a C."

Each student's statement reflects an underlying goal and definition of success that implies a belief about how this upcoming task might reflect on their ability (Molden & Dweck, 2000). What are these belief patterns? How will they differentially affect beliefs and behaviors such as effort, help seeking, engagement, self-efficacy, interest anxiety, and response to mistakes? How does the classroom context affect the underlying purpose for a goal?

Types of Achievement Goal Orientations

Initially, two general classes of goal orientation in an achievement situation were identified (learning and performance goals). Based on recent theory and research, performance goals have been expanded to two types, performance approach and performance avoidance (e.g., Elliot, 1999; Elliot & Harackiewicz, 1996; Pintrich, 2000b). The original goal models were distinguished as:

- learning and performance goals (Dweck, 1986, 1992; Dweck & Leggett, 1988; Dweck & Sorich, 1999, respectively),
- mastery and performance goals (C. Ames, 1992; C. Ames & Archer, 1988, respectively), and
- task-involved and ego-involved goals (Nicholls, 1983, 1990, respectively).

For simplification, the terms *learning* and *performance* are used in this text.

In one sense, the two classes of goals were described as "seeking to prove one's competence versus seeking to improve one's competence" (Dweck, 1992, p. 165). Based on recent theory and research, the classes of goals have now been expanded to three with two types of performance goals: performance approach and performance avoidance (e.g., Elliot, 1999; Elliot & Harackiewicz, 1996; Pintrich, 2000b). Although the terms describing the goal orientation patterns from these goal theorists differ, there is a basic agreement on the nature of the goals (Pintrich & Schunk, 2002; Urdan, 1997). What are the distinguishing patterns of the classes of goals?

Learning Goals

Students with a personal *learning goal* pattern are seeking to understand the material they are learning, master a skill, and increase their competence through their own effort. Their judgment of ability is more likely to focus on their improvement from a previous performance or the use of a standard or target goal as a criterion for evaluating their progress. Chandra's response in the previous example reflects a learning goal orientation. A learning goal is more likely to be associated with positive educational outcomes such as task engagement and an intrinsic value for learning (e.g., C. Ames, 1992; Elliot, 1999; Linnenbrink & Pintrich, 2002; Meece, 1991). As an adaptive motivation, it also provides resiliency in the face of failure (Grant & Dweck, 2003; Molden & Dweck, 2000).

Performance Goals

Performance goals are less straightforward than learning goals in their effects on student outcomes. As a general rule, students with a *performance goal* pattern are more concerned with their ability, how their performance compares to others, and extrinsic incentives (Anderman, Austin, & Johnson, 2001). Attributions for success are more likely to focus on their ability, not effort. As stated previously, however, performance goal orientation has been expanded to include both approach and avoidance goals. In either case, one's judgment of competence is based on comparisons with the performance of others (Pintrich, 2000a).

With a *performance approach*, the students' concerns are about the extent to which they appear as competent (to look smart, like Latrell). The goal for students with a *performance avoidance* orientation is to protect themselves from the perception that they have low ability similar to self-worth protection (not looking incompetent, like Stephanie). The research consistently indicates that performance avoidance goals are maladaptive (E. Anderman & Wolters, 2006).

Although the performance approach is more adaptive for learning than is performance avoidance, can performance-approach goals have a positive effect on motivation and learning? The research findings are less clear and the debate continues (E. Anderman & Wolters, 2006). Positive findings were found among college students under conditions of comparative grading. However, a performance approach focused on comparisons with others can have negative effects on involvement due to distractions related to anxiety or negative judgments of self (Brophy, 2005; Pintrich, 2000b).

Can one have both a learning goal and a performance goal? The answer is yes. The two goal orientations are not mutually exclusive (e.g., Pintrich, 2000a). A person can be motivated to learn and perform. The deterrent to motivation occurs when the concern for performance is stronger than the concern for learning or mastery. Pintrich (2000b) pointed out that two students can have the same target and achieve at the same level, but with different side effects. Midgley, Kaplan, and Middleton (2001) concluded, regardless of level of emphasis on performance goals, more energy should be focused on enhancing mastery goals. Characteristics of performance and learning goal orientations toward academic tasks are shown in Table 3.1.

Influences on Achievement Goals

What influences whether students are more likely to approach a task with a learning or a performance goal orientation? The particular goal that a student is pursuing can be influenced by the personal theory of intelligence held by the student or by contextual influences such as classroom structure.

TABLE 3.1
Contrasting Goal Orientations

Characteristic	Learning/Mastery	Performance/Ego
Value of learning	Has an intrinsic value for learning in itself. Goal to increase learning.	Learning is not an end in itself. Focus on looking smart.
Ability/competence	Effort attributions. Increases with effort.	Is seen as one's capacity, attributions to ability most frequent.
Error/failure	Learns from mistakes.	Doubts ability.
Feedback	Used to judge progress.	Used to compare performance with another.
Strategies	Cognitive and metacognitive.	Surface/rote.
Challenge	Seeks challenge.	Avoids risk taking and challenge.

Source. From C. Ames and Archer (1988), Dweck and Leggett (1988), and Nicholls (1983, 1990).

Theory of Intelligence

The theory of intelligence, entity or incremental, held by students influences whether a performance or learning goal is adopted (Dweck & Leggett, 1988; Elliott & Dweck, 1988; Molden & Dweck, 2000). According to this explanation, some individuals believe that intelligence is "something you have"—an entity. Other people believe intelligence is incremental and malleable, continuing to develop as one gains skills and knowledge. Stipek and Gralinski (1996) found that children with an entity belief also believe that levels of intelligence and performance are stable over time. Children with an entity view are more likely to pursue a performance goal, protecting their ability or demonstrating that they are smart. This can be particularly maladaptive when a child fails and attributes it to low ability. In contrast, children who have an incremental view of ability are more likely to adopt a learning goal focus with an emphasis on developing their ability (Dweck & Leggett, 1988; Dweck & Sorich, 1999). High effort is believed to increase ability; in contrast to performance goals, however, high effort often means one lacks ability. The teacher's role in beliefs about intelligence will be addressed in Chapter 6.

Does this mean there are no ability differences? Nicholls (1989) pointed out that, although children are aware of each other's competencies, it is a motivation problem only when there is a performance/ego-involvement focus. Children should learn, and teachers should keep in mind, that differences in ability should not be interpreted as superiority of the person with higher ability. The important understanding is that beliefs about intelligence facilitate or limit success in all academic subjects (Stipek & Gralinski, 1996).

REFLECTION.   In the previous chapter, Exhibit 2.2 asked you to compare your views about the importance of effort and ability. How did you judge these? Do you see contradictions in your beliefs? Are they related to your views of intelligence?

Classroom Contextual Influences

To what extent do classroom contextual factors affect personal goal orientations? Nicholls (1990) found that student conceptions of ability are influenced by the cues in a given classroom situation. The structure of a classroom and messages conveyed by teachers are the cues that influence whether a student might have more of a learning goal or a performance goal (C. Ames, 1992; Meece, 1991; Pintrich, 2000b; Turner et al., 2002). Classroom dimensions that convey messages about the purpose and meaning of achievement include teacher expectations for learning, what is rewarded, the type of feedback and evaluations, how students are grouped, and the extent to which students have opportunities for decisions.

Linnenbrink (2005) set up three goal contexts (mastery, performance approach, and combined mastery–performance approach) to compare the influence on students' motivation and behaviors. The students were in upper elementary classrooms engaged in mathematics group work. Teachers in each goal condition were given guidelines for the particular goal conditions. Goal orientation was assessed before the intervention and five weeks later. The conditions appeared to influence the goal orientations; students in mastery condition had higher master scores and those in performance approach had higher performance. Linnenbrink concluded that the classroom environment can influence student goal orientation.

TABLE 3.2
Context Factors that Contribute to a Learning Goal Environment

Classroom Structure or Message	Example
Opportunities to develop an increased sense of competence	Made sure that students not only had basic understanding in the content, but also developed competencies in other areas
Opportunities for self-directed learning	Helped students evaluate their own work; transferred responsibility to students as they gained competence
Emphasis on expectations and intrinsic value of learning	Emphasized the value and interest, and application, of what students are learning, and expected that all students would learn
Opportunities for cooperation and collaboration	Group work with emphasis on working together effectively and on helping each other
Ability/effort messages	Recognized progress; allowed students to retake test for improvement

Source.   From Meece (1991) and Turner et al. (2002).

It is not likely that a classroom structure is pure performance or learning goal oriented. Context factors of classrooms that contribute to a learning goal environment are shown in Table 3.2. Keep in mind that it is not just the classroom structure and the messages, but the students' perceptions, that determine the type of goal environment.

Goal Orientation Effects on Student Cognition and Behaviors

Research indicates that the particular goal orientations held by students is associated with a variety of behaviors and beliefs from elementary school through college. Major areas influenced by a learning or performance goal include cognitive strategies and engagement, and motivational beliefs and actions.

Cognitive Strategies and Engagement

Learning goals foster cognitive engagement and effort (Meece, Blumenfeld, & Hoyle, 1988). Fifth- and sixth-grade science students who placed greater emphasis on learning goals also reported more active cognitive engagement. Students with performance goals (pleasing the teacher or seeking social recognition) had a lower level of cognitive engagement. Wolters, Yu, and Pintrich (1996) found that task value and interest were related to learning goals.

The use of cognitive strategies and information processing is related to goal orientations of students at different levels of schooling. Learning that is potentially more meaningful or complex, requiring deep-level processing, appears to be the most vulnerable to the negative effects of performance goals (Graham & Golan, 1991). When the emphasis was on ability, as in the performance goal situation, there was interference with memory for tasks that required a great deal of cognitive effort. Performance goals also undermined the problem-solving strategies of children (Elliott & Dweck, 1988; Bereby-Meyer & Kaplan, 2005).

In contrast, learning goals were the strongest predictor of seventh- and eighth-grade students' cognitive strategy use (Wolters et al., 1996) and junior high students' more frequent use of metacognition strategies for studying (Wolters, 2004). These goals were also predictive of deep processing, persistence, effort, and exam performance of college students (Elliot, McGregor, & Gable, 1999).

Motivational Beliefs and Actions

The particular goal orientation affects motivation beliefs such as the role of effort in learning, self-efficacy beliefs, the tendency to use self-handicapping strategies, help seeking, and helpless patterns.

Self-Efficacy.   Overall, a learning goal orientation was found to be associated with higher self-efficacy. Wolters et al. (1996) reported that seventh- and eighth-grade students who reported greater endorsement of a learning goal also tended to report higher levels of self-efficacy. Learning goals were also positively related to self-efficacy in the subjects of writing and science (Pajares, Britner, & Valiante, 2000) and fifth and sixth graders in mathematics (Linnenbrink, 2005). In contrast, the fifth and sixth graders with performance goals reported higher anxiety. Performance goals were also related to low self-efficacy in college students (Pintrich, Zusho, Schiefele, & Pekrun, 2001).

Self-Handicapping. Self-handicapping strategies, such as low effort, are associated with performance goals (Midgley & Urdan, 2001). Elliott and Dweck (1988) found that children with performance goals were more likely to avoid challenge and exhibit low persistence, strategies that undermine student achievement. Another type of self-handicapping strategy associated with performance goals is cheating (E. Anderman, Griesinger, & Westerfield, 1998; E. Anderman & Midgley, 2004). Anderman and Midgley found higher levels of cheating associated with goal orientation before and after the transition from middle school to end of ninth grade. Similar to self-worth protection, the authors explained that cheating allows students to protect themselves against perceptions of low ability.

Help Seeking. The particular goal orientation was also found to influence help-seeking behaviors (Butler & Neuman, 1995). Second- and sixth-grade students were more likely to seek help when the task was presented to them as an opportunity to develop competence. When tasks were presented to students as a measure of their ability, they were less likely to seek help. Students were more likely to seek help in classrooms with a learning goal focus and to avoid help seeking in a performance goal structure (Butler & Neuman, 1995; Ryan, Gheen, & Midgley, 1998). Similar findings were reported for high school students in a computer science course (Cheong, Pajares, & Oberman, 2004).

Helpless Patterns. Finally, one of the most debilitating effects of performance goals is the vulnerability to helpless patterns (Dweck, 1986). Goals that focus students on using performances to judge their ability can make them vulnerable to a helpless pattern in the face of failure (Dweck & Sorich, 1999; Heyman & Dweck, 1992; Midgley et al., 2001).

There is continued agreement that the learning goal pattern is the more adaptive one, fostering long-term achievement that reflects intrinsic motivation (C. Ames, 1992; Heyman & Dweck, 1992; Kaplan & Middleton, 2002; Linnenbrink, 2005; Meece, 1991; Midgley et al., 2001). As Kaplan and Middleton asked, "Should childhood be a journey or a race?" A summary of the research indicates that cognitive strategy use and adaptive motivational beliefs are more associated with learning goals.

Linnenbrink concluded that, for classroom practice, "there needs to be an emphasis on learning and understanding in the classroom environment" (2005, p. 210).

Classroom Practices that Foster Learning Goals and Positive Competence Evaluation

Classroom practices make learning and performance goals noticeable to both students and teachers (Urdan, Kneisel, & Mason, 1999). First, it is important for teachers to be aware of the beliefs and behaviors of students that suggest clues to a performance or a learning goal. By recognizing student goal orientations, teachers are in the position to better understand and address students' motivation and to assist parents in understanding their children's motivation. Second, an awareness of communication and instructional practices will help teachers to avoid negative practices and use more positive ones.

What student behaviors may indicate their particular goal orientation? Clues to beliefs and behaviors that may indicate a performance or learning goal are listed in Strategy 3.2.

Strategy 3.2. Recognizing Student Goal Orientation

The following examples may indicate performance goals:

- Students or teachers believe that high achievers lose something when low achievers are successful like in cooperative learning.
- Students keep track of their GPAs to compare rankings, not as a way of tracking their learning.
- A student is visibly upset about receiving a grade of B on an essay exam and exclaims to her teacher, "But, I'm an A student."
- A middle school student, who makes low grades for not turning in assignments, tells his mother that "the work is too easy; I already know that."
- A student is heard to say to her friend: "You make good grades, you're so smart."

A focus on learning/mastery goals may be indicated by the following examples:

- The friend of the above student replies, "I work hard for my grades."
- A student compares his most recent test grade to previous grades to see if he improved.
- Students do extra work to improve without expecting a better grade.
- A student used the feedback on the first draft of the paper to revise.

What factors in a classroom context contribute to a negative motivation pattern such as self-worth protection and performance goals or an adaptive pattern? R. Ames and C. Ames (1991) identified practices that contribute to a negative motivation pattern. These practices include:

- "Communicating low expectations"
- "Reinforcing ability instead of effort"
- "Reinforcing performance instead of learning"
- "Public evaluations" such as posting the highest scores
- "Excessive emphasis on grades" (p. 255).

What are the strategies and guidelines that can reduce failure-avoiding strategies and performance goal orientation? Although the classroom environment may be too complex to implement a precise goal structure (Urdan et al., 1999), it is possible to implement instructional practices and communication to cultivate a learning environment. Strategy 3.3 presents recommendations for fostering positive competence evaluations and Exhibit 3.1 describes a successful intervention to promote adaptive goal orientation.

Strategy 3.3. Fostering Positive Competence Evaluations

Characteristics of classroom climate that foster development of competence:

- Effort and strategies are emphasized and respected.
- Learnable intelligence is emphasized.
- Improvement is recognized in evaluation.
- Failure does not mean dumb.
- Meaningful learning is emphasized.
- All students are valued and treated with dignity.
- Social comparison through public recognition and comparative grading is deemphasized.

Specifically:

- Introduce attributional antecedents that ability increases as one gains in knowledge and skills.
- Give students opportunity to improve knowledge and skills through retesting and revising.
- Instruct students in learning strategies.
- Emphasize student progress. Give feedback that indicates progress in skill development.
- Emphasize that effort is critical for improving ability.
- Avoid labels and statements (*smartest, slowest*) that can be interpreted as a ranking by ability.
- Use rewards to emphasize the learning accomplished by students. Arrange rewards so they signify individual accomplishment, not in competition with another person. Use noncompetitive or cooperative learning structures to provide more possibilities for students to gain rewards.

Exhibit 3.1. A Successful Intervention

Bell and Kanevsky (1996) designed an intervention in a regular Grade 2 classroom to promote adaptive learning responses associated with a learning goal orientation. A purpose was to "develop a strong foundation of positive motivation resilient to the undermining forces of evaluation and difficulties, inherent in academic achievement situations" (p. 2).

The intervention took place in math lessons with pattern-recognition tasks. The motivation instruction had three components occurring in seven sessions:

Learning goal. Students were told throughout the training that the goal was for them to learn. An example is "What is important when you are working with me is that you don't give up and that you practice so you can learn" (p. 3).

Nature of learning was used to support the learning goal. An example is, "It often takes lots of hard work and lots of tries and lots of time and lots of mistakes before something is learned" (p. 3). These were referred to as good or helpful learning behaviors and listed on a poster called good learning reminders.

Attribution training was used to increase awareness of the role of effort and to assist students in using effort in learning. This had four parts represented on a poster: (a) I can learn, (b) Where to start?, (c) What do I already know?, and (d) Help.

The results indicated that the training was effective. Compared with the nontrained group, the trained group (a) chose more challenging tasks on the posttest than on the pretest; (b) increased in effort attributions, whereas the nontrained group declined; and (c) increased their pattern-recognition scores, whereas the scores did not change for the nontrained group.

Competence and Achievement Anxiety

Self-evaluation of competence is also related to achievement anxiety. Test anxiety is aroused when students believe that their competencies may not be up to the demands of the task (Zeidner, 1998). Pekrun, Goetz, Titz, and Perry (2002) identified anxiety as one of the emotions directly linked to achievement. Anxiety has long been identified as a factor that can have debilitating effects on school performance (Hill & Wigfield, 1984). Test anxiety tends to correlate negatively with achievement at all ages and grade levels (Pekrun et al., 2002; Zeidner, 1998). It increases as students move through elementary into high school (Hill, 1984) and can interfere with learning and testing. As anxiety increases, it is more likely that students will have lower achievement. Jones et al. (1999) reported that test anxiety is a common complaint in regard to high-stakes testing. However, Sloane and Kelly (2003) contend that it is not clear whether this is due to the tests or to inadequate preparation. Key questions that relate to anxiety and achievement are (a) What are the current explanations of the relationship of anxiety and performance? and (b) What can teachers do to help alleviate debilitating anxiety?

Explanations of Achievement Anxiety

Although a number of models have been proposed to explain the causes and effects of anxiety, no one model can account for the complexity (Zeidner, 1998). The explanations include cognitive, affective, and motivational factors. Cognitive interference and skill deficit, and motivational explanations appear to be most relevant for educators.

Cognitive Interference and Skill Deficit

How does cognitive interference work? Self-defeating thoughts divert needed attention from the task (Zeidner, 1998). The already limited capacity of humans to process information is further limited by distracting and self-defeating thoughts at every phase of learning (Tobias, 1985). In a testing situation, students with a high level of anxiety focus on themselves, worrying about the outcome and spending less time focusing on the task, resulting in poorer performance. Contrary to popular beliefs, test taking is only one phase affected by anxiety. Attention is affected prior to study and self-defeating thoughts interfere with information processing during study.

A cognitive skill deficit explains poor performance as resulting primarily from inadequate study in the first place (Culler & Holahan, 1980; Tobias, 1985). The student is aware that he or she is unprepared for the test. In this case, anxiety does not directly cause poor performance. High-anxiety students have deficits in several study habit areas:

- self-monitoring—judging whether they are ready for an exam (Covington, 1992);
- organizing information into more meaningful patterns

(Steiner, Wiener, & Cromer, 1971; Zeidner & Matthews, 2005); and

- distractibility—classroom disruptions and students' own worries (Eysenck, 1988).

A student experiencing cognitive interference needs to avoid distracting thoughts and focus on the task. From a skill deficit point of view, high-anxiety students need study and organization skills to overcome these deficits (see self-regulation strategies in Chapter 5).

Motivational Explanations

According to Pekrun et al. (2002) anxiety is triggered when students envision a possible failure. Students with a learned helplessness belief experience anxiety and do not have a sense of control in the situation. Similarly, students who have a low sense of self-efficacy are more likely to experience the negative effects of achievement anxiety. However, high efficacy appears to protect a student from anxiety (Bandura, 1993). This reemphasizes the importance of identifying maladaptive attributions and low-efficacy judgments and providing attribution retraining and strategies to increase students' efficacy (Pekrun et al., 2002).

Goal orientation and self-worth protection are also related to anxiety. Students who have an entity view of intelligence with a performance goal can easily have high levels of anxiety about performing poorly because they fear they lack ability (Molden & Dweck, 2000). This may lead to performance avoidance motivation. Linnenbrink (2005) stated that performance avoidance goals had a detrimental relation to test anxiety. From a self-worth perspective, Covington (1992) theorized that achievement anxiety is a reaction to the threat of failure. A student who has not performed well in the past fears repeating the failure and being thought of as incompetent. Students who have good strategies and perform well can also be affected by anxiety. Their self-worth is more dependent on perfection, and they are more concerned with looking smart. A failure would destroy the perfection and their image. Covington characterized these students as overstrivers. They know how to get good grades, but this does not alleviate their fear that they may not really have ability.

This brings us to the following question: What can educators do to address the debilitating effects of anxiety?

Strategies for Alleviating Debilitating Test Anxiety

In view of the nationwide increase in high-stakes testing of students and teachers, it is imperative that teachers and schools develop strategies to minimize debilitating anxiety and help students manage achievement anxiety. The beginning step is a classroom climate that emphasizes learning goals more than performance goals (Pekrun et al., 2002). This includes adolescents with learning disabilities who are subject to high-stakes testing (E. W. Clark et al., 2005).

An important aspect is how teachers interact with students through expectations and feedback (Zeidner, 1998). This means teachers must be especially cognizant of the attributional feedback given. Helping students handle debilitating anxiety in the face of high-stakes testing involves interventions that help students to develop information-processing and test-taking strategies (Hill & Wigfield, 1984; Tobias, 1985; Wigfield & Eccles, 1989) and to develop coping strategies and learn to deal with

---

Strategy 3.4. Strategies to Reduce Debilitating Test Anxiety

1. Attitudes and beliefs

- Explain the purpose for the tests, emphasizing the learning aspect.
- Emphasize the importance of "doing your best."
- Use learning goal statements.
- Emphasize that test-taking skills are something we learn in school.

2. Cognitive strategies

- Teach students study skills as part of the curriculum.
- Teach students how to activate prior knowledge.
- Set up practice tests.
- Emphasize cognitive strategies that are aligned with the type of test.

3. During test taking, remind students:

- to sit where they can write easily,
- to pay attention to instructions both from teachers and provided with the tests,
- what they are allowed to do (i.e., whether they can make notes, underline, or highlight),
- to go back and check their answers if they finish before time is up, and
- to pace themselves, neither rushing nor working too slowly. If they cannot answer a problem, move on and come back to it later. (Clark et al., 2005; Hill & Wigfield, 1984)

failure in constructive ways (Rohrkemper & Corno, 1988). Specific guidelines for helping students handle achievement anxiety are found in Strategy 3.4. Additional suggestions for a supportive classroom climate are provided in Chapters 6, 7, and 8.

CONCLUDING THOUGHTS

The concepts of ability that are described in this chapter have important implications for educators. Resnick (1999) proposed effort-based schools as a way to achieve excellence and equality. Regardless of ability level, the important goal is to assist all children to reach their potential. This is the real meaning of *motivational equality* (Nicholls, 1989). Finally, "merely having ability or having potential is not enough to enjoy success in school or in life. Talent and potential will be wasted unless children believe they possess ability and have the freedom to use and develop their talents" (Miserandino, 1996, p. 210).

REVIEW OF MAJOR POINTS

1. How students evaluate their ability has important implications for academic motivation and expectancy for success. The prevalent view today is that perceptions of competence are not only domain specific, but distinct for different subject areas.

2. Self-efficacy is a judgment that individuals make about

their own capability to accomplish a future task. It is not just a reflection of one's ability, but the beliefs one holds about that ability. Self-efficacy judgments influence which activities we choose to undertake and which to avoid, how much effort we expend, and how long we persist in the face of obstacles.

3. Beliefs about one's capabilities come from four sources of information: task accomplishments, vicarious experiences (observing others), verbal persuasion, and physiological states. The most powerful source is task accomplishments or direct evidence.

4. Strategies that can increase self-efficacy are goals and feedback, rewards, self-instruction for verbalization of strategies, participant modeling, and various combinations of these strategies. Coping models that demonstrate the task, along with the difficulties experienced and strategies to succeed, are more likely to increase self-efficacy than mastery or expert models. Peer models have been found to be more effective than adult models in raising children's self-efficacy.

5. The self-worth motive is based on the need for students to maintain a positive image of their competence and ability. Students often see ability and self-worth as synonymous. Their motive then becomes one of avoiding failure and protecting their self-worth from the perception that they have low ability.

6. Students protect their self-worth through the use of failure-avoiding strategies: low effort, self-handicapping behaviors (procrastination, goals that are too high, and academic wooden leg), and success guarantee strategies (cheating and goals that are too low). The tendency toward self-worth protection is influenced by classroom practices that promote competition among students. Practices include insufficient rewards that force students to compete or give up, rewarding student ability but not effort, and evaluation systems where grades are based on how students rank in comparison to other students.

7. For minority students, the focus on ability may lead to vulnerability to racial stereotypes, which leads to disidentification with school and self-worth protection. Minority students may protect self-worth by resisting the values and goals of school, purposefully choosing behaviors that are detrimental to academic success. It is important that teachers and schools incorporate practices so that all students can identify with the goals of educational attainment.

8.   Two contrasting achievement goal orientations—learning and performance—refer to the underlying purposes behind actions. Students who have a learning focus are seeking to develop their skills; their feelings of competence come from improvement. Performance goals (approach or avoidance) refer to the performance of others. A performance approach focus is concerned with demonstrating student ability in comparison to others. A performance avoidance focus is on avoiding the perception of lack of ability and is more maladaptive. The learning goal is the more adaptive motivation pattern in most circumstances. Classroom context influences the type of goal orientation.

9.   A primary source of the particular goal orientation is whether intelligence is an inherent, fixed entity or incremental and malleable, continuing to develop as one gains skills and knowledge. Learning goals are associated with the latter although a person can be motivated for learning and performance. Learning goals have been found to be positively related to seeking help, self-efficacy, and cognitive strategy use.

10.   Two prevailing explanations for achievement anxiety are cognitive interference and skill deficits in strategy use. Poor performance is thought to result from self-defeating thoughts that interfere with test preparation and test taking and inadequate study. Students who have low self-efficacy are more likely to experience the negative effects of achievement anxiety, whereas high efficacy appears to protect a student from anxiety. Interventions that assist students to develop information-processing and test-taking strategies help students handle debilitating anxiety in achievement situations such as high-stakes testing.

Motivational Toolbox

1. Important points to think about and lingering questions

2. Strategies I can use now

3. Strategies I want to develop in the future

CHAPTER 4

Goals and Goal Setting

"Would you tell me, please, which way I ought to go from here?" asked Alice. "That depends a great deal on where you want to get to," said the Cheshire Cat.

—Carroll (1963, p. 59)

Have you used terms such as *aim, aspiration, purpose,* or *intent*? These are terms we often hear that imply goal setting. *Goals* have been defined simply as "something that the person wants to achieve" (Locke & Latham, 1990, p. 2). "Goal setting theory assumes that human action is directed by conscious goals and intentions" (Locke & Latham, 1990, p. 4). There is an important distinction between goal-setting theory and goal orientation (Chapter 3). *Goal setting* refers to a specific outcome that an individual is striving to achieve, whereas *goal orientation* refers to a type of goal orientation or underlying purpose behind the strived-for goal (Dweck, 1992). The focus of this chapter is on the importance of goal setting for achievement outcomes.

A coach would not think of starting a season without emphasizing both team and individual goals. Goals are a standard component of many, if not most, employee evaluation criteria. What about goal setting in classroom learning? Although teachers have goals in mind, how often are these made explicit? How often are students encouraged to set goals for themselves? From a motivational viewpoint, goals and goal setting play a central role in self-regulation (Schutz, 1991). Goal setting influences learning and motivation by providing a target and information about how well one is doing. This chapter describes the motivational effects of goals, types of goals, the properties of goals that

106

enhance motivation, the relation between goals and feedback, and applications of goal setting to the educational settings.

MOTIVATIONAL EFFECTS OF GOAL SETTING

Goals are cognitive representations of a future event and, as such, influence motivation through five processes (Locke & Latham, 1990; Locke, Shaw, Saari, & Latham, 1981). More specifically, goals:

- direct attention and action toward an intended target. This helps individuals focus on the task at hand and organize their knowledge and strategies toward the accomplishment of the goal;
- mobilize effort in proportion to the difficulty of the task to be accomplished;
- promote persistence and effort over time for complex tasks. This provides a reason to continue to work hard even if the task is not going well;
- promote the development of creative plans and strategies to reach them;
- provide a reference point that provides information about one's performance.

In sum, goals provide standards for knowing how well one is doing, thus activating a self-evaluation process. As Bandura (1997) stated, "simply adopting a goal without knowing how one is doing, or knowing how one is doing in the absence of a goal, has no lasting motivational effect" (p. 128).

GOAL CONTENT AND MULTIPLE GOALS

When an individual sets a goal, what is the focus of the goal? A goal may be a vague idea that is difficult to communicate or it may be a clear vision. The focus of a goal can be a product, such as designing a multimedia display of the life of a president, or a process, such as the strategies needed to complete the display. Although a number of goals may be operating at the same time, people tend to function with core goals—a set of one to five personal goals that guide behavior (Ford, 1992). Schutz (1994) identified three core goals that tended to be the most important for preservice teachers—family, occupation, and education. Most of their reported activities centered around these three goals.

What is the importance of this multiple goal perspective? When we set one goal, others may be activated (Ford, 1992). For example, when an adult returns to school to pursue a master's degree, the goal is to attain a degree. This goal may activate others at the same time, such as moving to a better pay scale, expanding social contacts, and learning new ideas to improve teaching. As this example demonstrates, the activation of one goal does not preclude the activation of another.

However, multiple goals can be especially problematic among adolescents (Wentzel, 2000). Wentzel (1989) asked adolescents to list what they try to achieve in their classes. From these responses, she compiled a list of 12 goals. Students were then surveyed to determine how often they tried to achieve each of the 12 goals in their classes. Comparisons made between low, medium, and high grade point average (GPA) groups indicated that the groups valued goals differently. The high GPA group ranked being a successful student, getting things done on time, and being dependable and responsible highest among the 12 goals. In contrast, the low GPA group ranked having fun and friends highest. Only 19 percent of the low GPA group indicated that being a successful student was a goal. Although some students can coordinate social (friends) and academic goals (completing homework) with no problem, other students are unable to coordinate these goals. This raises important questions. How can the school or teacher influence student goals? Can the low GPA group who ranked fun as the highest goal be encouraged to put more emphasis on goals associated with achievement?

One possibility for teachers is to emphasize that learning tasks may have multiple outcomes or goals. As goal rankings in the previous study indicate, high GPA students were more likely than low and medium GPA students to try to accomplish several goals at the same time. Ford (1992) pointed out that when a person has more than one reason for participating in an activity, motivational power is increased, providing a type of motivational insurance. For example, in a second study, Wentzel (1991) concluded that a goal of trying to interact with peers is not, in and of itself, detrimental to classroom learning. The pursuit of both social responsibility and academic goals was most related to achievement. Thus, for students who generally focus more on fun and friendships than on learning and self-improvement, it may be possible to use the multiple goals principle to facilitate meaningful engagement. For example, cooperative learning provides opportunity for multiple goals—academic, social skills, peer interaction, and responsibility. Cooperative learning in the social context is further explained in Chapter 7.

Some educators are beginning to broaden the possible types of goals by expanding the types of learning outcomes that are possible in school. Ellison (1992) used the seven types of intelligence—logical/mathematical, linguistic, musical, spatial, bodily/kinesthetic, interpersonal, and intrapersonal—proposed by Gardner (1983) as goal targets for fifth graders. The steps included the following:

- Goal-setting conferences with students began in September by asking, "Have you thought about your goals for the year?" Gathered information from parents about their children's strengths and areas of difficulty.
- Goal setting began with intrapersonal intelligence (capacity for understanding self), focusing the goals on confidence, responsibility, and self-management.
- Self-evaluation of goals occurred in February with affirmation, refocus, and celebration of goals followed by teacher redirection where indicated.

Exhibit 4.1 shows an example of a student goal (Ellison, 1992).

If multiple goals are to be productive, they must be coordinated and not in conflict. When people attempt more goals than they can handle, one or more of the goals may result in failure or one may become dominant. For example, fun may overcome being a successful student. The crucial factor is helping students balance their goals. Goals are most likely to contribute to students' academic competence when they correspond with the teacher's goals and expectations (Wentzel, 2000).

Exhibit 4.1.   Goal Setting: A Student–Parent–Teacher Process

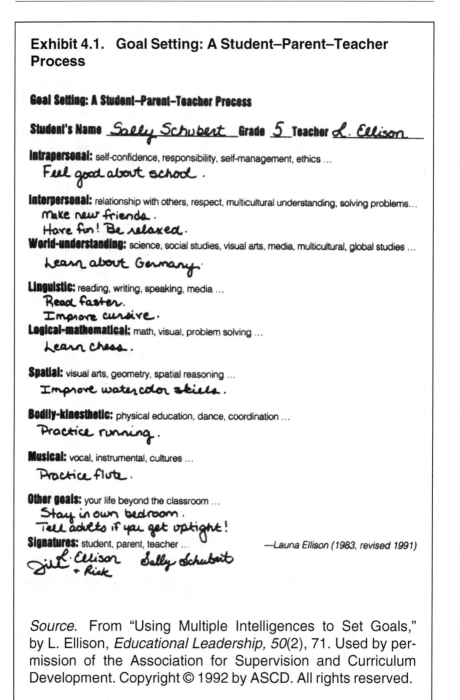

Goal Setting: A Student–Parent–Teacher Process

Student's Name _Sally Schubert_ Grade _5_ Teacher _L. Ellison_

Intrapersonal: self-confidence, responsibility, self-management, ethics ...
   Feel good about school .

Interpersonal: relationship with others, respect, multicultural understanding, solving problems...
   Make new friends .
   Have fun! Be relaxed .

World-understanding: science, social studies, visual arts, media, multicultural, global studies ...
   Learn about Germany.

Linguistic: reading, writing, speaking, media ...
   Read faster.
   Improve cursive.

Logical-mathematical: math, visual, problem solving ...
   Learn chess.

Spatial: visual arts, geometry, spatial reasoning ...
   Improve watercolor skills .

Bodily-kinesthetic: physical education, dance, coordination ...
   Practice running .

Musical: vocal, instrumental, cultures ...
   Practice flute .

Other goals: your life beyond the classroom ...
   Stay in own bedroom .
   Tell adults if you get uptight!

Signatures: student, parent, teacher ...   —Launa Ellison (1983, revised 1991)

   Jill L. Ellison   Sally Schubert
   + Rick

Source. From "Using Multiple Intelligences to Set Goals," by L. Ellison, *Educational Leadership, 50*(2), 71. Used by permission of the Association for Supervision and Curriculum Development. Copyright © 1992 by ASCD. All rights reserved.

PROPERTIES OF GOALS THAT
ENHANCE MOTIVATION

How difficult or specific should goals be? Goals by themselves do
not automatically lead to more effective task performance. However, certain properties of goals affect task performance: distal
or proximal, difficult or easy, specific or general, assigned or self-
chosen, and commitment to the goal.

Long- and Short-Term Goals

What is the relation between long- and short-term goals? Target
goals, mission goals, ultimate goals, end goals, distal goals, and
"begin with the end in mind" (Covey, 1989, p. 97) are all phrases
that imply long-term goals. Long-term or distal goals keep us
directed toward our ultimate target. Short-term goals, also
known as proximal goals or subgoals, are the stepping stones to
the long-term goal. Bandura (1997) suggested that without proximal goals, people fail to take the necessary steps to accomplish
the distal goal. As stated previously, the content of a goal is something we want to accomplish. The issue is not whether a long- or
short-term goal is more effective. Each has a role, and they com-
plement each other in contributing to achievement and self-regulation. This relation is illustrated in Fig. 4.1.

The interrelationship of these goals is illustrated in a study
that compared the effects of proximal and distal goals on children's self-efficacy and mathematics performance (Bandura &
Schunk, 1981). Third graders were assigned to one of three
groups:

1. Proximal goal group: Children were told they could consider
   setting a goal of completing at least six pages of work each
   session.
2. Distal goal group: Children were told they might consider
   setting the goal of completing the entire 42 pages by the end
   of the seventh session.
3. No goal group: Goals were not mentioned to the children.

The results indicate that children who set attainable subgoals
progressed at a more rapid pace, achieved mastery in math, and

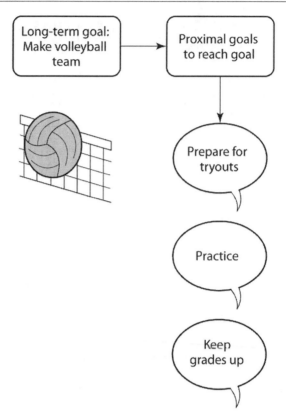

FIG. 4.1. Proximal goals leading to long-term goals.

increased their self-efficacy. The proximal group also displayed more competence and displayed the most intrinsic interest in solving the problems. The authors concluded that:

> Self-motivation can best be created and sustained by attainable subgoals that lead to future larger ones. Proximal subgoals provide immediate incentives and guides for performance, whereas distal goals are too far removed in time to effectively mobilize effort or direct what one does in the here and now.
>
> (Bandura & Schunk, 1981, p. 587)

Points to keep in mind for goal setting include the following:

- Distal goals help keep the larger picture in mind. However, focusing on the distant future may lead one to procrastinate more.

- When one sets distal goals, there is a tendency to break them up into proximal goals, but teachers cannot assume all students will do this (or even ourselves).
- When planning long-term projects, students need to see the relationship between what they are doing in class from day to day and the long-term goal.

In summary, both proximal and distal goals affect motivation and performance. Exhibit 4.2 shows a form for setting long-term goals. Exhibit 4.3 is a form for proximal goals that can be adapted for various age groups. Strategy 4.1 gives ways the forms can be used.

Exhibit 4.2. Long-Term Achievement Goal Form

LONG-TERM GOAL

Long-term goals keep us focused, give us direction, and provide a purpose for accomplishing the short-term goals. State a long-term goal using the following format.

1. One important goal I want to accomplish in the next six months to two years:

2. This goal is important to me because:

3. Specific steps I will take to accomplish this goal are:

4. Possible blocks, both external and personal, to accomplishing this goal are:

5. What I can do to lessen these blocks:

6. Who I can go to for help:

Exhibit 4.3. Proximal Goal Form

PROXIMAL GOALS AND PROGRESS

This form is a way to set goals for each week and to monitor your progress. Make the goals as specific as possible.

PLANNING

1. My specific learning goals for this week are:

2. Actions or steps I will take to accomplish these goals:

3. How I will know I have accomplished my goals:

4. Possible blocks, both personal and external, that may interfere with my accomplishing these goals and how I can overcome them:

5. Who I can go to for help with my goals:

6. How confident I am that I will accomplish these goals:

   not confident   very confident
   0 _____ 25

EVALUATING

7. How satisfied I am with my previous goal accomplishment:

   dissatisfied   neutral   highly satisfied
   0 _____ 12 _____ 25

8. Reasons for accomplishing or not accomplishing my goals are:

Strategy 4.1. Using Goal Forms

- *Long-Term Form.* Students can be asked to complete this form at the beginning of a semester. It might be used to help students think about multiple goals and their priorities.
- *Proximal Goal Form.* This form can be adapted as needed for different age levels. I have had undergraduates use this form weekly. For the first few times, the teacher gives feedback. As students learn criteria for effective goals, they might be paired as *goal buddies* to give feedback to each other. Feedback is most often needed for making the goal more specific and specifying action steps. The identification of how to overcome blocks is very important. The evaluation phase elicits attributions for why they did or did not attain the goals.

Goal Difficulty and Challenge

Which is more effective, easy or difficult goals? Did you predict easy goals? Surprisingly, harder goals lead to a higher level of performance than do easy goals if the task is voluntary and the person has the ability to achieve the goal (Locke & Latham, 1990). People tend to expend more effort to attain a goal they perceive as difficult. However, the goal must not be so difficult that it seems to be unachievable because most people will avoid an impossible task.

In a study with school children, Schunk (1983a) investigated the effects of goal difficulty on the performance of children who were deficient in arithmetic division skills. One group received difficult goals and another group received easier goals. The children in the more difficult goal group solved more problems and sustained greater task motivation than the less difficult goal group.

Establishing the level of goal difficulty—challenging, yet realistic—that will help students perform their best is a balancing act for teachers. Goals should not be so rigid that necessary adjustments cannot be made. If the standard for goal attainment is too difficult or rigid, there is likely to be a drop in motivation. As described in Chapter 3, setting an unachievable goal is one mechanism that individuals might use to protect a sense of self-worth. In addition, students may need help in setting realistic goals. Schunk (1991) recommended setting upper and lower limits and goal conferences as means of helping students set realistic goals.

REFLECTION.   Think about what a realistic goal means to you. How much risk is involved in your personal and professional goals?

Goal Specificity

Specificity is another property of goals that affects performance. Specific goals have clear standards for accomplishment (e.g., "My goal is to read and understand the story and have my summary finished for literature class tomorrow"). General goals are vague, with a nonspecific outcome (e.g., "My goal is to catch up with my assignments"). It has been demonstrated that specific goals result in higher performance than either no goals or general goals (Locke & Latham, 1990). A descriptive analysis of weekly goals set by college students in learning logs over the course of a semester found differences in types of goals by student grades (Alderman et al., 1993). The A group had more than twice as many specific goals as the B and C groups. Examples were (a) specific goals (e.g., "I want to make 36 out of 40 on the next test"), and (b) general goals (e.g., "I want to make a good grade on the next test"). The reason that specific goals increase task performance is because they provide a guide for the type and amount of effort needed to accomplish the task (Bandura, 1986). A specific goal is more likely to motivate an individual to higher performance than are good intentions. The proximal goal form (Exhibit 4.3) is useful for helping students learn to set specific, short-term goals.

Goal Commitment

Goal commitment is our determination to pursue a course of action that will lead to the goal we aspire to achieve (Bandura, 1986). How does this affect goal attainment? Strength of goal commitment will affect how hard one will try to attain the goal.

Commitment is most important when goals are difficult (Locke & Latham, 2002). What affects strength of commitment for goals? Goal commitment is affected by self-efficacy and the properties described thus far: difficulty and specificity. For example, when goals are too difficult, commitment declines, followed by a drop-off in performance (Locke & Latham, 1990). Commitment is also affected by goal intensity, goal participation, and peer influence.

Goal Intensity. Commitment is related to goal intensity, or the amount of thought or mental effort that goes into formulating a goal and how it will be attained (Locke & Latham, 1990). This is similar to goal clarification because, when we clarify a goal, we are involved in a conscious process of collecting information about the goal and task and our ability to attain it (Schutz, 1989). In a study of fifth graders, Henderson (cited in Locke & Latham, 1990) found that students who formulated a greater number of reading purposes with more detail and elaboration attained their goals to a greater extent than did students with superficial purposes. Although there was no difference in IQ scores of the groups, the students who set more goals with elaboration were better readers. It stands to reason that the more thought that is given to developing a goal, the more likely one will be committed to the goal.

Goal Participation. How important, motivationally, is it for people to participate in goal setting? This is an important question because goals are often assigned by others at home, school, and work. The state imparts curriculum standards or goals to teachers, who in turn impose them on students. Having individuals participate in setting goals can lead to greater satisfaction, and also telling people to achieve a goal can influence self-efficacy because it suggests they are capable of achieving the goal (Locke & Latham, 1990).

To investigate the effects of assigned and self-set goals, Schunk (1985) conducted a study of sixth-grade students with learning disabilities (LD) who were learning subtraction. One group was assigned goals (e.g., "Why don't you try to do seven pages today?"). A second group set goals themselves (e.g., "Decide how many pages you can do today"). A third group worked without goals. Students who self-set goals had the highest self-efficacy and math scores. Both goal groups demonstrated higher levels of self-regulation than the control group without any goals.

Nevertheless, Locke and Latham (1990) concluded that self-set goals are not consistently more effective than assigned goals in increasing performance. The crucial factor in assigned goals is acceptance. Once individuals become involved in a goal, the goal itself becomes more important than how it was set or whether it was imposed. Because, at work and in schools, goals are often assigned by others, it is important that the purpose of assigned goals be explained to participants. Joint participation in goal setting by teachers and students may increase the acceptance of goals.

Peer Influence.   One factor where teachers might be influential in promoting goal acceptance and commitment is peer influence. Strong group pressures are likely to increase commitment to goals (Locke & Latham, 1990). This group cohesiveness is more often found on athletic teams. Obviously, the coach wants a strong commitment to the team goals. In the classroom, group goals may aid the commitment of students working in cooperative learning groups and thus lead to a higher quality of work.

RELATION OF FEEDBACK AND GOALS

It is important to reemphasize that goals initiate a self-evaluation process that affects motivation by providing a standard to judge progress (Bandura, 1986). This simply means two comparative processes are needed: goal and feedback or knowledge of results about progress. For goals to be effective, individuals/teams need to know where they are in relation to the goal. The relationship between goals and feedback is as follows:

1. Goals tell students what type of performance is to be attained, and a way of evaluating actions and efforts.
2. Feedback then is used to track progress in relation to the goals and adjust or self-correct (Locke & Latham, 1990). This process is shown in Fig. 4.2.

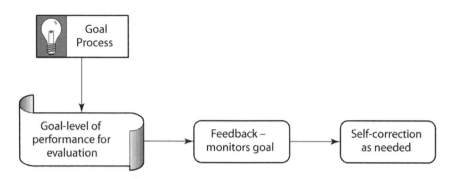

FIG. 4.2. Process: Goal setting, monitoring, feedback process.

What factors make it more likely that feedback will occur? Proximal goals give more opportunity for knowledge of results because individuals can monitor their performance and make corrections as needed. When people see a discrepancy between their goal and their performance, what are the effects on subsequent performance? It usually increases performance (Locke & Latham, 2002). Research by Bandura and Cervone (1983, 1986) investigated the effects. The results indicate that the more dissatisfied high self-efficacy individuals were with their performance, the more they increased their effort for future tasks. The motivational influence of goal discrepancy is apparent in the log entry in Exhibit 4.4 when the student said, "I didn't finish two of my goals. I think I have to get a few priorities straight."

Exhibit 4.4. Log Entries Showing the Relation Between Goals and Feedback

Third Week

Got 32/40 on exam. First read chapters, then did reviews in study guide. Reviewed class notes but should have done before last night. Know I could have done better if I had put more time in it. I know B in any course is OK, but for me an A is my goal.

Next Entry

My first chance to do homework all week. I worked on my bulletin boards [for another class]. I guess setting achievable goals does help. It's kind of like giving a test to yourself. Even though no one else knows about it you still feel like you failed if you don't achieve it. Next week I'm going to achieve these goals:

1. Have my correct chapters read for each class.
2. Get all the information I need for my bulletin board.

Next Entry

So far so good. I've kept up on my reading and finished two out of three programs. My goals from last week are almost achieved. On to new ones. I'm going to actually start my bulletin board. I've discovered that setting achievable goals makes you realize that even though it seems like there is a mountain of work, you can get it done, one step at a time.

Next Entry

I didn't finish two of my goals. I think I have to get a few priorities straight.

Next Entry

• I started to implement the PQ4R technique we were taught in class. I read the overview, topic headings, and the summary. I didn't ask questions, but I did use the study guide. I improved my grade to a 36 this time. I'm very happy about that, not only because of the score, but because I tried to use this technique and it started to work.

Source. From Alderman, M. K., Klein, R., Seeley, S., & Sanders, M. (1993). "Preservice Teachers as Learners in Formation: Metacognitive Self-Portraits." *Reading Research and Instruction, 32*, 38–54. Reprinted by permission.

Which should be the focus of feedback—achieved progress or deficiencies? Bandura (1993) emphasized feedback on progress. When feedback emphasizes progress, personal capabilities are highlighted. This enhances self-efficacy and aspirations. In contrast, feedback that emphasizes deficiencies undermines the self-regulatory processes.

CLASSROOM INTERVENTIONS
IN GOAL SETTING

What types of goal-setting interventions have been applied in classroom settings and what was the outcome? Interventions conducted at elementary, secondary, and college levels with students from another culture and with students with LD are described in the following sections.

Elementary and Secondary Interventions

White, Hohn, and Tollefson (1997) conducted research to determine the extent children in Grades 3 through 6 could set realistic goals—a goal that was challenging but achievable. The children were taught realistic goal setting through a basketball and a baseball game using bean bags, (see Strategy 4.3 for the training process). The training also included achievement contracts in spelling. After training, students were classified as realistic and nonrealistic goal setters. By the second semester of Grade 2, children appeared to be able to set realistic goals. A notable finding was that young children in Grades 2 and 3 were able to assess their own ability in relation to the difficulty of a task.

Goals were used to help students in a middle school English as a second language class self-evaluate portfolios (Smolen, Newman, Walthen, & Lee, 1995). Based on self-evaluation of their work, students established personal goals. Index cards were distributed to students every Monday. The students wrote a new goal on one side of the card and the evaluation on the other side. After several weeks of modeling, demonstration, and practice, students were able to write their own goals. They were encouraged to choose goals from strategies that were posted in the room. The student goals gave the teacher a window into the students' progress. An example of a student's goal is shown in Exhibit 4.5.

Gaa (1973, 1979) investigated the effects of individual goal-setting conferences on both elementary and secondary students' achievement. First- and second-grade children were assigned to one of three experimental conditions: conferences with goal setting, conferences without goal setting, and no conferences. All students received the same reading instruction. The children in the goal conference group met with the experimenter once a week and received a list of reading skills. In each conference, children

---

Exhibit 4.5. Bao's Goal Card.

The Front of Bao's Card

Bao Le

4-12-95   **A**

1. "My goal for this week is to stop during reading and predict what is going to happen next in the story."

2. "My goal for this week is to finish writing my Superman story." Ⓙ🅛

The Back of Bao's Card

I met my goals for this week. The first goal help me understand a lot when I'm reading.

Source. From "Developing Student Self-Assessment Strategies," by L. Smolen et al., 1995. *TESOL Journal,* 51(1), 22–26. Copyright © 1995 by Teachers of English to Speakers of Other Languages, Inc. Reproduced by permission.

---

checked the goals (skills) they would work on during the week and rated their confidence in their ability to achieve goals. Children in the no-goal conference group also met weekly with the experimenter, but they did not set goals or receive feedback. On follow-up assessment, the goal-setting group scored higher on the reading achievement posttest, set fewer goals, and achieved more of the goals they set. Gaa concluded that practice and feedback in goal setting leads to more realistic goals and helps students be more accurate goal setters. He explained that the goal conference group may have set fewer goals because they had learned to focus their effort on the goals to be accomplished.

Gaa (1979) conducted a second study with high school students. The focus for this study was process goals. Process goals were the actions or steps to accomplish the product (e.g., the paper). In comparison to the group who had individual conferences but set no goals, the goal-setting group that had conferences scored higher on an English achievement test and viewed themselves as more in control of their achievement outcomes. Their attribution for goal attainment was more to themselves than to external factors.

These studies support the positive effects of goal-setting strategies for various ages. White et al. (1997) concluded there is value in direct instruction for realistic goal-setting strategies for elementary students. Two ways of assisting elementary students are shown in Strategy 4.2.

Strategy 4.2. Goal Setting for Elementary Students

- Lois Peak (1993) described a way that goal setting is taught to children in Japan. At the beginning of a new term in elementary schools, students are encouraged to think about their past performance and set a personal goal for the coming term. Next they develop a plan for reaching it, write their goals down, and post them on classroom walls. Students are periodically assigned a brief essay to describe their progress toward their goal of self-improvement. At the end of the term they write a final essay describing their success and the difficulties they encountered and read it to the class. When the students have finished reading their essay, the teacher finds a few words of praise and the entire class applauds.

- *Goal Interview.* Five steps are used to assist children to formulate a goal; ask students:

  1. to tell or write a story about something they want for themselves (e.g., a dog, complete chores, be friendly);
  2. to tell why they want the particular thing (motive);
  3. to tell how they will attain the goal;
  4. what could stop them from getting the goal (obstacle);
  5. to tell about overcoming the obstacle. (Goldman, 1982)

College Students' Interventions

Which will enhance college students' performance more—being trained in goal setting or time management? At the undergraduate level, Morgan (1985, 1987) conducted two experiments to determine whether goal setting could enhance the performance of college students. In the first study, there were four groups (Morgan, 1985):

1. The subgoal group was trained to set and monitor study subgoals for concepts from assigned readings (e.g., "My goal is to learn the difference between assimilation and accommodation").
2. The time group was trained to monitor time spent studying.
3. The distal group focused on a single goal.
4. The control group met only to take the assessment.

The group that self-monitored the concept subgoals outperformed groups that monitored time, study, or distal goals. Although the group that self-monitored study time actually increased study time and spent more time than the subgoal group, their performance was not significantly better than the control group. Morgan explained this surprising outcome as: Although subgoals bring about more effective use of time, it is what one does with the time that is most important. In reference to these results, Winne (2001) maintained that goals framed in terms of the amount of time to study do not provide standards.

In the second study, Morgan (1987) compared groups on goal setting alone, self-monitoring alone, and a combination of self-monitoring and goal setting and two control groups. All three experimental groups performed better than the control groups. However, contrary to expectations, the combination goal-setting and self-monitoring group did not perform better than either goal setting or self-monitoring. Morgan's explanation for the latter finding was that goal setting and self-monitoring are intertwined and difficult to separate from each other. If one component is in place, it sets the other in motion.

Students with LD Interventions

The positive effects of goal setting have also been found to work with students who have LD in studies by Tollefson and colleagues (Tollefson, Tracy, Johnsen, & Chatman, 1986; Tollefson, Tracy, Johnsen, Farmer, & Buenning, 1984). Seventh-, eighth-, and ninth-grade students with LD were trained to set realistic goals and expend effort to attain goals (Tollefson et al., 1984). Students were first taught goal setting by how many basketball goals they could make. Following goal-setting training, students set goals in spelling or math—their most difficult subject. Goal contracts were combined with attributional retraining. Initially, the students did not set realistic goals (only 19 percent were classified as realistic goal setters). After the training, a significant number (79 percent) set realistic goals. Students also increased their attributions to effort and decreased their attributions to luck. The training process is described in Strategy 4.3.

In another study, Graham, MacArthur, Schwartz, and Page-Voth (1992) taught fifth-grade students with LD a strategy for

---

Strategy 4.3. Learning to Set Realistic Goals

- **Basketball game.** There are three choices for distance: long, medium, and short. Each student selects a preset distance and is allowed three tosses of a bean bag into a wastebasket, predicting in advance how many baskets they would make. They keep records of their predictions and scores.
- **Baseball game.** Four lists of words were made for each student: easy (a single), moderately difficult (a double), difficult (a triple), and very difficult (a home run) words. Students were then given words that matched their level of spelling ability. To begin an inning, students chose the type of hit they wanted and recorded their prediction. Students then spelled the word orally; correct words were a hit and incorrect words an out. The students kept records of their actual outcomes. Each team is given 2 min at bat or three outs, whichever comes first. (Tollefson et al., 1984)

setting both product and process goals for writing an essay. The plan the students followed indicated:

1. Choose a product goal (e.g., purpose of the paper).
2. Develop a process goal for how the product goal would be attained.
3. Write while continuing the plan.
4. Develop and organize notes prior to writing.
5. Evaluate progress in meeting goals.

A mnemonic was used to help students remember: *PLANS* ("*P*ick goals, *L*ist ways to meet goals, *A*nd make *N*otes, *S*equence Notes"; Graham, MacArthur, et al., 1992, p. 327). After students learned the strategy, they wrote longer essays with improved quality. This study confirmed the effectiveness of both process and product goals. Goal setting was also found to positively affect the writing performance of seventh- and eighth-grade students with LD (Page-Voth & Graham, 1999). The goals clearly specified what to include in the essays.

Goal-Setting in Other Cultures

Are the goal-setting strategies valid for other cultures? Shih and Alexander (2000) investigated this matter in Taiwanese schools where social comparison is emphasized more than self-referenced comparison. In one treatment condition, students set goals for working fraction problems and were given either self-referenced comparison feedback or social comparison feedback. The group with goals/self-referenced comparison feedback resulted in higher self-efficacy and learning goal orientation; the group with goals/social comparison feedback scored higher on performance goals. The authors concluded that, even in competitive classrooms, self-referenced comparison feedback can lead students to concentrate on improvement and that these self-regulatory mechanisms are applicable to Taiwanese students in general.

Setting a goal is the first step, but a key is the implementation of the goal so it becomes a binding one (Oettingen, Honig, & Gollwitzer, 2000). The authors conducted a research study with the purpose of turning a goal desire into a binding goal. The research involved fifth-grade students in Germany who were learning English as a second language. The students were asked to contrast, by writing a story, how they would feel about achieving the goal of learning English with how they would feel about not achieving it. The contrast group was compared with a group who wrote a positive story and a group who wrote a negative story. The results indicated that students who contrasted positive and negative goal outcomes with high expectations reported stronger effort and stronger performance in learning English. The authors concluded the mental contrasting of the desire with a negative outcome turned the desire into a binding goal.

GUIDELINES AND STRATEGIES FOR GOAL SETTING IN THE CLASSROOM

Positive effects of using goal setting in classrooms have been described. However, how proficient are students at goal setting if they are not taught? Bergin (1989) studied high school students' goals in out-of-school learning activities. The findings indicate that few of the students used effective goal-setting techniques. Only 12 percent listed subgoals that would be necessary to attain the goal. In addition, the majority of the goals were general, not specific.

Goals can play an important role in increasing student competence and motivation. Teachers or coaches should not assume that students know how to set effective goals. Strategy 4.4 presents guidelines for using goal setting and describes a lesson.

Strategy 4.4. Guidelines for Using Goal Setting in the Classroom

- Present tasks and assignments to students as goals to be accomplished. These can be broken down into proximal goals.
- Have students keep a record of goals set and their performance (e.g., their test scores) so they can monitor their performance. Graphing their performance allows students to see their progress (Harris & Graham, 1985).
- Help students identify obstacles that might interfere with goal accomplishment.

- Teach students who are procrastinators to set proximal goals and monitor them.
- Have cooperative learning groups set goals for their next work sessions and evaluate their goals from the most recent work sessions.

Goal-Setting Lesson

This is a lesson I have used to teach proximal goal setting to teachers, undergraduates, and high school students, including those with developmental handicaps. The steps are based on a model for stating and refining goals (Doverspike, 1973).

1. First the teacher models with a think-a-loud. "Here is a goal [on transparency or chalkboard] that is too general and idealistic. You are to help me revise it so it is cognitive, realistic, and specific. The goal is 'I want to have great study habits.'"
2. Students give ideas for the revision by identifying general terms and substituting new ones. Mark out the original terms as new ones are decided on.
3. The revised goal might read: "I will improve my reading comprehension by learning PQ4R." Possible subgoals are "I will practice each part one at a time" or "I will monitor my progress after each test."
4. Have each student write a goal, then, in pairs or triads, help each other refine their goals to be more cognitive, specific, and realistic.

REFLECTION.   How do you feel when you accomplish a goal? Why might goal setting sometimes be scary for students? For yourself?

COMBINING MOTIVATIONAL PROCESSES

Motivational processes were examined in Chapters 1, 2, and 3. Principles from these processes can be combined as strategies for interventions. The LINKS model is one such combination.

The LINKS model was designed to break the low-expectation cycle associated with learned helplessness (Alderman, 1990). The steps combine goal setting, attributional retraining, self-efficacy, and learning and metacognitive strategies as sequential steps. These steps are shown in Fig. 4.3.

A key assumption of this model is that a successful experience is not enough. Students must attribute success to controllable factors—their ability or operationalized effort—if their expectations and confidence are to increase.

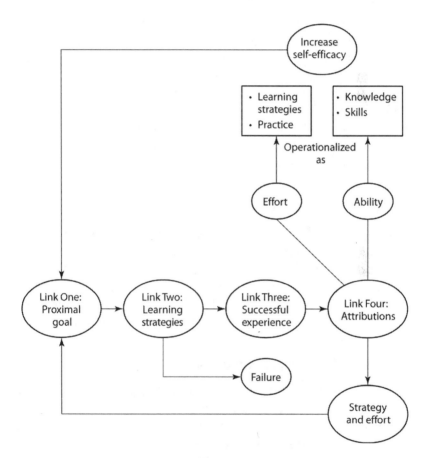

FIG. 4.3. LINKS to success. From "Motivation for At-Risk Students," by M. K. Alderman, *Educational Leadership, 48*(1), 27–30. Used by permission of the Association for Supervision and Curriculum Development. Copyright © 1990 by ASCD. All rights reserved.

Link 1: Proximal Goals

The first link to success is to set a goal for performance. How does a teacher decide this starting point or proximal goal? Determine where students' performance levels are or establish a baseline. The baseline can be determined by pretests (formal or informal), teacher observation, and the analysis of student errors. Teachers and students can then jointly decide on the proximal goal.

Link 2: Learning Strategies

The students' second link to success is to develop the necessary learning strategies to accomplish the task. It can be assumed that low-achieving students fit the category *inefficient learners* (Pressley & Levin, 1987). An inefficient learner is described as any student who fails to apply learning strategies where they would be beneficial. In this link, the student is taught the necessary learning strategies to accomplish his or her goal. Examples are memory strategies, reading comprehension strategies, and metacognitive knowledge about when to use them.

Link 3: Successful Experience

Success in this link is defined as a learning goal rather than a performance goal. The focus is on "how much progress I made," not on "how smart I am." The proximal goal serves as the criterion for successful experience. Success is not the final link, however. The student's attribution for the success must link his or her personal effort or strategy to the successful outcome.

Link 4: Attribution for Success

In Link 4, students attribute success to their personal effort, strategies, or ability. The teacher's role is to help students make the appropriate attribution. Internal-unstable attributions are easiest to change. Because students control their own effort, this is the likely starting point for attribution for success. For this attribution to be effective, effort must be operationalized. What did the student do when he or she tried? Effort might be completing all homework, correcting errors, extra practice, redoing an assignment, going to a help or review lesson, or using the appropriate learning strategies. Students must also attribute success to ability operationalized as knowledge or skills. This model then goes full circle. Students who have succeeded and attributed the success to their own effort or ability have concrete performance feedback that, in turn, will lead to increased self-efficacy. Increased self-efficacy, in turn, leads to increased confidence about goal accomplishment with an increase in teacher efficacy.

CONCLUDING THOUGHTS

Goal setting has long been recognized as important by coaches in athletic endeavors. It is also a strategy that is useful in motivation for learning and achievement and is appropriate for students from elementary to college age. When students (or teachers) are overwhelmed, goals are the beginning step.

REVIEW OF MAJOR POINTS

1.   Goals and goal setting play a central role in self-regulation, influencing learning and motivation by affecting motivation through five processes: directing attention and action; mobilizing effort; promoting persistence and effort over time; promoting the development of creative plans and strategies to reach them; and providing a reference point that provides information about one's performance. The focus of a goal can be a product or process.

2.   People tend to function with core goals—a set of one to five personal goals that guide behavior. This multiple goal perspective is important because when we set one goal, others may be activated. If multiple goals are to be productive, they must be coordinated and not in conflict.

3.   Properties of goals that affect task performance are distal or proximal, hard or easy, specific or general, assigned or self-chosen, and commitment to the goal. The distal long-term goals keep us on our ultimate target. Short-term goals, also known as proximal goals or subgoals, are the stepping stones to the long-term goal. Harder goals lead to a higher level of performance

than do easy goals if the task is voluntary and the person has the ability to achieve the goals. Specific goals result in higher performance than either no goals or general goals.

4.   Goal commitment is our determination to pursue a course of action that will lead to the goal we are aspiring to achieve and is related to goal intensity. Intensity is the amount of thought or mental effort that goes into formulating a goal and how it will be attained.

5.   Although letting individuals participate in setting goals can lead to greater satisfaction, telling people to achieve a goal can influence self-efficacy because it suggests they are capable of achieving the goal. The crucial factor in assigned goals is acceptance. Once individuals become involved in a goal, the goal becomes more important than how it was set or whether it was imposed.

6.   Feedback is important because goals initiate a self-evaluation process that affects motivation by providing a standard to judge progress. Feedback allows the students to set reasonable goals and track their performance in relation to their goals so that adjustments can be made in effort, direction, and strategies as needed. When feedback emphasizes progress, personal capabilities are highlighted. This enhances self-efficacy and aspirations.

7.   Goal setting has been found to be effective at all levels of schooling, in other cultures, and with students with LD. However, some research indicates that few students use effective goal-setting techniques. An important role for the teacher is to teach students how to set goals.

8.   The LINKS model is a comprehensive system integrating goal setting, strategies, attributions, and self-efficacy.

Motivational Toolbox

1. Important points to think about and lingering questions

2. Strategies I can use now

3. Strategies I want to develop in the future

CHAPTER 5

Developing Student
Self-Regulatory Capabilities

The best moments occur when a person's body or mind is stretched to its limits in a voluntary effort to accomplish something difficult and worthwhile. Optimal experience is thus something we make happen. . . . These periods of overcoming challenges are what people find to be the most enjoyable times of their lives. . . . By stretching skills, by reaching toward higher challenges, such a person becomes an increasingly extraordinary individual.

—Csikszentmihalyi (1990, p. 6)

This chapter focuses on the personal capabilities needed for motivation to learn. *Self-agency*, *self-motivation*, *self-determination*, and *empowerment* are terms used to describe the personal capabilities that enable students to be independent learners and develop a core of resiliency. A framework for the development of personal capabilities is a social-cognitive perspective of *self-regulation*. This refers to the degree to which "students are metacognitively, motivationally, and behaviorally active participants in their own learning process" (Zimmerman, 2001, p. 5).

There is increasing research on the importance of self-regulation in academic success from young children to college students. The use of self-regulatory capabilities was found to differentiate between underprepared and regular admission college students (Ley & Young, 1998), high and low achieving high school students (Zimmerman & Martinez-Pons, 1986), and at-risk and non-at-risk young children (Howse, Lange, Farran, & Boyles, 2003). Self-regulatory strategies were also found to improve performance of students with learning disabilities (LD)

(Graham, Harris, & Troia, 1998). Although the self-regulatory capabilities are important for school success and life, according to Zimmerman (2002) few teachers prepare students for these capabilities. Furthermore, Dembo (2004) suggests that self-regulated learning of the student has been overlooked in the school reform movement.

SELF-REGULATORY CAPABILITIES AND ACADEMIC SUCCESS

How much do capabilities such as concentration, self-discipline, effort, planning, determination, and patience contribute to a student's academic success? To what extent does the absence of these qualities contribute to a student's academic failure? The contrast between two first-grade students illustrates the importance of these qualities for school success (Greenspan & Lodish, 1991). Albert and Angela are first-grade students seated at their desks working with colors.

Albert	*Angela*
• is circling letters that go with pictures (with obvious pride);	• is scribbling different colors on her paper and is restless when finished;
• is attentive, smiles warmly as Ms. Miller walks by;	• is sitting half on, half off her chair with a puzzled expression on her face and doesn't ask Ms. Miller what to do;
• even though he can't quite read directions, figured out what to do from teacher's facial expression, posture, and words.	• grabs Brad's marker, pesters him, and is sent to timeout.

Albert clearly has an edge over Angela in behaviors that will help him be academically successful. He demonstrated capabilities characterized by Greenspan and Lodish (1991) as the "ABCs of school learning." The ABCs have four elements: (a) attending and focusing, (b) establishing positive relationships, (c) communicating, and (d) being able to observe and monitor oneself.

Many students like Albert first learned these qualities at home. What is the school's role with the Angelas who lack these qualities? Although teachers value personal qualities such as attentiveness and concentration, effort and persistence, self-restraint, and punctuality, Sockett (1988) suggested that there does not seem to be a concerted effort by schools to help students develop them. Instead there is often a belief that these qualities are unteachable.

REFLECTION. What are your beliefs? Are qualities such as these teachable? Should they be taught? Do you teach any of these qualities?

Let us look at another student. The following description is from a college application written by Lilia, who overcame insecurities of parental divorce, bulimia, and a short time in Juvenile Hall.

> With the help of AVID [a program designed to help students have a greater chance to go to college] I am taking two AP classes which I never dreamed possible. I know the joy of learning and the sense of accomplishment which comes with doing the best I can. One of my philosophies is if at first you don't succeed, keep trying until you do, which is one of the reasons I have taken the ACT once and the SAT twice—I plan to apply the strength and determination that have enabled me to be successful in high school throughout my college career.
>
> (Mehan et al., 1996, pp. 1–2)

Lilia demonstrated personal characteristics and behaviors of self-regulation. Yet self-regulation is a social-cognitive phenomenon that also includes the environmental influence, in this case the social context. The school had a role in providing the supportive environment for Lilia's development of the capabilities that enabled her to have a chance to go to college. (The AVID program is further described in Chapter 9.) Chapters 6, 7, and 8 describe the teaching motivation, social climate, and instructional practices that help cultivate students' development of self-regulated learning characteristics.

OVERVIEW OF SELF-REGULATED LEARNING

What are the personal capabilities that will help students seize and make the most of their opportunities? Although there are a number of models of self-regulated learning, the models share general assumptions: active participation by learners in goals, monitoring their motivation and learning by comparison against some criteria or standard, and mediating between their beliefs, behaviors, and the environment (Pintrich, 2003; Zimmerman, 2001).

Zimmerman (2001) describes a three-phase model of self-regulation that acts in a cyclical process (see Fig. 5.1). The three phases are:

1. *Forethought*—planning, goal setting, and beliefs that precede learning and set the stage. This includes adaptive beliefs about the role of ability and effort, positive self-beliefs for accomplishing the task, and intrinsic value of the task.
2. *Performance or volitional control*—processes that occur during learning to help the learner stay on the task. These include self-monitoring, attention focusing strategies, and self-instruction.
3. *Reflection*—evaluating the outcome of a task which, in turn, cycles back and influences forethought. Types of reflection include an evaluation of the outcome according to some criteria, an attributional analysis of the causes, and using these to make decisions about whether an adjustment is needed.

FIG. 5.1. Phases of self-regulated learning. Adapted from Zimmerman, B. J. (1998). "Developing Self-Fulfilling Cycles of Academic Regulation: An Analysis of Exemplary Instructional Models." In D. H. Schunk & B. J. Zimmerman (Eds.), *Self-Regulated Learning: From Teaching to Self-Reflective Practice* (pp. 1–19). New York: Guilford Press.

One example where the cyclical phases of self-regulatory strategies play an important role is the approach used by skilled writers during the writing process (e.g., planning and setting goals, making outlines, monitoring by keeping daily records, and revising: Graham & Harris, 1994).

The cognitive processes, strategies, and beliefs presented in Chapters 2, 3, and 4 form basic blocks of self-regulation. These include: (a) a belief that effort will lead to increased success and a strong sense of self-efficacy; (b) tools for setting effective goals and monitoring progress, and seeking help when needed; and (c) adaptive attributional beliefs, accepting responsibility for one's learning. Other qualities of self-regulated learning presented in this chapter are a vision of the future, volitional control strategies, cognitive and metacognitive strategies, and the essential tools of self-instruction (self-coaching), self-monitoring and self-evaluation, and time and resource management.

Are these qualities of self-regulated learning universal to all cultures? According to Paris, Byrnes, and Paris (2001), there is not a universal list of self-regulated strategies that all students will follow. Social norms in the culture denote which aspects of self-regulated learning are important. For example, the emphasis on independence may vary depending on the cultural norms.

VISION OF THE FUTURE AND POSSIBLE SELVES

How important is a vision of the future in self-regulation? Students in a high school dropout-prevention program (Farrell, 1990, 1994) were asked this question: What expectations do you have for yourself? The following are responses from three students in the program:

Cathy: "I want to . . . I don't know what profession I want to be . . ., but whatever I choose to do I wish to succeed and to have a family and to be the best I can be" (Farrell, 1994, p. 15).

Roberta: "There are so many things. I want to be a singer or a teacher, a stewardess, psychologist" (Farrell, 1994, p. 15).

Michael: "The thing that scares me most is . . . having no future. That really scares me. One of my greatest fears is growing up and bein [sic] a bum" (Farrell, 1990, p. 14).

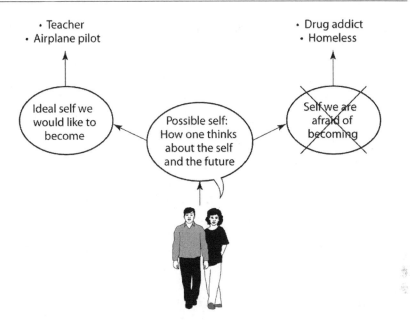

- Teacher
- Airplane pilot

- Drug addict
- Homeless

Ideal self we would like to become

Possible self: How one thinks about the self and the future

Self we are afraid of becoming

FIG. 5.2. Possible selves.

Cathy and Roberta have a positive vision of what they want their futures to be like. In contrast Michael is fearful about his future prospects. The views of the future expressed by these students illustrate the concept of *possible selves*. Possible selves are how we think about ourselves and our future (Marcus & Nurius, 1986). As depicted in Fig. 5.2, possible selves include the ideal selves we would like to become as well as a self we are afraid of becoming. For example, African-American adolescents were asked to list hoped-for possible selves and feared selves (McCready, 1996). Hoped-for selves included doctor, dancer, cosmetologist, and social worker. Feared selves included drug dealer, homeless, and working at McDonald's. The possible self we envision can be seen as a symbol of hope, as it is for Cathy and Roberta, or a reminder of a bleak future, as it is for Michael.

How Important is the Vision of the Future for Motivation?

A vision of a possible self is the first step in developing self-regulation. It sets planfulness in motion and acts as an incentive for present behavior (Borkowski & Thorpe, 1994; Marcus & Nurius, 1986). Sometime in your past, *teacher* became a possible self for you. Your hopes of becoming a teacher guided decisions such as choosing to go to college and sacrificing financially in order to do so. Or, if you are now teaching, your vision of becoming an even better teacher is guiding your decision to continue to learn.

What if a student has a fearful view of the future as Michael does? The absence of possible selves is viewed as a serious motivational problem affecting other components of self-regulation. A primary characteristic of underachieving older students and adults is the absence of a vision of the future (Borkowski & Thorpe, 1994). When students' views about the future are unclear, their current behavior is more likely to be governed by whatever is happening at the moment. Remember the students in Chapter 4 whose primary goal in school was *fun*? Their immediate concern with fun deters them from the academic preparation needed for college preparation or work opportunities. If students have not developed a future vision or are not committed to academically supportive short- and long-term personal goals, they are likely to show little self-regulation of their study behaviors. The failure to develop multiple, positive selves in early childhood may create a condition in which there is little long-term motivation for pursuing current and complex problem-solving activities (Borkowski & Thorpe, 1994).

How are Possible Selves Developed?

The formation of possible selves is influenced both by developmental and sociocultural factors (Day, Borkowski, Dietmeyer, Howsepian, & Saenz, 1992; Yowell & Smylie, 1999). For young children, the future is vague. However, as they develop, the future becomes more clearly defined. Interactions with our social environment—including parents, media, people we admire, peers, and school experience—have a formative influence on possible selves.

Homer Hickham (1999) envisioned becoming a rocket scientist when he saw Sputnik cross the sky over Coalwood, West Virginia: "I let my imagination wander, seeing the first explorers on the moon . . . an inspiration came to me. At the supper table that night, I put down my fork and announced, I'm going to build a rocket" (pp. 38–39).

The influences of others can have positive or negative effects on possible selves. The track star Carl Lewis formed an image based on Jesse Owens (Marcus & Nurius, 1986). Many track athletes probably formed an image of a possible self based on Carl Lewis. However, students in the potential dropout population were viewed neither as student nor as worker by the peers and adults in their lives (Farrell, 1990). Consequently, these students did not see themselves in these roles. Welch and Hodges (1997) contended that if an academic identity is not in place, students will be limited in their expectations for themselves. Perhaps Cathy and Roberta were influenced by someone in their family or school to form the positive vision of the future, whereas Michael did not have this positive influence. In fact, Usinger (2005) investigated parental expectations for their seventh graders' future. The analysis of the responses found a continuum from no response by some parents to a clearly stated vision of their child's role in the future by other parents.

Possible selves are also influenced by our attributional history and self-efficacy judgments. A combination of ability and effort attributions for success is thought to help create more positive possible selves (Borkowski & Thorpe, 1994). If our prior explanations for success and failure were primarily attributed to uncontrollable factors, we are not likely to envision the future with much hope. In addition, the possible self may be dominated temporarily by negative possibilities resulting from a defeat, loss, or lapse of will power. Seeing these setbacks as temporary is essential for our motivation for the future (Marcus & Nurius, 1986).

Self-efficacy beliefs that are linked to an envisioned possible self are likely to be influential for career choices (Borkowski & Thorpe, 1994). A student who has a strong belief in his or her math ability is more likely to expend the effort and persist and is more likely to include math in his or her career aspirations. The importance of helping students develop adaptive attributions and strong self-efficacy beliefs is underscored by their influence on a positive view of the future.

Helping Students Develop a Vision of the Future

What role can schools and teachers play in helping students develop possible selves or a vision of the future? When students have expectations for hoped-for selves, they also must have the knowledge, beliefs, and skills to enact what it takes (Yowell & Smylie, 1999). Two programs designed to help students develop a vision of the future are described: a project to help make possible selves more concrete for elementary children and a project designed to help Hispanic students succeed at college.

Possible Selves Project: Elementary Students. An intervention was designed specifically to help elementary age (Grades 3–5) Mexican-American students think about their hopes and fears as they related to academic and occupational achievement (Day et al., 1992; Day, Borkowski, Punzo, & Howsepian, 1994). The intervention consisted of three critical components across eight lessons, with Lesson 1 composed of ground rules.

- *Lesson 2.* The metaphor "possible-me-tree" was used to make possible selves concrete for the students. The possible-me-tree has four strong branches that represent four areas of life: (a) family and friends, (b) free time, (c) school, and (d) work. Each type of branch had two types of leaves: green for hopes for the future and red to represent their fears of the future. The possible-me-tree was introduced through artwork by asking students to imagine they were trees and explaining a growing tree as having a strong trunk made of healthy parts of the self (knowledge and skills), sturdy branches (the four areas of their lives), and the two types of leaves to represent their hopes and fears for the future (motivational aspects of hopes and fears were explained). Students then constructed a tree out of felt material, generated leaves for each branch, and discussed why unhealthy trees (weak trunks, fragile branches, few leaves) hindered their ability to reach their goals. The students added leaves to their trees as they saw new possibilities and fears for themselves.
- *Lessons 3–6.* Students were given instruction and practice in three self-regulatory strategies to achieve their goals: "Think ahead to the schoolwork you need to do; think while

doing school work; think back over what you have learned"
(Day et al., 1994, p. 80) (notice, these reflect the phases of
self-regulation). Students contrasted good and poor learners,
and they used the concrete representation of a time machine
to practice the three strategies. Enacting a situation where
students forgot a homework assignment, failed the test on it,
and had a consequent discussion of failure followed this.
Finally, students were given an assignment to use the time
line, practice the three strategies, and discuss their feelings
of success.

- *Lessons 7 and 8.* The focus was on the connection between
hoped-for and feared selves and doing well in school. The
time machine was used to project their future to the year
2010 and what they hoped to be doing then. The students
role-played specific jobs they might be doing—both enjoyable
jobs and jobs they might hold as a result of not graduating
from high school.

Throughout all lessons, students were helped to form linkages
between what they were doing in school currently and future
occupations, and between proximal and distal goals.

The results revealed that students who received the intervention increased their understanding of the characteristics of good
learners and the three self-regulatory strategies of think back,
think now, and think ahead. Furthermore, they improved their
knowledge of the importance and value of education for future
occupations and financial security. Their hoped-for future selves
increased for prestige jobs.

The possible-me training was adapted by J. D. Gibson (1998)
for seventh-grade students. The results indicated that the students listed fewer hoped-for future selves after training, but
their future selves were more realistic.

A Program for High School Students. At the secondary level,
Programa: Latinos Adelantan De Nuevo (PLAN) was developed
to help Hispanic students develop a vision of the future (Abi-
Nader, 1990). This was a comprehensive program designed to
address the belief held by many inner city minority students that
they have no control over their lives and are, therefore, powerless to shape their future. Consequently, these students lack

motivation, are unable to set goals, and are indifferent about the importance of school. This may have been the case with Michael.

One implicit goal of PLAN was to help students create a vision of the future. Several components of the program were used for this goal: assignments with stories in literature, mentors, and future talk. For example, students read *The Monkey's Paw* by William Jacobs (1979). This is a story about a family who used a mysterious paw to get wishes to come true, but with ill-fated results. Students were given a follow-up assignment to present 3-minute speeches about their own dreams and wishes. In the speech, they were to imagine their future, talk about their dreams, and explain how they would achieve them.

PLAN also provided mentors and models for the students by having Hispanic college students and professionals make presentations once a month for seniors. Mentors were former PLAN participants, and they attributed their success to the skills they learned in the program. Hearing these stories helped students see that it was possible for people like themselves to go to college.

An important role for teachers in the PLAN classroom was the initiation of a pattern of future-oriented classroom talk. Teachers focused on the future during discussions in four types of activities:

- *preparation* (e.g., planning a visit to a local university and learning how to fill out a financial aid form);
- *description* of situations students are likely to encounter in college (e.g., in reference to a term paper assignment, "I just want you to learn how to do it—I don't want surprises when you go to college": Abi-Nader, 1987, p. 195);
- *storytelling* about PLAN graduates and their success in college. Teachers told stories and provided examples of role models who successfully completed the program. The examples included a display of good papers by former students. Because some students had difficulty identifying with success, a story of a student who struggled and finally made it was included (a coping model);
- *providing a rationale* for PLAN's skill-building exercises (e.g., giving students an example of why public speaking is an important skill for college and work interviews).

The teacher's talk during these activities took place in the indicative mode, "when you go to college," rather than conditional mode (e.g., "if you go to college"). The PLAN approach has been effective. Students in PLAN graduate from high school and most earn full-tuition scholarships to college (Abi-Nader, 1991).

One strategy that can help students develop a vision of the future is the use of models. Suggestions for using models to help students develop a vision of the future are shown in Strategy 5.1. Both of these programs go beyond learning about careers to providing knowledge, beliefs, and skills needed for achieving goals.

Strategy 5.1. Providing Students with Models for a Vision of the Future

1. Do not assume that all students will identify positive models on their own, as one teacher discovered. Students were asked to look in the newspapers to find examples of successful people. The teacher was surprised to find that the largest number of examples selected by students was a professional athlete who had been arrested on drug charges and a movie actress who had been arrested for fighting with police. Expose students to positive models and have them identify characteristics and strategies of the model that led to success.
2. Bring in people with whom students can identify as models of success. Be sure the models describe the strategies that helped them achieve their success.
3. Use stories of inspiration from fiction, autobiography, and movies for discussion.

REFLECTION. What stories with examples of personal capabilities have inspired you? What stories might inspire your students?

VOLITIONAL CONTROL: DIRECTING MOTIVATION AND EFFORT

One of the most important components of self-regulation is volition. *Volition* is a form of action control, "the tendency to maintain focus and effort toward goals despite potential distractions" (Corno, 1994, p. 229). In everyday life, we use a number of terms that imply volition: *will*, *will power*, *discipline*, *self-direction*, and *resourcefulness*. These terms all imply the ability to buckle down to difficult tasks (Corno, 1993). However, current volitional theory is more about strategies to control personal behavior and lead to effective work habits (Corno, 2004). The following example illustrates volition:

> Elissa, a college student, is a single parent with a 7-year-old child, Shanell. She finds it very difficult to study in the evening. There are constant distractions, such as her child needing help with homework. She remembers that the Urban League Center has a program of supervised homework for students in the evenings. She takes Shanell to the center two evenings a week while she studies in the library.

Elissa demonstrated the use of volitional strategies by finding a way to study while providing a resource for her child.

The Function of Volition in Self-Regulation

Volitional strategies protect goals by directing and controlling one's energy toward them. Elissa was protecting two goals at the same time: her need to take care of her family responsibilities and her need for academic success. Refer to the proximal goal form in Exhibit 4.3. First you planned a goal. According to Corno (1993), this is the motivational aspect. The volitional component, Step 4 in Exhibit 4.3, asked you to list possible blocks and how you will overcome them. The actions you take to overcome the barriers are volitional strategies. Volition is responsible for making sure the goal is enacted. When goals are easy, volition is not necessary. Volitional strategies protect goals by (a) focusing attention, (b) prioritizing and completing goals, (c) handling distractions, and (d) managing effort (Corno, 1993, 2001).

What are volitional challenges faced by students? There are many distractions in and outside of school, including social pressures, that can deter students from goal accomplishment. Challenges and distractions include the following:

- juggling athletic or musical practice with time needed for homework;

- the belief that a task is too easy, too difficult, or boring;
- goals that are not valued;
- staying on task during cooperative learning;
- complex assignments and long-term projects;
- doing homework;
- accommodating work hours and academic responsibilities;
- distractions on the computer such as web surfing; and
- classroom or home environment with distractions.

Some of these items may seem trivial to adults, but such distractions and conflicts can have serious effects on the volition of children and their performance in academic areas.

Homework presents students with difficult volitional challenges because of many possible distractions; its success depends on students being able to handle distractions. Homework distractions were the subject of a study by Benson (1988), who asked sixth-grade students to list distractions that disturbed them the most when doing homework. At that time, the phone and television were the most frequent distractions listed by students (currently, it is likely cell phones and computers). Others were people, general noise such as appliances, and background music. Students were also asked to list solutions for the distractions. A primary solution suggested by students was to get their parents to help them. The researchers concluded that the students tended to place the responsibility to control distractions on others or the environment, not on themselves. However, the act of listing the distractions and solutions appeared to help students see how they could be more responsible for finding solutions.

Baird (2002) surveyed tenth-year students in Australia on their homework, volitional control strategies, and their teachers' perceptions of the strategies. One strategy used by students was a set time for completing homework. The survey of teachers, however, indicated that they ignored two important aspects for volitional control that would help students: strategies to control distractions and strategies for effective learning.

Guthrie, Van Meter, et al. (1996) suggested that children reading at home need volitional strategies such as having a system with a time and place, finding and keeping materials, decisions about what and what not to read, and knowledge of potential obstacles.

Increasingly, an area where self-regulatory volitional control strategies are important is effectively using the Internet (Rogers & Swan, 2004). Whipp and Chiarelli (2004) found that graduate students in a web-based technology course used self-regulated learning strategies and adapted them as needed for the web-based course.

Volitional Control Strategies

What are volitional control strategies? They are strategies that exercise overt and covert control over our actions and thoughts. Covert control of metacognitive, emotional, and motivational strategies is used to control self-defeating thoughts and to remind oneself to focus on the goal or task. Overt strategies control the self by controlling the environment, including persons within that environment (Corno & Kanfer, 1993). Examples of each of the five types of strategies reported by seventh-grade students and teachers are shown in Table 5.1 (Corno & Kanfer, 1993).

If students are to be academically successful, they need volitional strategies to keep them working at goals although there are other things they want to do. Garcia, McCann, Turner, and Roska (1998) found that volitional strategies were strongly related to college students' use of cognitive strategies. However, Wolters (1998) found that college students responding to a hypothetical problem relied on their will power rather than on volitional strategies. The students may not be aware of the need for conscious control of volitional strategies to maintain intentions to complete a task. How can teachers help students develop volitional strategies to manage distractions?

Helping Students Acquire Volitional Strategies

Interventions to help students acquire volitional strategies have been conducted from the first-grade level to the community college level. First-grade students were taught to reduce distractibility during reading group work (McDonough, Meyer, Stone, & Hamman, 1991). The students were taught how to set goals, avoid distracting themselves, and avoid distracting their classmates. Manning (1988) taught first and third graders to control

TABLE 5.1
Volitional Control Strategies Exemplified by Students and Teachers

Strategy	Student	Teacher
Covert		
Metacognitive Control	Think of first steps to take and get started right away. Go back over my work before I turn it in to make changes that will improve it.	Keep a running tab of times I have to speak to X about behavior. Reflect immediately after a lesson on how it went and make mental notes on what to do differently next time.
Motivation Control	Pat myself on the back for good work. Tell myself, "Concentrate on this work because . . ." Think through ways to carry out this task that will be more fun, more challenging, or more reassuring to me.	Keep my mind on grading these papers when I'd rather be doing something else. Plan ways to make my teaching better whenever I have spare moments for thought (e.g., while driving, walking).
Emotional Control	Count to 10 before I blow up. Remember I have lots of things I can draw on to help myself; I've done this kind of thing before.	Wait 5 seconds before speaking when angry. Marshal my inner resources and remember I've been through more than this and made it.
Overt		
Control the Task Situation. Control Others in the Task Setting	List the things I can do to get to where I want to go. Move away from noise and distractions. Ask friends for help.	Redefine my goals so they are more realistic for me. Establish rules for student behavior and enforce them. Call teacher study groups to cooperatively resolve problems. Give roles to students who need special attention.

Source. From Corno, L. & Kanfer, R. (1993). "The Role of Volition in Learning and Performance." In L. Darling-Hammond (Ed.), *Review of Research in Education* (Vol. 19, pp. 53–90). New York: American Educational Research Association. Adapted by permission of the publisher.

off-task and disruptive behaviors in the classroom using cognitive self-instruction, which is described later in this chapter.

A volitional enhancement program was implemented to help community college students develop volitional strategies (Trawick, 1991). The program consisted of four 70-minute lessons geared toward the control of external and internal environments. The four lessons were (a) control of task and setting, (b) control of others in the task situation, (c) self-monitoring to control attention, and (d) motivational control such as attributional statements.

Interviews with eight subjects found that the most important change students made was gaining control over their study environment. They were better able to handle distractions from friends, siblings, and others. Changing the external environment was easier for students than changing their covert metacognitive processes. From this finding, it is suggested that when helping students acquire volitional control, they need more time and practice for covert metacognitive strategies.

A planned volitional curriculum to help students in acquiring strategies was described by Corno (1994). Class activities developed for the curriculum are shown in Strategy 5.2. These can serve as a starting point for helping students acquire volitional control strategies.

Strategy 5.2.   Activities in Volitional Enhancement Curriculum

1. Teacher and students list possible distractions when studying.
2. Teacher and students make a master list of the most frequent distractions and categorize them as to where they occurred or if they were distracting thoughts.
3. List ways students usually handle distractions; then match the response with the distraction. Evaluate how well it works. The most effective way is to refocus on the task.
4. Teacher models and demonstrates both effective and ineffective responses to a distracting situation.
5. Teacher leads students through 20-item quiz requiring identification and classification of more effective strategies.
6. Using written scenarios, small groups of students role play more effective strategies for handling distractions. Peer audience evaluates actor's strategies.
7. Teacher reminds students that he or she will be looking for evidence of using strategies to handle distractions and doing their work. Select key tasks to observe. Record amount of

time on tasks by groups and individuals. Students self-evaluate; then results are discussed with students.

Source. From Corno, L. (1994). "Student Volition and Education: Outcomes, Influences, and Practices." In D. H. Schunk & B. J. Zimmerman (Eds.), *Self-Regulation of Learning and Performance* (pp. 229–54). New York: Taylor & Francis. Adapted with permission.

As educators we have the potential to teach students volitional control when we cannot change the prior experience of students (Corno, 2001). For example, volitional control can mediate maladaptive attributions. Although volitional strategies are necessary for negotiating our busy work and academic lives, can there be a negative side? Yes, they become maladaptive when the goal is no longer appropriate (Corno & Kanfer, 1993).

LEARNING AND METACOGNITIVE STRATEGIES

Self-regulated learners know a large number of learning strategies such as reading comprehension and memory strategies. They also understand how learning strategies work, know when to use them, and can evaluate their effectiveness. These latter processes are known as metacognitive strategies (Borkowski & Muthukrishna, 1992). Learning and metacognitive strategies enable students to acquire and master academic content. Although it is beyond the scope of this text to make a full description of learning strategies, a basic set of learning and metacognitive strategies is presented in the following sections.

Learning Strategies

Two lists of learning strategies are presented. The first list contains the eight categories of learning strategies proposed by C. E. Weinstein and Mayer (1986) that form a useful starter set. These strategies are listed in Table 5.2. This list ranges from simple strategies like rehearsal to elaboration, which is essential for deep-level processing.

TABLE 5.2

Eight Categories of Learning Strategies

Strategy	Description
1. Basic rehearsal strategies	Repetition
2. Complex rehearsal strategies	Copying or highlighting
3. Basic elaboration strategies	Creating a mental image or pictures that connect items
4. Complex elaboration strategies	Extending learning by summarizing or relating to prior knowledge
5. Basic organization strategies	Grouping or categorizing items
6. Complex organization strategies	Creating outlines and graphic organizers that show relationships
7. Comprehension monitoring	Self-questioning to check understanding
8. Affective and motivational strategies	Use of self-talk to reduce anxiety

Source. From Weinstein, C. E. & Mayer, R. E. (1986). *The Teaching of Learning Strategies*. In M. C. Wittrock (Ed.), *Handbook of Research on Teaching* (3rd ed.). New York: Thomson. Reprinted by permission.

The second list contains cognitive strategies that really work for elementary school students in reading comprehension. This list was identified by Pressley, Johnson, Symons, McGoldrick, and Kurita (1989):

- summarization—the ability to make a concise summary by constructing a sentence, short paragraph, or visual map;
- mental imagery—constructing a visual representation of the content;
- story grammar—the knowledge of how a story is structured;
- question generation—constructing questions that capture main ideas;
- question answering—answering questions on content such as at the end of the chapter; and
- prior knowledge activation—strategies to recall previously acquired knowledge.

Keep in mind that many secondary and even college students may not be proficient in these reading comprehension strategies. In this case, the teacher's role is one of helping students become self-regulated learners by explicitly teaching these strategies, beginning with one at a time. For more explicit descriptions of learning strategies, see Gaskins and Elliot (1991); Gettinger and Seibert (2002); Pressley, Johnson, et al. (1989); Pressley, Woloshyn, and Associates (1995); and Wood, Woloshyn, and Willoughby (1995).

Metacognitive Strategies

From a self-regulation standpoint, metacognition is the integration of cognitive, motivational, and situational characteristics (Borkowski & Thorpe, 1994). The cognitive aspect of metacognition generally refers to the knowledge and beliefs about one's cognitive processes and the monitoring and control of these processes (Flavell, Miller, & Miller, 1993). If students are to learn independently and manage their lives, metacognitive strategies are essential.

Metacognitive knowledge and strategies can be subdivided into three categories: person, tasks, and strategies (Flavell et al., 1993). Examples in each category are as follows:

- *Person.* Knowledge and beliefs about memory and how it works; beliefs about intelligence (e.g., some students believe a good memory is something you have or do not have).
- *Tasks.* An awareness that some tasks are more difficult than others and the evaluation of task difficulty and amount of time needed for task completion (e.g., planning a project and estimating the time needed and comparing it with the time available).
- *Strategies.* Decisions concerning which strategy will work the best for different types of tasks (e.g., which strategy is best for an essay test and which for mastering the table of elements in chemistry).

Metacognitive strategies that help students take control of their learning are often lacking in low-achieving students (Gaskins & Elliot, 1991). As teachers, we often do this metacognitive work for students instead of helping them acquire the strategies to help themselves.

SELF-REGULATION THROUGH
SELF-INSTRUCTION AND SELF-MONITORING

Tools used by self-regulated learners to regulate actions and thoughts are self-instruction and self-monitoring in the performance phase, and self-evaluation in the reflective phase. As humans, we use self-instruction when we talk to ourselves to guide our behavior. Self-monitoring occurs when we observe and evaluate our progress. These two strategies are often used in tandem. For example, a student might use self-instruction to remember how to carry out a series of steps in a problem and then use self-monitoring to keep track of his or her progress and evaluate the outcome.

Self-Instruction

An important tool in cognitive self-regulation is self-directed talk to control thought and actions (K. R. Harris, 1990; Rohrkemper, 1989). Self-instruction can be covert, silently talking to ourselves, or overt, speaking out loud. It is useful for control of behavior, development of metacognition, and treatment of academic problems (Meichenbaum, 1977). Examples of self-instruction are (a) Elissa silently reminding herself not to panic when she sees a test question that is unfamiliar; and (b) Angela repeating out loud, "I must stay in my seat until I finish my colors."

What is the source of self-directed speech? Its roots are in Vygotsky's (1962) explanation of the development and role of speech in children. It begins in early childhood, when young children talk out loud to themselves, even in the presence of others. This is initially guided by others' speech. Vygotsky explained that young children talk to themselves or use private speech to direct their own behavior. At about age 6 or 7, children become aware that it is not appropriate to talk out loud to oneself. Self-speech then becomes covert or silent (see Fig. 5.3).

As a self-regulatory process, self-instructional speech can take six forms (Graham, Harris, & Reid, 1992). These forms can help students understand the task, generate strategies for accomplishing the task, manage anxiety, and evaluate progress. These forms may be used independently or in combination as needed. Table 5.3 shows the forms with examples of each.

FIG. 5.3. Overt and covert self-instruction.

TABLE 5.3
Forms and Examples of Self-Instruction

Forms	*Examples*
1. Problem definition statements	I made a D on my first exam. What can I do? Was it how I studied? How can I improve?
2. Focusing attention and planning	I have to figure out a better way to study. The text is hard for me so I have to find a way to understand what I'm reading.
3. Strategy statements	I will try the SQ3R that the teacher gave us.
4. Self-evaluation and error correction statements	I tried to summarize what I have read so far and I still don't understand. I need to call one of my classmates to see how she is doing with this.
5. Coping and self-control statements help students overcome difficulties or failure.	Although I don't understand it yet, I don't need to panic. I can always ask my teacher.
6. Self-reinforcement	My friend asked me questions and I could answer them. I'm ready for this test.

Source. From Graham, S. & Harris, K. R. (1996). *Making the Writing Process Work: Strategies for Composition and Self-Regulation.* Cambridge, MA: Brookline Books. Adapted by permission.

Teaching Students to Use Self-Instruction

Self-instruction has been used for a variety of goals, including positive classroom behavior, composition skills, and problem solving. It is particularly useful for helping students with LD to develop academic competencies (Graham et al., 1992). The instruction for self-talk can be geared to an entire class or to individual students (Manning, 1991). Self-instructional training typically begins with modeling by the teacher, followed by practice by the students. The steps for teaching are described in Strategy 5.3.

The following research study shows the effectiveness of self-instructional training. First- and third-grade students who had a history of inappropriate classroom behavior were selected for the intervention to increase appropriate classroom behavior (Manning, 1988). The training targeted behaviors that students needed to decrease (e.g., out of seat, daydreaming, disturbing

---

Strategy 5.3.   Steps for Teaching Self-Talk

1. Explain the importance of self-talk. Discuss with students how talking to ourselves can be either positive or negative. For example, self-statements such as "I can't do it" are self-defeating. "I'm not stupid, I just didn't use the right strategy" is a step in a positive direction. Ask students to give examples of their self-talk and classify them according to whether they are positive or negative.
2. Model self-instruction. A coping model, teacher or peer, can show how they have used self-talk to improve performance. Students might be given a self-talk script and then develop their own.
3. Select tasks and have students practice self-talk. Gradually fade the modeling and prompting as they can do it on their own. Cues are provided through cue cards and posters until students perform independently.

Source.   Based on Graham, Harris, et al. (1992) and Manning (1991).

---

others) and behaviors that students needed to increase (e.g., staying seated, listening, concentrating, keeping hands and feet to self). The training was conducted two times per week, 50 minutes per session, for 4 weeks. The training components were:

- *Modeling.* Students viewed adult models in class and video tapes of peers. The models used self-instruction to improve work habits like raising a hand instead of screaming out an answer.
- *Guided practice.* Students practiced behaviors through games, role play, and the completion of incomplete scenarios.
- *Cueing.* Students were given cue cards with reminders to do the behaviors in the classroom. Cueing was continued until students used behaviors without prompts.

The self-instruction training group was compared with a control group that did not receive self-instruction at three time periods—immediately following training, after 1 month, and after 3 months. The experimental group demonstrated greater on-task and less disruptive behavior at all three intervals than did the control group. The teachers also observed the improved behavior.

Do students with LD benefit from training in self-regulation strategies? The answer is yes, based on a training research study by Miranda, Villaescusa, and Vidal-Abarca (1997). Two groups of fifth- and sixth-grade students with LD were taught self-instruction as a basis for training in reading comprehension and metacognitive strategies. One group was also given attribution retraining. Both training groups scored as well as a normally achieving control group on the comprehension posttest and both had adaptive attributional profiles.

There are many ways students and teachers can use self-instruction as a self-regulatory strategy. Self-instruction can be used as follows:

- as a volitional strategy to remind oneself to concentrate on work;
- to remember steps in academic tasks like problem solving or writing;

- to control attention and on-task behavior;
- to cope with anxiety and failure; and
- as part of attributional retraining.

Self-Monitoring and Self-Evaluation

Self-monitoring (or self-observation) requires a student to selectively attend to specific actions such as on-task behavior or processes such as attributional thoughts. It contains two components that go hand in hand: self-recording and self-evaluation (Zimmerman, 1995). Self-recording is a record of cognitions or actions being monitored by a student. The methods of recording include tally sheets, charts, graphs, and narrative logs. A student can evaluate the frequency or duration of a behavior like how long he or she was able to stay at his or her desk studying or a student can evaluate accuracy by rechecking his or her solutions before turning in the homework. Zimmerman and Martinez-Pons (1986) found that self-regulated students systematically checked their work before submitting it. An example of a form for self-monitoring of homework goals is shown in Exhibit 5.1.

Exhibit 5.1.   Self-Monitoring Homework

1. Did I write my assignment down?   Yes   No

2. What do I need to take home?

    a.——————————————————————

    b.——————————————————————

    c.——————————————————————

3. Time I will do my homework———————

4. Completion of my homework   Yes   No

5. What did I not understand?

Students who cannot monitor their own learning are at a great disadvantage. They are likely to continue to make the same mistakes. Self-monitoring serves as a tool for self-improvement and enhances learning in several ways (Zimmerman, 1995). It:

- increases selective attention by focusing students on a limited number of responses;
- helps students determine how effective a performance was;
- lets students know how effective a learning strategy was and encourages them to find a better one; and
- enhances management and use of time.

Record keeping was a strategy used by inner city students who demonstrated characteristics of self-regulation (Wibrowski, 1992). One student reported the following:

> I keep a list of the words, I got wrong. . . . When studying from a textbook, if I find something important, I get a piece of paper and just write down the name of the person and what he or she did or something like that and I have a study sheet.
>
> (p. 78)

Self-monitoring and recording are particularly important for students who have difficulty paying attention. Fifth- and sixth-grade students were taught to self-monitor study strategies in an individualized mathematics program (Sagotsky, Patterson, & Lepper, 1978). They periodically recorded "+" on a grid if they were actually working on the math and "−" if they were not. Students increased in study behaviors and math achievement.

> *Personal Note: I kept a daily log while writing this text. I recorded such things as literature sources and note-taking completion, work on drafts, where I should begin the next work session, and ideas. When I began a new work session, I knew where to begin; this kept me from repeating a task. More important, it led to better organization, goal setting, and use of my time.*

Self-monitoring of progress is essential for self-evaluation. The work or the processes monitored provide the information as basis for comparison with a criterion such as the goal or the standard expected (Zimmerman, 1998). The self-evaluations then become a source for attributional explanations and an ensuing adaptive or maladaptive response to the feedback.

RESOURCE MANAGEMENT STRATEGIES: TIME AND ENVIRONMENT

Self-regulated learners manage their time and environmental resources to accomplish their goals. Strategies to budget time and manage resources are presented in this section.

Time Management

The term *time management* is somewhat misleading. There are only 24 hours in a day and we cannot change that. We can only manage ourselves in how we use the time. Covey (1989) reminded us that the most important factor is how we prioritize time use. Does a high level of motivation ensure that students will manage their time well? The answer is no, according to research findings from studies of college students (Zimmerman, Greenberg, & Weinstein, 1994). Students often failed to regulate time even when they were motivated. Self-reports of time management were more strongly related to the achievement of college students than were their Scholastic Aptitude Test (SAT) scores (Britton & Tessor, 1991).

Time use was also found to be the second most important self-regulated learning strategy used by inner city high school students interviewed by Wibrowski (1992). Students reported two types of time strategies: time budgeting (planning time use) and time accounting (awareness of time use). The following report reveals one student's use of time:

> After school, I usually go home, I relax for about one hour and then I do my homework until I'm finished and if it is before 8 or 9 o'clock, I just relax and then go to sleep at around 10 o'clock. Or I just get up at about 6:30 and about 6:45, I call my mom, then I have breakfast, then I leave, then I get on the train for about 30 minutes, then I get to school, I go the cafeteria and talk to my friends till about 8:40.
>
> (p. 75)

Successful students indicated the time they spent studying or the time of day they studied. They were also aware of specific times that different activities took place.

Time budgeting is related to the processes of attributions for success and failure and self-efficacy perceptions (Zimmerman et al., 1994). A student who believes he or she is failing math because of ability is not likely to plan time to study math. However, a student who believes that writing improves through the process of feedback and revision will plan time for this to occur. An important factor in the self-regulation of time use is the quality of self-monitoring. When students are not aware that they are not learning, they are not likely to plan or adjust their use of time.

Our use of time is frequently based on habits, not on specific plans. Training students in time-budgeting strategies requires helping them become aware of their use of time and strategies to plan and prioritize their time use. Strategies for helping students learn how to use time effectively are found in Strategy 5.4.

Strategy 5.4. Strategies to Help Students Learn Effective Time Use

1. Discuss time use with students. The statement "I don't have time" can be discussed for attibutional meaning.
2. Have students record their time use both daily and weekly to determine how they are using time.
3. Next, have students make a personal time schedule.
4. Ask students to estimate time needed to complete various types of activities in and out of school.
5. Give examples of how you plan time for your lesson planning, grading, and other responsibilities.
6. Use computer software with calendars where available.
7. Make a calendar for your students to fill in with assignments for their classes.

Environment Management

Environmental control is concerned with study areas, noise levels, appropriate materials, and people (Gaskins & Elliot, 1991). Environmental management includes effective strategies to assist learning and strategies to reduce interference with learning. Organization is a crucial strategy that helps students control environmental factors. Some students need explicit instruction in organizational strategies. For example, when teachers at The Benchmark School initially generated a list of strategies needed by middle school students, organization was overlooked. However, they found that students needed to be taught how to organize their notebooks, notes, and handouts. Although several class periods were devoted to this early in the school year, the students were found to need a "refresher course" after 1 month or so. Explicit teacher explanations for organization can be found in Gaskins and Elliot (1991).

Organizational strategies are taught early in Japanese elementary schools (Peak, 1993). During the first weeks of first grade, students are taught a series of steps by which they prepare themselves to study. For example, they are first taught how to lay out materials on their desk and then they practice laying out the materials. They are also taught a routine to use at home in the evening to be sure all their equipment and book bag are ready for the next morning.

Management of study areas requires establishing a place where one can concentrate. One characteristic of self-regulated high school students was the arrangement of the physical setting where they studied (e.g., "isolate myself from anything that distracts me": Zimmerman & Martinez-Pons, 1986, p. 618). Teachers can have students discuss and generate a checklist for a home and classroom study environment, then have the students evaluate how their personal environments compare with the master list.

SELF-REGULATION IN CLASSROOM CONTEXTS

Self-regulation strategies are learned through instruction, experience, and students' own invention (Paris et al., 2001). Teachers play an important role in helping students acquire self-regulated strategies. Boekaerts and Niemivirta (2000) cautioned that an obstacle to self-regulated learning is the belief by many students that it is the teacher's role to motivate them to engage in the learning activity. Teachers then must convince students that self-regulatory strategies will be beneficial in and out of school, and then teach them strategies as needed.

In this section, two classroom interventions are described— one at elementary level and one at secondary level—that establish an environment with opportunities to develop self-regulated skills and provide explicit instruction on how to be a self-regulated learner. In both interventions, the teachers and researchers collaborated on the design. A third intervention describes teachers' role as self-regulated learners.

Elementary Classroom Context

N. E. Perry (1998) first identified differences between low and high self-regulated students in Grades 2 and 3. Strategies used by high self-regulated students were planning writing by constructing semantic webs, self-monitoring and self-correcting, self-evaluation, and asking for help with challenging tasks. In contrast, students with low self-regulation were characterized by defensive behaviors and self-handicapping. N. E. Perry and VandeKamp (2000), in collaboration with teachers, then created a classroom context that supported self-regulated learning for Grades 2 and 3. The features included:

- complex, open-ended reading and writing activities with choice about what to read;
- choice about what to read with teacher support; and
- tasks that provide an optimal level of challenge with the accompanying beliefs that challenge is important for learning and that one can learn from error.

The results indicated positive effects on students' self-regulated learning. Students had high levels of self-efficacy for reading and were able to use effective strategies for reading and writing.

Secondary Classroom Context

A classroom environment was created by Randi and Corno to promote self-regulated learning through literature in a Latin class (Corno & Randi, 1999; Randi & Corno, 2000). This was done on two levels:

- The enduring themes of self-reliance and independence in the humanities literature were explored with students.

Literature was chosen in which characters displayed characteristics such as quest, persistence, resiliency, and courage, in order to exemplify personal traits and characteristics of self-directed learners. One example was using the story, Virgil's *Aeneid*, to have the students create an imaginary character who symbolized three Roman qualities the hero represented: loyalty, purposefulness, and perseverance.

- Explicit instruction to students on how to be successful as learners (e.g., planning and monitoring, resource management, help seeking, homework partners, self-evaluation) was provided. In addition the importance of grades was minimized, whereas challenges gradually increased.

The strategies included overt and covert strategies that were listed in Table 5.1. The results indicated that students demonstrated their understanding of self-management strategies in their written essays.

Physical Education Class

Self-regulatory components were used by Alderman (1985) to prepare high school seniors for a final exam in physical education (Exhibit 5.2).

Exhibit 5.2.   Physical Education: A Self-Regulated Structure

First Day of Class

- *Self-Evaluation and Goal Setting.* Students completed a self-evaluation of health/physical fitness, competence level, and interest in various activities and then set goals for the year.

First 9-Week Grading Period

- *Weekly Self-Tests and Record Keeping.* Students completed tests in physical fitness and recorded scores in team notebook.
- *Goals for Final Exam.* Based on feedback from self-tests. Students were asked to set a realistic aerobic goal. Choices

---

included jog, walk, or jump rope. Instructor met with each to discuss the goal.

Second 9-Week Period

- *Practice Schedule.* Students practiced three times a week and recorded practices on individual record cards.

Final Evaluation

- *Self-Evaluation.* Students evaluated learning with comments such as, "I learned to set a goal and accomplish it."

Source. Adapted from Alderman (1985).

Preservice Teachers as Self-Regulated Learners

Randi (2004) contended that, if self-regulated learning is important for students, it also applies to teachers because a teacher's role is to assist students with strategies of self-regulation. Teachers may use strategies themselves, but do not explain them to students. Randi developed an approach to prepare preservice teachers as self-regulated learners in a teacher education program.

In one aspect of the program, preservice teachers developed literature-based instructional units integrating reading and writing. Character traits from the literature were emphasized to promote self-regulated learning, specifically volition. For example, a unit for a fifth-grade class used the book *Hatchet*, by Gary Paulsen (1999), for the theme of survival. Students identified traits of survival in the main character and applied them to their own lives.

An important step would be for teachers to begin to make their own self-regulatory strategies explicit for students. There are also many opportunities for teachers to incorporate self-regulatory components into their content area.

SELF-REGULATION FOR FAILURE ADAPTATION AND RESILIENCY

One of the most important aspects of self-regulatory capabilities is the potential for dealing with failure and building resiliency to setbacks. Bandura (1997) reminded us that our pathways to goals and tasks are likely to be strewn with obstacles. It is not the failure and disappointments that are crucial, but the response to the setbacks. Failure is a part of school—failing tests, not being the valedictorian, not placing in the state music competition, not making the starting team or the drill team, criticism of one's work in art, losing the election for student council representative, and not understanding the reading time after time. A student's failure might be small—making his or her first B—from the view of a teacher, but a crisis from the student's perception.

One factor that elevates the importance of helping students develop and maintain confidence is the increased pressure on students from the emphasis on standards and high-stakes testing (Stiggins, 1999). As described in Chapter 2, when setbacks occur, some individuals abandon their efforts, prematurely giving up their goals, whereas others look for more effective strategies and try harder. Students who react by using mindful effort will continue striving (Boekaerts & Niemivirta, 2000). One important role for teachers is to help students develop adaptive strategies to handle failure. What are these strategies?

Bandura (1997) contended that an optimistic belief in one's efficacy is a necessity in dealing with setbacks. This is related to adaptive attributions for success and failure—a learning goal view of ability and intelligence, volitional strategies to overcome obstacles, positive self-talk, and support from key people. As Rohrkemper and Corno (1988) contended, "Rather than shielding students from learning stress, we seek to teach them how to adaptively respond and learn from it" (p. 311).

Self-regulatory capabilities that have been described are not magical, and they are not learned simply by attending school. Examples of students who did not possess these capabilities have been presented in this and previous chapters:

- students in Ms. Foster's ninth-grade class, who did not have the goals or learning strategies or the social skills for cooperative learning;
- Angela, a first grader who was inattentive and off task; and
- community college students who lacked volitional strategies.

Self-regulatory strategies for students like Angela need to begin in the early grades. If there is no intervention, her inattentive/withdrawn and disruptive behavior will likely continue and it will become increasingly difficult for her to be engaged in learning (Finn, Pannozzo, & Voekle, 1995). Three components of self-regulation are particularly important for focus in the early years: self-control processes, beliefs about personal control, and hoped-for future goals (Borkowski & Thorpe, 1994).

Students who have developed these personal capabilities have also been presented:

- Albert, a first grader who is attentive and independent in figuring out what to do;
- Lilia, who has a vision of college and has determination to succeed; and
- inner city students with self-regulatory strategies.

REFLECTION. Make a list of your own self-regulatory strategies. Describe or envision the characteristics of a self-regulated learner in your classroom.

The capabilities of self-regulation are needed by all students whether they are high or low achievers. Students who have these qualities of personal capability will have a foundation for resiliency. Resilient students possess qualities such as a sense of purpose and future planning, social and help-seeking skills that enable them to gain support, and the ability to act independently (Benard, 1993). A role of the school is to establish a quality environment with factors that promote resilience (Benard, 2004). These factors are: (a) caring, supportive relationships; (b) high expectations; and (c) opportunities to participate in school. The key factor according to Benard (2004) is, "schools are made up of students whose innate resilience is promoted rather than dampened by the people and conditions they encounter there" (p. 86).

Teachers can influence the development of these capabilities by working directly on (a) intellectual skills, (b) self-evaluation, (c) skills in interpersonal relations, (d) activity levels, and (e) self-efficacy and hopefulness (Reynolds, 1994).

CONCLUSION

For competence development and motivation, students must have a responsive environment, but personal agency beliefs are often more fundamental (Ford, 1995). In this chapter we saw interventions that attempted to do both. Classroom climate and instruction that supports the development of these personal capabilities are presented in Chapters 7 and 8.

REVIEW OF MAJOR POINTS

1. *Self-regulation* refers to one's own learning through metacognitive, motivational, and behavioral participation. It is composed of three phases acting in a cyclical fashion: forethought, volitional control, and self-reflection.

2. A vision of a possible self—how we think about ourselves and the future—is the first step in developing self-regulation. Motivationally, possible selves act as incentives for future behavior, with the absence of possible selves viewed as a serious motivational problem. Development of possible selves is based on social environment, attributions, and self-efficacy beliefs. Interventions to help students develop possible selves or visions of the future have been developed at elementary and secondary school levels with promising success.

3. *Volition*, the "tendency to maintain focus and effort toward goals despite potential distractions," is important for self-regulation because it protects goals (Corno, 1993, p. 229). Students encounter many volitional challenges such as homework; its success depends on students' handling of distractions. Volitional control strategies are covertly used to control self-defeating thoughts and covertly and overtly used to control the self by controlling the environment. Interventions to help students acquire volitional strategies have been developed from the first-grade level to the community college level.

4. Self-regulated learners possess learning and metacognitive strategies. Learning strategies range from simple strategies like rehearsal to elaboration, which is essential for deep-level processing. Metacognitive strategies include knowledge and strategies of the person (knowledge and beliefs about memory

and how it works), tasks (evaluation of task difficulty), and strategies (decisions about which strategy will work the best for different types of tasks).

5. Self-regulated learners use self-instruction and self-monitoring to manage actions and thoughts. Self-instruction is used when we talk to ourselves to guide our behavior and can be covert (e.g., silently talking to ourselves) or overt (e.g., speaking out loud). Six forms of self-instructional speech can help students understand the task, generate strategies for accomplishing the task, manage anxiety, and evaluate progress. Self-instruction has been used for a variety of goals, including positive classroom behavior, composition skills, and problem solving; it is particularly useful for helping students with LD develop academic competencies. Self-instructional training typically begins with modeling by the teacher, followed by practice by students.

6. Self-monitoring is the observation and evaluation of our progress and the outcome. It contains two complementary components: self-recording and self-evaluation. It requires a student to selectively attend to specific actions, such as on-task behavior, or processes, such as attributional thoughts.

7. Self-regulated learners manage their time and environmental resources to accomplish their goals. Students can be motivated but fail to regulate their time. Training students in time-budgeting strategies requires helping them to become aware of their use of time and to develop strategies to plan and prioritize their time use.

8. Environmental control is concerned with study areas, noise levels, appropriate materials, and people, as well as strategies to reduce interference with learning. Organization is a crucial strategy that helps students control environmental factors.

9. Classroom approaches to developing self-regulation have been developed for elementary and secondary grades and for preservice teachers. Self-regulatory strategies for students need to begin in the early grades with self-control processes, beliefs about personal control, and hoped-for future goals. Students who have these qualities of personal capability will have a foundation for resiliency. Resilient students possess qualities such as a sense of purpose and future planning, social, and help-seeking skills that enable them to gain support, and the ability to act independently.

Motivational Toolbox

1. Important points to think about and lingering questions

2. Strategies I can use now

3. Strategies I want to develop in the future

PART III

THE CLASSROOM CLIMATE FOR OPTIMAL ENGAGEMENT AND MOTIVATION

This part moves from motivational processes to the classroom context. A classroom in which students are engaged does not just happen; it is the result of interactions among students, teachers, and curriculum. The following four chapters focus on teacher expectations and confidence, the social climate of the classroom, and instructional components that affect engagement.

Teachers' beliefs about their potential effectiveness in teaching in various conditions and their expectations about abilities of diverse students have been identified as powerful influences on the achievement of students. An essential element is for students of diverse cultures to experience a shared sense of membership with the school and classroom. Challenges for the teacher are to establish conditions that allow for optimal work conditions and provide safety for all students while facilitating the development of personal responsibility. Three interrelated components comprise the classroom instructional focus: task, incentives, and evaluation.

CHAPTER 6

Teacher Motivation: Expectations and Efficacy

Miss Bailey, a language arts teacher in a high poverty middle school believes "The average student, no matter what his social or economic status, wants to be better when he leaves the classroom than when he walked in. . . . I try to provide the tools for them to do that. I teach every student like I was teaching the president of the United States. . . . when more than half of our students are at risk, we are all at risk."
—Rust (1992, pp. 1G, 6G)

Currently, many educators advocate for or embrace beliefs such as "all students can succeed (or learn)." What does this statement really mean in terms of practice? How do teachers' beliefs about students and their ability to teach them affect their teaching practice and student motivation and achievement? This chapter focuses on two related areas that reflect teacher confidence: teacher expectations and teacher efficacy. *Teachers' expectations* reflect teachers' beliefs about student capabilities to learn. *Teachers' sense of efficacy* refers to their confidence about how effective their teaching will be to bring about desired student achievement.

TEACHER EXPECTATIONS

Since the publication of Robert Rosenthal and Lenore Jacobson's (1968) *Pygmalion in the Classroom*, the topic of teacher expectations and self-fulfilling prophecy has been of great interest and controversy. The Rosenthal–Jacobson research was designed to manipulate teacher expectations and determine if these manipulations affected student achievement. Students were given a general achievement test, but teachers were told that it was a test that would identify certain students as late bloomers—students who would make large achievement gains during the year. In fact, the students identified as late bloomers had been chosen at random, not on the basis of any test scores. At the end of the year, those students who had been labeled late bloomers showed greater gain on achievement test scores than did the others. Rosenthal and Jacobson explained this gain as a self-fulfilling prophecy. A self-fulfilling prophecy occurs when "an originally erroneous expectation leads to behavior that causes the expectation to come true" (Good & Brophy, 1994, p. 84). This interpretation meant that the gains students made on achievement test scores were a consequence of expectations the teachers held for the students. There was much criticism of this study when later research failed to find the same results (Claiborn, 1969). Because this study did not include classroom observations, further research was conducted to determine how teachers' expectations influenced their instruction for different students.

Teacher Expectations and Teacher Expectation Effects

Good and Brophy (1994) differentiated teacher expectations and teacher expectation effects. *Teacher expectations* are defined as "inferences that teachers make about the future academic achievement of students based on what they know about these students now" (Good & Brophy, 2003, p. 67). *Teacher expectation effects* are defined as "effects on student outcomes that occur because of actions that teachers take in response to their expectations" (p. 67). Teacher expectations can lead to positive or negative effects. Two types of teacher expectation effects have been identified: self-fulfilling prophecy effect and sustaining expectation effect (Cooper & Good, 1983; Good & Brophy, 1994).

The Self-Fulfilling Prophecy Effect. The self-fulfilling prophecy effect occurs when a teacher forms different expectations for students early in the year and uses different instructional practices with different results. Good and Brophy (1994) described the process as follows:

1. The teacher forms different expectations based on some student characteristic.
2. Because of these different expectations, the teacher behaves differently toward various students.
3. The teacher's behavior tells students what behavior and achievement the teacher expects from them.
4. If this treatment persists and if students do not resist or change it in some way, motivational patterns, such as their aspirations and self-efficacy, are likely to be affected.
5. With time, students' achievement and behavior will conform more and more closely to that originally expected of them: High-achieving students continue to achieve, whereas low-achieving students gain less.

The fact that teachers have different expectations for students does not by itself lead to a self-fulfilling prophecy. According to Good and Brophy, if any one of these elements is missing, differential effects may not occur. In addition, teacher expectation effects can be moderated by home influences (Alvidrez & R. S. Weinstein, 1999).

The Sustaining Expectation Effect. A sustaining expectation effect occurs when a teacher has an existing expectation about a student and continues to respond to the student in the same way although the student's behavior has changed. This response maintains the behavior. An example is one in which a student has a history of misbehavior and then begins to behave more positively. The changes go unnoticed by the teacher, who continues to respond to the student in the same way, reinforcing the old behavior (Good & Brophy, 2003). Sustaining expectation effects are the most frequent type of effect and may become stronger as children advance through the elementary grades (Kuglinski & R. S. Weinstein, 2001).

Expectations need not become sustaining or self-fulfilling effects. Brophy (1985) explained that a low expectation may have a positive outcome when a teacher is aware of low academic performance of a student, but is unwilling to accept it. The teacher may take extraordinary measures to see that the student achieves some success. Rose (1995) described a teacher who was aware of the low performance level of students but was not willing to accept it: "Teachers will say either 'we can't lower our standards' or 'this poor child is reading below grade level so I'll need a third- or fourth-grade book.' But what you need to do is to make that eighth-grade book *accessible*" (p. 17).

Although as a teacher you will be aware of student behavior and achievement, it is how you respond to students and how you teach as a result of the awareness that make the difference. Consider the examples of two first-grade students. In one example, low expectations led to high performance and, in the other, high expectations led to declining performance (Goldenberg, 1992). Marta and Sylvia were Spanish-speaking children from low SES families in a bilingual education program. Both students were in a reading program for children who were at risk for reading failure. The case of Marta and Sylvia is described in Exhibit 6.1.

Exhibit 6.1.   How Low Expectations Can Lead to High Performance and High Expectations Can Lead to Declining Performance

Marta: Low Expectations

Marta's teacher initially predicted that she would be among the lowest 5 of 29 students, primarily because of her attitude, low effort, inattention, and careless work. However, because the lack of effort bothered the teacher, she kept Marta after school and told her she needed to improve her behavior and attitude and needed to be more careful and neat, and met with Marta's mother and told her the same thing and that Marta needed more practice at home.

Marta made slight improvement by making more of an effort, resulting in the teacher revising her prediction upward. After a one-month break in school, Marta began to do much better, with the most observable changes in her attitude and behavior. She was more task oriented and seemed more confident. When Marta had setbacks, the teacher viewed them as temporary (unstable) and thus not serious. By February, she referred to Marta as a *wonder child*; by April, Marta could do anything.

Marta succeeded because the teacher took positive and decisive steps toward changing her behavior early in the year, instead of using actions that would lead to the self-fulfilling prophecy effect.

Sylvia: High Expectations

Sylvia's teacher had high expectations for her achievement in first-grade reading. Early in first grade, the teacher referred to Sylvia as a *whippy kid* because her hand was frequently up, she usually answered correctly, and she did not forget homework or lose her syllable cards. The teacher was very satisfied with Sylvia's progress and had high expectations for first grade.

By December, the teacher said Sylvia was out of it most of the time and was not progressing as previously. She did not finish seatwork assignments that were piling up and hindering her progress. Sylvia was a slow worker and, when left to work alone, she rarely finished any assignment, resulting in a drop in the teacher's expectation. Sylvia's uncompleted work increased while her phonic skills fell below first-grade norms; she was now described as one of the *unsuccessful* readers.

As the year progressed, the children got longer assignments and were expected to complete more. Sylvia's uncompleted work increased. Because the teacher assumed that Sylvia was working at her limit, she did not see a need to intervene. Goldenberg (1992) suggested that the teacher consider:

- reducing Sylvia's workload and telling her exactly how far she was expected to get in completing an assignment;
- giving her an amount that seems reasonable and holding her accountable, gradually increasing the work.

Several weeks later, the teacher reported that Sylvia was finishing everything, with time on task increasing to 65 percent and 70 percent of the time. Sylvia began to proudly announce each day how much she finished. In addition, the teacher's aide had expected Sylvia to finish her work before she was allowed to color—an activity she enjoyed.

Goldenberg concluded that the teacher's initial high expectations had led her to assume that Sylvia would do well on her own without explicit monitoring and/or action.

FIG. 6.1. Sources of expectation.

Sources of Teacher Expectations

It is important for teachers to be aware of the potential sources of expectations that could affect their interaction with students. What factors influence the expectations teachers form about students? A primary source is the teacher's perceptions of student ability (Alvidrez & R. S. Weinstein, 1999). This judgment may be based on actual student performance. Other potential sources of expectations are shown in Fig. 6.1.

Note that the sources are potential ones. As stated earlier, awareness of differences does not automatically lead to self-fulfilling prophecies. Teachers who focused on only one characteristic tended to have lower expectations while teachers who considered multiple dimensions had higher expectations (Timperley & Phillips, 2003).

REFLECTION.   Which of these student characteristics will be more likely to influence you? What preconceived notions will you need to guard against? Your evaluation of these potential sources of expectations can help you become more aware of biases that may lead to differential practices.

Beliefs about the nature of intelligence are powerful sources of teacher and school expectations. Two conceptions of intelligence—entity and incremental (Elliott & Dweck, 1988)—were presented in Chapter 3. If teachers view intelligence as an entity that is fixed and stable, they are likely to see students as *smart* or *dumb* and teach them according to the label. However, if teachers believe that intelligence is composed of many dimensions and is incremental, and that learning strategies can be taught, they will be more concerned with how much they can teach students.

How influential are SES and ethnicity on forming expectations? R. S. Weinstein (2002) pointed out that limited attention has been paid to expectancy effects and the increasing diversity of students in schools. However the evidence suggests that teachers underestimate the ability of Black and lower SES students although their achievement may be equal to that of Whites (R. S. Weinstein, Gregory, & Strambler, 2004). Social class and ethnicity were singled out as the two most observable characteristics that are likely to influence teacher beliefs (Baron, Tom, & Cooper, 1985). These two variables are often interrelated because low-SES groups are overrepresented by minority groups. One of the few studies on expectations for young children examined teacher beliefs about former Head Start and non-Head Start students from White, African-American, and Hispanic groups, and how their beliefs related to test performance (Wigfield, Galper, Denton, & Sefeldt, 1999). The findings indicated that teachers held positive beliefs about Head Start and non-Head Start groups, but that White children were rated more favorably than African-American or Hispanic children for next year's grades.

Some high-poverty classrooms were found to have negative teaching practices (Shields, 1995). Shields observed that a small percentage of teachers believed that students from certain cultural or economic groups possessed significant limitations that could not be overcome, and this affected how they taught. One example of a negative practice occurred in a first-grade reading class in which half the students were Hispanic and half were White. The low reading group, composed of Hispanic students, was turned over to an aide for instruction instead of being taught by the regular teacher. Negative practices such as this were thought to be based on negative stereotypes about ethnic or SES background of students and what they could accomplish, and affected teaching practices. Jussim, Eccles, and Madon (1996) concluded that low-SES and minority students are more susceptible to negative teacher expectancy.

How do Teachers Communicate Expectations to Students?

Expectations are communicated to students by a variety of teaching practices. Table 6.1 presents a list of differential expectations as summarized by Good and R. Weinstein (1986). Selected classroom practices are described in greater detail.

Questioning Strategies. Teachers may use different questioning strategies for students thought to be low ability compared

TABLE 6.1
General Dimensions of Teachers' Communication of Differential
Expectations and Selected Examples

	Students believed to be *MORE* capable have:	Students believed to be *LESS* capable have:
Task Environment Curriculum, procedures, task definition, pacing, qualities of environment	More opportunity to perform publicly on meaningful tasks.	Less opportunity to perform publicly, especially on meaningful tasks (supplying alternate endings to a story vs. learning to pronounce a word correctly).
	More opportunity to think.	Less opportunity to think, analyze (since much work is aimed at practice).
Grouping Practices	More assignments that deal with comprehension, understanding (in higher-ability groups).	Less choice on curriculum assignments—more opportunity to work on drill-like assignments.
Locus of Responsibility for Learning	More autonomy (more choice in assignments, fewer interruptions).	Less autonomy (frequent teacher monitoring of work, frequent interruptions).
Feedback and Evaluation Practices	More opportunity for self-evaluation.	Less opportunity for self-evaluation.
Motivational Strategies	More honest/contingent feedback.	Less honest/more gratuitous/less contingent feedback.
Quality of Teacher Relationships	More respect for the learner as an individual with unique interests and needs.	Less respect for the learner as an individual with unique interests and needs.

Source. From Good, T. L. & Weinstein, R. (1986). "Teacher Expectations: A Framework for Exploring Classrooms". In K. K. Zumwalt (Ed.), *Improving Teaching (The 1986 ASCD Yearbook)* (pp. 63–85). Alexandria, VA: ASCD. Reprinted by permission.

with students thought to be high ability (e.g., Allington, 1980). Typically, low-ability students were called on less often and given less time to answer (Good & Brophy, 2003). Teachers were also more likely to give low-ability students the answers or to call on another student rather than to provide hints or to rephrase questions to help them improve their responses. These low-ability students were less likely to be asked higher level comprehension questions. Questioning practices such as these communicate to students that they are less capable; they also deprive the lower-achieving students of an opportunity to develop higher-level comprehension skills.

Grouping Practices. The effects of grouping practices can occur in individual classrooms such as reading groups, and at the school level where tracking by ability is in place. Although more of the research has documented the negative impact of some types of grouping, there is also documentation of the positive impact.

A student's group assignment is likely to be the first factor that conveys a teacher's expectation for student achievement (R. S. Weinstein, 1993). Those expectations will be communicated by the curriculum, text, and instructional practices selected or designed by the teacher. What is the evidence about the effects of grouping practices on student achievement?

Group placement can communicate expectations, both directly and indirectly, to students (R. S. Weinstein, 1993). Giving different reading group assignment instructions to high- and low-ability groups conveys a direct expectation. For example, Good and Marshall (1984) found that low-ability groups spent much of their time in repetitive drill with inadequate instruction. An indirect way to communication expectations is the use of labels such as *special readers*, signifying the low reading group.

When students are segregated into separate classes, as in ability grouping (tracking), there are more opportunities for undesirable self-fulfilling prophecy effects (Brophy, 1985). A number of instructional practices have been identified whereby high- and low-track classes received differential instruction. In all cases, low-track classes seemed to have fewer opportunities to learn than did high-track classes. Examples of differential instruction are as follows:

- Teachers in low-track classes tended to be less clear about objectives, made fewer attempts to relate material to student interests and backgrounds, were less open to student input, and were not as clear in introducing material (Evertson, 1982).
- Low-track classes were taught less demanding topics and skills, especially those involving higher level thinking skills; had less experienced teachers; and had less active learning and more seatwork and worksheet activities in math and science (Oakes, 1985).

By the same token, teachers need to be aware of the subtle ways they lower achievement and achievement expectations when they think they are helping the student. A study of how teachers adapted instruction for at-risk students (LD in this case) was conducted by Miller, Leinhardt, and Zigmond (1988). They discovered teaching practices that did not require even moderate engagement by students. To the contrary, the practices acted as deterrents to students' developing more adaptive strategies. The practices included:

- shuffling of information without really processing it (e.g., transferring information from the chalkboard to a notebook, to homework, or to tests);
- teachers reading the text for students and extracting important information for students without requiring students to acquire information-processing or reading comprehension skills;
- giving tests where 81 percent of the items came verbatim from a review sheet.

On the other hand, placing lower achieving math students in a more advanced class found positive effects (Burris, Heubert, & Levin, 2006; Mason, Schroeder, Combs, & Washington, 1992). Both interventions placed students in Grades 6–8 (Mason et al., 1992) in with higher level curriculum and provided the necessary support such as expectations, effective instruction, and tutoring. The results indicated that students in both interventions chose to take more advanced math courses.

Student Awareness of Differential Treatment

To what extent are students aware of differential treatment by teachers within the classroom? R. S. Weinstein and colleagues (R. S. Weinstein, 1993; R. S. Weinstein & McKown, 1998) reviewed research that examined students' perceptions of their treatment by teachers. They described the students as "sophisticated observers" who draw from nonverbal and verbal cues. The findings indicated that students, ranging from first grade through sixth grade, were aware that teachers treat students differently. A typical response was "sometimes she [the teacher] says, 'Oh, that's very poor reading' to someone else and she says 'pretty good' to me . . . I kind of marked myself in the middle because—To other people, she says, 'excellent reading'" (R. S. Weinstein, 2002, p. 100). Reports by students indicate that they were aware that low achievers are likely to (a) receive more negative feedback, (b) get more rules and teacher directions, (c) receive lower expectations, and (d) have fewer opportunities or choices. Students were also aware of different qualities of praise and of frequency of being called on to give answers.

A relationship was found between students' perceptions about the value of study strategies and their perceptions about what their teachers wanted them to learn (Nolen & Haladyna, 1990). The findings indicate that when students thought that their teacher wanted them to think independently and thoroughly master the material to be learned, they were more likely to have a learning goal orientation rather than a performance orientation and thus value using learning strategies. The authors concluded that teachers' expectations can influence students to use study strategies.

R. S. Weinstein and McKown (1998) concluded that any understanding of teacher expectancy must recognize children's perceptions of what the teacher expects and of differential treatment accorded different students.

Level of Expectations

Which has more positive effects on student expectations: minimal requirements that all students are expected to reach or the most hoped-for level anyone can reach? A now-classic study compared achievement in low-SES African-American and White schools (Brookover, Beady, Flood, Schweitzer, & Wisenbaker, 1979). The most important differences affecting achievement were (a) the level of expectations teachers held for students, and (b) teacher commitment to ensuring that academics were learned. The more successful teachers established floor levels for student achievement rather than ceiling levels. A *floor level* was the minimal requirement that teachers expected *all* students to achieve; in this case, it was usually grade level. In contrast, teachers in low-achieving schools tended to have ceiling-level expectations. The *ceiling level* was the highest estimate of what students could be expected to learn because of their background (low SES), and no attempt was made to teach more than this. Thus a ceiling effect acted as a cap on learning, as shown in Fig. 6.2. Teachers in high-achieving schools who had floor-level requirements were largely successful at attaining the academic expectations.

Brookover et al. (1979) concluded that, although a student body composed of minority or low-SES students may predispose teachers and principals to accept low levels of achievement, this can be overcome through developing a positive academic climate with appropriate instruction.

Toward Positive Expectations

Moving toward positive expectations is a move toward developing the potential of students (R. S. Weinstein et al., 2004). Simply telling teachers to raise their expectations for all students—using phrases such as "All children can learn" or "success

Floor expectation

I expect my students
to make at least a
year's growth

Ceiling expectation

Because of these students'
homelife, I can expect only
so much from them

FIG. 6.2.   Floor and ceiling effects.

for all"—is not enough (Ferguson, 1998; Corbett, Wilson, & Williams, 2002). But there are practices that will help teachers raise expectations and achievement.

A starting point is to reduce the use of labels such as *low ability, slow, deprived, poor, LD,* for individual students and groups. Labels imply fixed abilities and deficits in the students and can lead to underestimating student potential and lowering expectations (R. S. Weinstein et al., 2004). Instead of concentrating on a student's low ability, concentrate on what the student needs to learn. A positive expectation is, "Jason may be a poor reader, but I know he will improve his comprehension after I teach him to find a main idea and to recall prior knowledge."

Wheelock (1992) found a number of ways that teachers communicated positive expectations (Exhibit 6.2). Teaching implications for expectations are listed in Strategy 6.1.

Exhibit 6.2. How Teachers Can Communicate High Expectations

Lessons can communicate high expectations if they:

- Build on and validate students' prior knowledge and experience
- Help students construct their own knowledge
- Communicate information in a variety of ways
- Engage in dialogue that evokes more than one-word answers
- Require thinking skills such as comparing, contrasting, and applying knowledge
- Incorporate students' own cultural backgrounds into learning
- Involve students through a variety of activities that engage different kinds of intelligence
- Involve all students, whether or not they volunteer comments

A teacher communicates high expectations for students by:

- Introducing activities in which every individual becomes invested in the group effort
- Communicating that making mistakes is part of learning and that practice and concentration promote improvement

- Creating an environment of mutual trust and cooperation among students and between students and the teacher
- Arranging seating in such a way that no student is "invisible" to the teacher or others

Permanent classroom "decorations" can convey high expectations so that:

- Students understand that learning continues beyond the completion of a classroom assignment and that extra time is still learning time
- Students work in an environment that stresses their responsibility for their own learning
- Teachers are relieved of the necessity of repeating directions related to assignments, allowing them to remain engaged in coaching or dialogue with students

A teacher can communicate high expectations by:

- Allowing students plenty of time to answer questions
- Giving hints and working with students if the answer does not come quickly
- Creating a student–teacher partnership in the uncovering of knowledge
- Putting students in the role of the teacher

A classroom environment can communicate high expectations by:

- Letting students know that their schoolwork is preparing them for life, not just for the next grade
- Providing images and information that encourage students to stretch their aspirations to include the possibility of a wide range of future options
- Distributing legitimate recognition to as many students as possible in as many ways as possible
- Assigning projects that require extended effort
- Providing examples of high-quality work as models of what is expected from the class

Praise from teachers can reinforce high expectations when:

- Praise informs students about the value of their accomplishments and orients them toward a better appreciation of their thinking and problem-solving abilities

- Praise focuses on the specifics of the accomplishment
- Praise is authentic and leaves students convinced that the teacher has given thoughtful consideration to performance and means what she says

A classroom can create high expectations through:

- A set of explicit guidelines that emphasize the school, parents, and students working together as a team
- Parental involvement in monitoring and supporting their children's work
- Provisions for keeping parents informed of student progress through regular and frequent reports, not just at report card time
- Regular face-to-face meetings between parents

Source. From Wheelock, A. (1992). *Crossing the Tracks.* New York: New Press. Adapted with permission.

Strategy 6.1. Teaching Implications for Expectations

The following recommendations are based on Brophy (1983), Good and Brophy (2003), Timberley and G. Phillips (2003), and R. S. Weinstein (2002).

- Focus on what students are to learn rather than their perceived deficiencies.
- Monitor student progress to keep expectations current. Be sure to note and take into account when students are improving. Emphasize the students' present performance over their past history of failure.
- Set standards at floor levels, not ceiling. As the class progresses, focus on how far they can go, not on limits that were established in the beginning.
- When giving individual students feedback,
  —Use individual comparison standards, not standards that compare their performance with other students.
  —Respond to success and failure with attributional feedback that gives the students information about why they were successful and how they can improve.

- Use different teaching strategies and supplementary materials when students have not understood a lesson.
- Focus more on stretching students' minds by assisting them to achieve as much as they can rather than protecting them from failure or embarrassment.
- Help the students develop self-regulated learning strategies such as self-monitoring, self-control, and help seeking.

In Exhibit 6.3, Isennagle (1993) describes how he set expectations for his elementary urban classroom.

Exhibit 6.3. Setting Expectations for an Elementary Urban Classroom

In setting up a structure for my class, I work to establish both an intangible framework of mindset and spirit as well as a tangible structure of set routines, customs, and classroom practices . . . Each student's heart must be caught up in the passion and enjoyment of learning and reading. This attitude is a mindset that must be nurtured daily. Time for this cultivating of spirit is set into every day's lesson plans. It is imperative that I teach each student that they can learn, regardless of whatever they believe hinders them . . . Teaching students to know they can learn requires that I couple an academic sense of identity with a sense of mission. This begins the first moment I meet my pupils.

Welcome, graduating class of the year 2001. Yes, you are all learners, discoverers, and future high school and college graduates. In June 2001, you will no longer be in second grade but you will be going to college. Why? Because I have some of America's finest, some of the brightest students in the nation. Not one of you cannot learn. Don't play games with me, your parents, or yourselves and pretend you can't because I know and you know that you can. You will graduate from college and do something special for the world. Each of you will make me famous. Why? Because of the great things that each and every one of you will do.

Source. Isennagle (1993, pp. 373–74).

R. S. Weinstein (2002) concluded that expectations of groups and individuals are a more powerful influence and more ecological in nature (interrelationship among characteristics of students, home, school, classroom) than had been acknowledged. It is unrealistic for teachers not to be aware of student differences. The important principle is to teach in ways that will help all students develop their abilities. In the next section, teacher efficacy and how expectations translate into teacher confidence and practice about various types of teaching assignments are discussed.

TEACHER EFFICACY

Teacher efficacy refers to "the extent to which teachers believe that they have the capacity to affect student performance" (Ashton, 1984, p. 28). It is the teacher's belief in his or her capability to enact the instruction needed in a given context to be successful (Tschannen-Moran, Woolfolk Hoy, & Hoy, 1998). Two Rand Corporation studies first introduced teacher efficacy by having teachers rate themselves on the following two questions (Armour et al., 1976; Berman, McLaughlin, Bass, Pauly, & Zellman, 1977):

1. "When it comes right down to it, a teacher can't do much because a student's motivation and performance depends on his or her home environment."
2. "If I really try hard, I can get through to even the most difficult or unmotivated students." (Berman et al., 1977, pp. 159–60)

Based on the Rand studies, the authors concluded that a teacher's sense of efficacy was one of the best predictors of increased student achievement and the extent of teacher change. Ashton and Webb (1986) continued self-efficacy research, focusing particularly on teachers' confidence about teaching low-achieving students.

Similar to self-efficacy, teacher efficacy has two components (Ashton & Webb, 1986). The first is general teaching efficacy or beliefs about what teachers, in general, can accomplish despite obstacles. This refers to beliefs about the teachability of students or subjects and is reflected in the first question cited previously.

Personal teaching efficacy is a judgment about the extent the teacher, personally, can affect student learning. This is reflected by the second question, which is the one that is most related to how teachers teach. Teachers reflecting high- and low-efficacy beliefs have been identified at all levels of schooling: elementary school (Brownell & Pajares, 1999), high school and middle school (Ashton & Webb, 1986; Warren & Payne, 1997), special education (Podell & Soodak, 1993), preservice teachers (Hoy & Woolfolk, 1990), and college developmental math (Klein, 1996). Teaching beliefs and practices that differentiate high- and low-efficacy teachers, effects on student achievement and motivation, influences on efficacy, and factors that increase efficacy are described in the remainder of this chapter.

Beliefs Related to Teacher Efficacy

How do teachers with a high sense of efficacy differ from those with low efficacy? They differ in their beliefs about students' capabilities, their capability to teach them, and how they teach them.

Beliefs about Intelligence. As in teacher expectations, a belief about the nature of intelligence strongly differentiates high- and low-efficacy teachers. One of the biggest deterrents to high efficacy is the belief that intelligence is a fixed, stable ability (Ashton, 1984; Klein, 1996; see also entity and incremental views in Chapter 3). The following two statements recorded by Ashton and Webb (1986) illustrate this difference:

- Teacher A, Low Sense of Efficacy: "I don't know if they [low-achieving students] will ever get it [basic skills] no matter how hard you work them. Partially [that's due to] immaturity and lack of motivation. I'm sure some of it has to do with their mental ability and capacity. I'm sure of that" (p. 68).
- Teacher B, High Sense of Efficacy: "I don't believe it's right to give up on anybody. I guess that's why I keep trying. A student can fail every day in the week [but] I'm not going to accept it. Most students start doing some [work] and they ... see results. They're not going to be math wizards, but they're going to be able to do something [before they leave this class]" (p. 72).

Teachers with a high level of personal teaching efficacy, like

Teacher B, are more likely to believe that all students can learn and to feel responsible for their learning than are teachers with low efficacy, like Teacher A. Teachers who have low efficacy are likely to believe that it is hopeless to attempt to teach students believed to have low intelligence. However, "Efficacy influences teachers' persistence when things do not go smoothly and their resilience in the face of setbacks" (Tschannen-Moran et al., 1998, p. 223).

Beliefs about Student Culture and Ethnicity. Although little research has examined the relationship between teacher efficacy and student culture, student ethnicity may be a factor that influences efficacy. One study compared preservice and in-service teachers on their efficacy for teaching African-American students (Pang & Sablan, 1998). Overall, the teachers did not feel confident in their ability to teach African-American children, with preservice teachers reporting stronger efficacy than in-service teachers. An important finding is that the predominantly White sample had limited knowledge of African-American students and their culture. The authors believe that this is a factor that contributed to low efficacy.

Irvine (1999) asserted that explanations for why "poor children of color can't succeed in schools" minimize the role of efficacy and agency (p. 245). As one African-American teacher with high-efficacy beliefs expressed, "students must know that they can succeed if they set their goals, and that it is my job to help them meet the goals" (G. H. Lee, 2002, p. 73). Irvine explained that teachers and schools can offset the effect of negative influences by their beliefs about their ability to teach these students and their challenging and effective teaching techniques.

Beliefs about Student Motivation. Contrasting examples reported by Rosenholtz (1989) illustrate how teacher beliefs about student motivation influence their teaching practices:

- Teacher A: "I think the caliber of [the third-grade] students generally has been the same [over the years]. Of course, there have been some students who didn't progress. Some students didn't progress because they didn't want to improve. That's their own decision. You can't do much about them; you can't really help them" (p. 117).

- Teacher B: "I guess I pressure my [first-grade] children a lot in the beginning. They find out that this is what she wants. She wants me to read. She wants me to like reading. She wants me to think school is fun. I want to do a good job. I think I do. I've had students say 'I can read all through the years.' . . . It's important for me to do this for *all my* students. Some first graders are not ready for this yet. I try to keep the environment hopeful, give them special help, and they will come around. If they have special learning problems, I always try to help" (p. 118).

Teachers also may have a tendency for self-worth protection (see Chapter 3). When a teacher attributes a student's low achievement to lack of ability or low stable effort, the teacher protects himself or herself from feeling responsible for the student's learning. Attributing poor achievement to a student's lack of ability or unwillingness to work, as Teacher A did, may lead teachers to use failure-avoiding strategies to protect their self-worth (Rosenholtz, 1989). These self-protective strategies may include accepting normally unacceptable work and then not persisting in instruction for these students. The critical difference is that Teacher A uses student motivation to justify students' poor performance, whereas Teacher B consciously cultivates student motivation.

Teaching Practices Related to Teacher Efficacy

What specific teaching behaviors differentiate between teachers with high- and low-efficacy beliefs? High- and low-efficacy teachers were found to differ in how they interact with students and in how they teach. High-efficacy teachers:

- tend to hold students accountable for their performance (e.g., insist that students attempt challenging questions and problems: Ashton & Webb, 1986);
- spend more time on academic learning in contrast to low-efficacy teachers, who spend more time on nonacademic pastimes (S. Gibson & Dembo, 1984);
- strive for higher goals for their students and set goals that are overall more ambitious than those with low efficacy (Allinder, 1995);

- develop supportive trusting relationships with students. Both practicing and preservice teachers reported themselves as more trusting of students, more able to give up their absolute control, and more willing to share responsibility with students for solving classroom problems (Ashton & Webb, 1986; Hoy & Woolfolk, 1990).
- work to build friendly relationships with low achievers and hold higher expectations for them (Ashton, 1984; Klein, 1996);
- are less likely to refer low-SES students to special education (Podell & Soodak, 1993);
- make fewer negative predictions about students based on their characteristics and are more likely to adjust when students change (Tournaki & Podell, 2005);
- are more confident in working with parents (Hoover-Dempsey, Bassler, & Brissie, 1987); and
- are less concerned about self-survival as teachers and the tasks of teaching (Ghaith & Shaaban, 1999).

A summary of teacher attitudes is shown in Table 6.2 (Ashton, 1984).

REFLECTION. The attitudes shown in Table 6.2 form a useful checklist to self-evaluate your own teaching beliefs. Think about each in your classroom. What insights were revealed?

Finally, and most important, high-efficacy teachers are more likely to innovate and change their teaching practice. Sparks (1988) reported that high efficacy leads to a greater willingness to try new methods, see the importance of training in new practices, and use these new practices in the classroom. A consistent finding is that teachers with high-efficacy beliefs are more likely to implement cooperative learning than are teachers with low-efficacy beliefs (Ghaith & Yaghi, 1997). After teachers received training on the Student Teams Achievement Division (STAD) model of cooperative learning, teachers with high-efficacy beliefs indicated a greater willingness to implement it in their classrooms. They considered STAD as more congruent with how they currently teach and as less difficult to implement than did teachers with low-efficacy beliefs. In another study, the teachers

TABLE 6.2

Eight Attitudes that Distinguish High from Low Efficacy Teachers

Teacher Attitude	High Efficacy	Low Efficacy
(1) A Sense of Personal Accomplishment	Feel their work with students is important and meaningful; that they have a positive impact on student learning.	Feel frustrated and discouraged about teaching.
(2) Positive Expectations for Student Behavior and Achievement	Expect students to progress and for the most part find students fulfill their expectations.	Expect students to fail and react negatively to their teaching effort and to misbehavior.
(3) Personal Responsibility for Student Learning	Believe it's their responsibility to see their students learn and, when students experience failure, look to their own performance for ways they might be more helpful.	Place responsibility for learning on students and, when students fail, look for explanations in terms of family background, motivation, or attitude.
(4) Strategies for Achieving Objectives	Plan for student learning, set goals for themselves and their students, and identify strategies to achieve them.	Lack specific goals for their students, uncertain about what they want their students to achieve, and do not plan strategies according to goals.
(5) Positive Affect	Feel good about teaching, themselves, and their students.	Frustrated with teaching and often express discouragement and negative feelings about their work with students.
(6) Sense of Control	Confident they can influence student learning.	Experience a sense of futility in working with students.
(7) Sense of Common Teacher–Student Goals; Democratic Decision Making	Feel they are involved in a joint venture with students to achieve goals they have in common. Involve students in decision making and strategies for achieving them.	Feel they are pitted in a struggle with students with goals and strategies in opposition to theirs. Impose decisions regarding goals and learning strategies on students without involving them in process.

Source. Ashton, P. (1984). "Teacher Efficacy: A Motivational Paradigm for Effective Teacher Education." *Journal of Teacher Education, 35*(5), 28–30. Reprinted by permission.

who implemented cooperative learning in their classroom expressed greater efficacy in promoting the learning of slow students compared with teachers who used traditional methods (Shachar & Shmuelevitz, 1997).

Teacher Efficacy and Student Self-Efficacy

Is student self-efficacy related to teacher efficacy? Teacher efficacy beliefs were found to have a stronger impact on the self-efficacy of low-achieving students compared with high-achieving students (Ashton & Webb, 1986; Midgley, Feldlaufer, & Eccles, 1989). A low-efficacy teacher is especially detrimental to the motivation of low-achieving students. In contrast, students have a chance to increase their self-efficacy with a high-efficacy teacher (Midgley et al., 1989).

Midgley and colleagues studied the influence of teacher efficacy on student self-efficacy in mathematics beginning the last year of elementary continuing through the first year of junior high school. Measurements taken in the spring of both years indicate that students who had higher efficacy teachers had higher expectancies for their own performance in math. Students who had low-efficacy teachers viewed math as more difficult. What if students moved from a high-efficacy teacher in elementary school to a low-efficacy teacher in junior high school? Compared to students with high-efficacy teachers, these students showed the most change. With a low-efficacy teacher, students declined in their expectancies and judgments of task performance whereas judgment of task difficulty showed an increase.

The effects of teacher efficacy on student outcomes on computer skills was investigated by Ross, Hogaboam-Gray, and Hannay (2001). The authors reported that a student with low confidence in computer skills had higher skills when they moved to a teacher with high-efficacy beliefs at the next grade level.

Sources of Teacher Efficacy Beliefs

The relationship between teacher efficacy and student confidence in academic performance underscores the importance of teacher efficacy beliefs. Because a sense of efficacy affects the instructional methods used by teachers, an important question is this: What influences teacher sense of efficacy and, especially, what increases it? These factors are described next.

School and Classroom Environmental Characteristics. Difficult-to-teach students are a challenge to teachers' sense of efficacy (Soodak & Podell, 1998). Ashton and Webb (1986) found that many teachers felt unprepared to teach students deemed at risk. In a study of secondary classrooms, the most important classroom variable affecting a sense of efficacy was the students' ability level and the extent to which the teacher felt prepared to teach the students (Raudenbush, Rowan, & Cheong, 1992). If teachers were able to keep students engaged in learning, however, the negative effects of tracking on efficacy disappeared.

The quality of teacher preparation differentiated preservice teachers' sense of efficacy about teaching students with LD (Brownell & Pajares, 1999). Preservice and in-service teachers reported stronger confidence for teaching mainstreamed students when coursework includes information about the characteristics of students, adaptation of instruction, and behavior management strategies.

A supportive school climate is one factor that influences a high sense of efficacy. The support of administrators and colleagues is important. Chester and Beaudin (1996) found that a collegial school culture was an important factor for new teachers in an urban district. Efficacy beliefs were higher in schools where there was a high level of collegial support.

One supportive school organization structure is interdisciplinary teams with common planning times, as found in many middle schools (Warren & Payne, 1997). Teachers in this arrangement had higher personal efficacy than teachers who were in content departmental teams. The authors concluded that the common planning time makes a difference in teachers' judgment about their competence because of the opportunity to collaborate and share problems and concerns with team members.

Teacher Experience.   It seems like an obvious assumption that more experienced teachers will have a higher sense of efficacy, but is this the case? Based on findings from research, the answer is yes and no. Teacher efficacy does tend to increase during preservice training and student teaching when new skills are being learned and practiced (Hoy & Woolfolk, 1990). A study by Benz, Bradley, Alderman, and Flowers (1992) compared preservice and experienced teachers on beliefs about their effectiveness in handling 15 teaching situations. Preservice teachers expressed a higher efficacy belief about handling difficult motivation problems, whereas the experienced teachers expressed higher efficacy beliefs on planning and evaluating lessons. The authors speculated that for the motivational problems, the preservice teachers were either idealistic or had learned strategies that were not available to the experienced group. The experienced teachers had a more extensive knowledge base in planning and evaluation and this likely led to their higher sense of efficacy. Ghaith and Yaghi (1997) also found efficacy differences between experienced and less experienced teachers in the implementation of the STAD cooperative learning approach. One difference was how compatible STAD was with their current teaching approach. Less experienced and high-efficacy teachers perceived STAD to be more compatible with how they taught. The more experienced teachers tended to rate the STAD as more difficult and less compatible with their teaching approach.

Personal teaching efficacy does ebb and flow across time (Ross, 1998). When a teacher is implementing a new strategy, confidence may decrease as one is unsure about the strategy, then increase as the skill improves (Tschannen-Moran et al., 1998). The converse may also happen. Confidence increases during student teaching, then decreases the first year of teaching, likely because the novice teachers found teaching more complex than they imagined (A.W. Hoy & Spero, 2005).

Subject Matter Preparation. Subject matter preparation is another factor that influences how effective teachers judge themselves to be. One problematic area for many elementary teachers is the teaching of science. For example, Ramey-Gassert and Shroyer (1992) found that many elementary teachers reported that they had inadequate backgrounds in science and consequently avoided teaching it when possible. Because of these findings, efforts are being made to enhance science teaching efficacy at both preservice and in-service levels. Subsequent research found an increase in a sense of efficacy for mathematics after preservice teachers completed elementary methods courses that promoted teacher beliefs (Wilkins & Brand, 2004).

How does knowing about the factors that influence efficacy beliefs help me as preservice or practicing teacher? It tells me that experience alone is not enough to develop a strong belief in my ability to promote academic learning. It tells me that if my subject area is one in which I have doubts about my ability to teach it well, I should seek to continue to develop my expertise in this area. The following section describes factors that enhance a sense of teacher efficacy.

Strengthening Teacher Efficacy

"The development of a strong sense of efficacy can pay dividends of higher motivation, greater effort, persistence, and resilience across the span of a teaching career" (Tschannen-Moran et al., 1998, p. 238). What factors lead to the development or enhancement of teaching efficacy? A beginning step in a program to promote a sense of teacher efficacy for teaching culturally diverse students was to help teachers understand that multiple factors can affect student achievement, thus each student must be taught accordingly (Tucker et al., 2005).

Ross (1995) concluded that preparation of beginning teachers and staff development for practicing teachers need to explicitly address teaching efficacy in addition to the enhancement of teaching skills. A staff development program that addressed both teaching skills and teaching efficacy resulted in increased feelings of confidence for the participants (Fritz, Miller-Heyl, Kreutzer, & MacPhee, 1995). Teachers who participated in the training increased their feelings of personal competence in meeting the needs of students and saw fewer barriers to learning.

Social and Skill Support.   Support from colleagues or supervisors was found to be important for developing a sense of efficacy for both preservice and in-service teachers. Preservice teachers who worked in teams in field experiences and worked together to develop and present lessons were found to have higher efficacy (Cannon & Scharmann, 1996; Wilson, 1996). The positive effect of collaboration was stated by one preservice teacher: "When you are in a group of people you tend not to be afraid because you know you are all working together" (Cannon & Scharmann, 1996, p. 432).

Another area where social support contributed to a sense of efficacy was planning and evaluating interventions for students with behavior problems (Kruger, 1997). Teachers' perception that their skills and abilities were appreciated by coworkers was the most helpful form of social support. The author concluded that, if teachers were reassured of their worth as professionals, they might feel more confident about working with children with behavior problems.

Support from knowledgeable colleagues was an important factor in increasing science teaching efficacy for elementary teachers (Ramey-Gassert, Shroyer, & Staver, 1996). Effective models were important for strengthening beliefs of teachers with a low sense of efficacy.

Social-Cognitive Factors. The same factors that increase student self-efficacy—competence feedback and vicarious experience through models—are likely to increase a sense of teacher efficacy. Three phases of self-regulation offer a plan for strengthening teacher efficacy beliefs:

- Forethought phase. Conduct a task analysis of present efficacy beliefs. Analyze the assignment or the teaching task for difficulties and resources (Tschannen-Moran et al., 1998). Set goals that are proximal, realistic, and specifically related to the development of new teaching strategies.
- Performance phase. View and seek help from effective models (Ramey-Gassert et al., 1996). Maintain an ongoing assessment of student progress to provide evidence of improvement (McDaniel & Dibella-McCarthy, 1989).
- Self-reflection phase. When you have experienced initial success for students, identify what you did that contributed to the successful outcome. This attribution will lead to a stronger sense of efficacy. If you are not successful, return to proximal goals and begin the cycle again.

As in self-efficacy, simply learning new skills is not sufficient to increase a sense of efficacy; teachers must also recognize when their skills are improving. The LINKS model (Alderman, 1990), introduced earlier, provides a sequence that teachers might use to enhance a sense of efficacy (see Fig. 4.3).

What can you do to develop your own teaching efficacy? Strategies and a planning and evaluation guide based on self-efficacy principles are presented in Strategy 6.2.

Strategy 6.2. Developing High Teaching Efficacy

- Have a learning goal orientation for yourself; this effort will pay off in increased skills. Acknowledge that setbacks or outright failure will be part of the learning process. Focus on your progress whether you are an experienced teacher implementing a new practice or a preservice teacher learning to teach. This will reduce discouragement.
- Collect data on student progress. As students gain in achievement, your efficacy should increase.
- Look to effective teachers as models of practice and for support. Use peer observation with feedback.
- Collaborate with peers who are interested in improving student achievement.
- Take advantage of professional development opportunities with colleagues so continuing support is available.
- The following steps can be used as a Planning and Evaluation Guide:

Planning

1. What knowledge or teaching skills do you now possess that will be useful?
2. What new teaching skills will you need to develop?
3. What are questions, unknowns, issues, or concepts that you may not fully understand? What major decisions will you need to make?
4. What are possible barriers to implementation—personal and external?
5. How can you try this on a small scale? Or what is your starting point?

Evaluation

1. Observation—who could observe you?
2. What student data will be important?
3. Self-evaluation—self-observation, keeping a journal.
4. My self-efficacy at this point for developing and implementing this strategy or project is:

Low confidence   High confidence
0 —— 1 —— 2 —— 3 —— 4 —— 5 —— 6 —— 7

COLLECTIVE TEACHER EFFICACY

Thus far, the discussion has centered on the individual efficacy of teachers. An overriding influence on student educational achievement may be the perceived collective efficacy of teachers. *Collective efficacy* is the sum of all teachers' efficacy and the sum of teachers' beliefs about their schools' capability to educate students (Bandura, 1993, 1997). Collective efficacy is concerned with the extent that the faculty as a whole believe they "can organize and execute courses of action required to have a positive effect on students" (Goddard & Goddard, 2001, p. 809).

A particular school organization appears to play a role in teachers' reported efficacy. Teacher efficacy is higher in schools where collective efficacy is stronger and this has an effect on student achievement. Collective efficacy was the strongest predictor of mathematics achievement in an urban high school; stronger than SES (Hoy, Sweetland, & Smith, 2002).

Lee and Smith (1996, 2001) investigated how the organization of high school teachers' work affected adolescent achievement. Regardless of the type of organization and decision making in schools, they found that the overriding factor related to student achievement was the teacher's perception of collective responsibility for student learning. Teacher beliefs about limitations of students' ability to learn and their ability to teach them were stronger than collaboration and teacher empowerment (Fig. 6.3).

FIG. 6.3. Collective/personal efficacy.

The high-achieving schools described by Brookover et al. (1979) can be considered examples of schools with a strong collective sense of efficacy.

In view of educational reform with increased standards, the collective beliefs of teachers that they have the capabilities to help all students meet the rigorous standards is important (Goddard, LoGerfo, & W. K. Hoy, 2004). The authors suggest this is more likely to happen when teachers are involved in the instructional decisions for achieving the goals.

CONCLUSION

Teacher expectations followed by a high sense of teaching efficacy are the starting points to make "all students can learn" more than a slogan. However, if this is to be more than a slogan, expectations must be combined with effective education for all students and schools (R. S. Weinstein, 2002). The academic rigor and thinking curriculum of an effort-based school as proposed by Resnick (1999) requires that we not accept the judgment that inborn aptitude counts the most and students who are not achieving do not have this aptitude. Instead, we must believe that "We can harness effort to create ability and build a smarter America" (Resnick, 1999, p. 38). Like Miss Bailey stated in the quote at the beginning of this chapter, we then have to provide the students with the tools to harness effort and to create ability.

REVIEW OF MAJOR POINTS

1.   Teachers' beliefs in students' abilities to learn and their confidence in their ability to promote academic learning both affect how they teach. This, in turn, affects students' motivation and achievement.

2.   Teacher expectations are inferences teachers make about students' future achievements, whereas teacher expectation effect is the actual effect on student outcome as a result of teacher actions. Sustaining effects—when a teacher's actions toward a student stay the same even when the student is improving—are more prevalent in the classroom.

3.   The fact that teachers have different expectations for students does not lead to a self-fulfilling prophecy. An expectation affects how teachers respond to the students; in turn, the students are more likely to behave in the expected manner.

4.   Expectations are influenced by labels assigned to students, teacher beliefs about intelligence, and student characteristics such as SES and ethnicity. Expectations are communicated to students through teaching practices such as questioning strategies, grouping, curriculum, and materials used, and the use of labels such as *low ability*.

5.   Students as young as elementary ages were found to be aware of teachers' differential expectancy beliefs. Students were aware of differential treatment such as who has more opportunities and choice and who receives more negative feedback.

6.   Establishing positive expectations includes setting standards at floor levels, not ceiling levels; reducing the use of labels for groups and individuals; and being aware of potential biases for low expectations.

7.   Personal teaching efficacy is a form of self-efficacy that refers to how effective teachers judge themselves to be in a given teaching situation. A teacher's sense of efficacy was found to be one of the best predictors of increase in student achievement, having stronger impact on the self-efficacy of low-achieving students compared with high-achieving students.

8.   High-efficacy teachers are more likely to develop supportive, trusting relationships with students; share responsibility; strive for higher goals for their students; spend more time on academic learning; and innovate and change their teaching practices.

9.   Teacher efficacy is influenced by support of the school climate, experience, and subject matter preparation.

10.   Teacher efficacy is positively influenced by improvement of teaching skills, competence feedback, social support by colleagues and supervisors, collaborative working relationships, and directly addressing efficacy. The three phases of self-regulation offer a viable model for addressing efficacy.

11.   Collective efficacy is concerned with the extent that a faculty as a whole believe they can have a positive effect on students and learning. It has been found to be a stronger predictor than factors such as SES on mathematics achievement.

Motivational Toolbox

1. Important points to think about and lingering questions

2. Strategies I can use now

3. Strategies I want to develop in the future

CHAPTER 7

Promoting Optimal Motivation and Engagement: Social Context

One of the greatest tasks of teachers is to help students learn how to be recipients of care. Those who have not learned to do this by the time they have entered school are at great risk and their risk is not just academic.
—Noddings (1992, p. 108)

Classroom learning and motivation are inherently embedded in a social context (Corno & Rohrkemper, 1985). Classrooms are composed of a teacher and individual students who are likely to be diverse in many ways (e.g., ethnicity, gender, ability, SES, skills of self-regulation, goals, interests, and special needs). Instructional groups are of varying sizes: whole group, small groups ranging from informal to well-planned cooperative learning groups, partners on the computer, and teams on the playground. Additionally, informal interactions such as students talking to each other, teasing, name calling, and comparing work are ongoing. In all cases, teachers are continually interacting both with individuals and groups of students. What is the relationship between social context and optimal student motivation and engagement?

Social context, in or out of school, influences motivation in a number of ways, both positive and negative. It has been found to influence academic engagement and effort, and subsequent success and failure at all levels of schooling. Social context was identified as a factor in the following situations:

- reduction of drop-out rate in secondary schools (Wehlage, Rutter, Smith, Lesko, & Fernandez, 1989);

205

- increased student engagement in secondary schools (Newmann, 1992);
- increased retention rates in college (Tinto, 1993);
- successful transition from elementary to middle school (Eccles & Midgley, 1989);
- level of engagement of urban middle and high school students (Goodenow, 1993); and
- successful elementary teachers of culturally diverse children (e.g., African-American children, Comer, 2005; Ladson-Billings, 1994; Latino children, Rueda & Moll, 1994).

If optimum motivation is to happen, a major priority is to build a classroom climate in which students support each other for learning and not only want to achieve, but also care about their classmates' achievement.

The following sections of this chapter explain the nature and importance of psychological membership or belonging for school adjustment and cognitive engagement, identify factors that build or hinder membership, and present environmental variables that can be altered by teachers in order to build a positive social context.

SENSE OF MEMBERSHIP AND BELONGING

Wehlage et al. (1989) asserted that a sense of school membership is the foundation on which educational engagement is built. What is school membership? Psychologically, Goodenow (1993) described *membership* as the "extent to which students feel personally accepted, respected, included, and supported by others in school environment" (p. 80). A sense of school membership is based on the satisfaction of three basic human needs: autonomy, competence, and belonging or relatedness (Connell & Wellborn, 1991). When students experience a sense of belongingness in a school context, they are more likely to adopt goals valued by the school. A sense of belonging had positive effects on the motivation variables of valuing school and self-efficacy for four different ethnic groups—African-American, Asian-American, Latino, and Asian descent (Faircloth & Hamm, 2005). Similarly, a sense of school belonging predicted academic motivation, effort, and absenteeism among Latino adolescents (Sanchez, Colon, & Esparza, 2005).

In contrast, a context that does not allow for satisfaction of the three basic needs will diminish motivation and lead to alienation and poor performance (R. M. Ryan & Stiller, 1991). L. H. Anderman (2003) found that students' sense of belonging declined across grades six through seven. To the extent that students feel disconnected to school, they are likely to reject school goals. For example, Steele (1992) proposed that one reason for the lower achievement of African Americans is that identification with school is missing. A low sense of school belonging and low school motivation was found among urban adolescents (Goodenow & Grady, 1993). What factors seem to be necessary for students to identify with schools and be willing to adopt the goals of school and work toward them?

Social Bonds

Wehlage et al. (1989) studied 14 schools that were successful with at-risk students. A common factor among all schools was the *social bonds* that connected students to the school. Four factors were identified that establish social bonds to the school:

- *Attachment*. Students are socially bonded to the extent that they have social and emotional ties to adults and peers in the school. This attachment is reciprocal: "The school/teacher cares about me and I care about my actions." Therefore, students have a vested interest in meeting expectations of others and abiding by the norms of behavior expected in the school.
- *Commitment*. Social bonds are formed by commitment—a conscious decision by students about what they have to do to achieve the school's goals (e.g., working in classes where they have no real interest). If students do not have hope for the future, however, commitment is more unlikely.
- *Involvement*. Student involvement in both academic and non-academic school activities increases the likelihood of bonding. If students are not active participants in school, they are more often disengaged, as evidenced by their passivity.
- *Belief*. Students' belief that an education is important and

their faith in the school to provide them with one is asserted by Newmann (1992) to be the bedrock of membership. The first three factors are somewhat dependent on this one. This is also a reciprocal relationship, requiring that teachers also believe that students are competent to learn and to achieve the goals of school.

Newmann (1992) identified four broad conditions for school that set the stage for social bonding. If in place, these four conditions—clarity of purpose, fairness, personal support, and success—are integrated into a climate of caring.

1. Clarity of purpose or agreement on goals by the school and community is important, and students need to see there is a serious attempt to accomplish the goals.
2. Fairness is necessary for a sense of membership because students may believe they are treated unfairly in areas of discipline, opportunities, and rewards. Although discrimination may not be blatant, students of low-SES and minority backgrounds may experience subtle inequity. Do all students have equal access to resources and the best teachers?
3. Personal support from teachers and students is essential if students are to attempt challenges in learning. When chances for success are risky and uncertain, students need support of both peers and teachers.
4. Successful experiences are necessary for students to experience a developing sense of competence. Newmann cautioned that a sense of membership will not be achieved by grade inflation nor by reducing the rigor of academic demands.

A caring environment with these four components communicates that students are worthy and important members of school and that the school is serious about helping them develop competence and academic achievement. Understanding the groups or categories by which students identify themselves (social identity) is important in building a climate for a sense of membership. The next section examines social identity and membership with motivational implications.

Social Identity and Membership

Students, adolescents in particular, define themselves by the groups with which they affiliate (Goodenow, 1992). This is the essence of social identity, an identity based on group membership. Students may experience a sense of membership or belonging at several levels: school, individual classroom, and subgroups (e.g., peer group, cultural or ethnic, athletic teams, religious affiliation). How does social identity affect a sense of belonging and engagement in school? Goodenow contended that the extent to which a group identifies with the goals and values of school, and/or devalues academic effort and achievement, affects engagement for learning. In view of the culturally diverse school population, it is important to understand the role and influence of social identity on motivation and achievement. When social interactions are negative, school can be a stressor or a source of vulnerability for students (M. L. Clark, 1991). By the same token, social identity and support networks (including interracial friendships) can serve as protective mechanisms that contribute to student adjustment.

Peer Group Influence and a Sense of Membership

Peer subgroup affiliation has a strong influence on a sense of school membership, either negative or positive. Peers may influence each other not to work hard to achieve or to work and achieve (Berndt & Keefe, 1992; B. B. Brown, 1993). An insightful view of social identity is reported by Farrell (1990), who interviewed urban students in a drop-out prevention program. The primary identity for these students was based on how others— family, friends, teachers, and other adults—responded to them. For example, although others might respond to the adolescent as a friend/peer, they made little response to the possible identity of these adolescents as a student or future worker. Adolescents in this program were less likely to think of student or potential worker as an identity for themselves. Because peers can encourage each other to view school experiences positively or negatively, a major task for teachers and parents is to understand the nature of peer relationships so this influence is directed toward engagement. How does negative peer influence work?

Negative Peer Influence.   Peer influence plays a major role in the extent to which the peer group values or devalues academic effort and achievement (Goodenow, 1992). Farrell (1990) observed this negative peer influence at work in the drop-out program where students got little support from their peers for liking classes. They hid their academic ability to keep from being ostracized by their friends. In fact, friends reinforced each other to avoid work and be disruptive.

B. B. Brown (1993) made a distinction between peer influence for academic achievement and academic excellence. He noted that, although there is positive academic peer pressure to graduate from high school, the pressure is more to get by academically rather than to excel. The emphasis is more toward getting good grades (performance goals) than on working hard and learning (learning goals). Brown concluded that the general peer norm is to strive for academic adequacy rather than academic excellence. Peer pressure seems to impose upper as well as lower limits on intellectual effort that students can put forth without fearing some sanctions. There is, however, a more direct anti-achievement influence at work in many school contexts.

Antiachievement.   What is the nature of direct antiachievement? Why are high-achieving students often the target of ridicule by peers, resulting in students either hiding their academic achievement or, as Fordham and Ogbu (1986) stated, "putting on the brakes" on academic effort (p. 191)? B. B. Brown (1993) identified several factors that lead to negative views of achievement:

1. There is a brain–nerd connection or peer distinction between students who excel and those who do not. The stereotypic image of *brains* is a label often carrying with it negative characteristics such as nerd, brainiac, and geek—all implying social misfit.
2. Because some students are excelling, teachers expect more from other students and they have to work harder.
3. Pressure for academics is often overshadowed by pressure toward nonacademic activities such as social activities and part-time work. Pressure to keep up with status symbols valued by peer groups leads to part-time jobs to buy symbols

like designer label athletic shoes. There is an inverse correlation between number of hours working and grade point average (GPA). The more hours worked (more than 15 hours per week is detrimental), the lower the GPA. In this way, peer pressure works indirectly by distracting students to other interests.

Adult Influence on Effort and Student Achievement. B. B. Brown asserted that teachers and other adults have the potential to influence peer culture both positively and negatively. There are several ways that teachers and adults may help teenagers justify limited effort toward achieving in school: Passive acceptance of the peer group structure. Teachers expect that students will behave in keeping with their peer group affiliations and make no attempt to intervene with the structure. In other words, teachers passively accept the brain–nerd differentiation.

- Favoritism toward athletes. Athletes often receive more esteem in school and are often seen by other students as receiving special treatment like more academic help from teachers.
- Peer group separation. Ability grouping forces isolation among students at different achievement levels, with each group forming its own peer culture (B. B. Brown, 1993). When students are grouped by ability tracks, low achievers are isolated from models of achievement motivation and more effective strategies.
- Blame or excuse the victim. Effort may be undermined when adults use stereotypical images to either excuse or blame students based on social identity categories and crowds to which they belong. For example, a teacher may excuse poor student test performance on the basis of family background. By the same token, a teacher may blame the family background for the performance. In either case, student achievement is undermined.

How can educators promote a positive peer culture? B. B. Brown recommended ways that educators can enhance rather than undermine the academic motivations of American adolescents:

1. Teachers should increase awareness of adolescent social systems. Be aware of the peer group social structure that operates in a particular school, the norms that operate within each group, the relationship of one group to another, and the loyalty students display to their own group. It is important for teachers to appreciate the dynamics of the brain–nerd connection and the burden of "acting White," as well as recognizing the hostility of groups to one another. At the same time, they must be careful not to reinforce stereotypes.

2. Avoid making achievement a game of winners and losers. Ability grouping and grading on a curve place students in competitive situations as winners or losers. Alternative grading systems are discussed in Chapter 8.

3. Enhance the status of academic achievement. B. B. Brown believed this is the most powerful influence on student achievement. Because there is a positive relationship between student achievement and popularity, schools should give more public recognition to high achievement. Schools can recognize academic excellence in areas that are outside the core curriculum, such as art shows and trade fairs. Avoid sending mixed messages about the relative merit of academic and nonacademic achievement. This often happens when more prominence is given to the school's athletic achievements than to academic achievements.

REFLECTION.   Think about the status of academic achievement in schools in your community. What is the status of academic achievement compared with the status of sports?

Cultural Identity and Identification with Academics

With the increasing cultural diversity in our society, the role of ethnic identity in school plays an increasing role in student engagement and achievement. A sense of membership and cognitive engagement is affected in important ways by the sociocultural orientations that students bring to school (Newmann, 1992). Students who identify with the expectation that working hard in school and achieving will lead to occupational success are likely to invest themselves in the academic work of school. In contrast, students who have little hope that academic performance will lead to occupational success are less likely to invest themselves in schoolwork. What are factors that affect identification with academic norms of schooling?

One explanation is stereotype threat (Steele, 1992, 1997) in which some minority students withdraw from identification with academics or devalue them (as explained in Chapter 3). The effects of academic disengagement may be more specific to ethnic minority boys than to girls because minority boys have been portrayed in more negative cultural stereotypes (Hudley & Graham, 2001).

Another view is Ogbu's (Ogbu, 1992, 2003; Ogbu & Simons, 1998) cultural-ecological explanation of school performance, that some minorities strive to do better in school than others because of their different historical and cultural experiences. Ogbu classified minority groups according to whether they entered a country voluntarily or involuntarily. *Voluntary* groups (e.g., Asians such as Japanese and Koreans, Europeans such as Irish) were seeking a better life; *involuntary* groups were brought into the country against their will (e.g., African Americans) or through conquests (e.g., Latinos, American Indians).

Ogbu (1992) contended that the different experiences have influenced the identification with norms of schooling and academics. Voluntary minorities more readily accept the relationship between hard work, academic performance, and occupational success, without seeing a conflict with their identity. Involuntary minorities have an ambivalent view: they believe hard work and education are necessary but their experiences have often been at odds with those beliefs. This view presents a conflict between cultural identity and the norms of schooling, especially for some minority adolescents. How does this dilemma affect school motivation and learning? Fordham and Ogbu (1986) found that school learning is equated with the acquisition of culture and language of the dominant culture, White Americans. This is seen as a loss of social identity, with negative consequences, and is known as "oppositional collective or social identity" (p. 181).

Adolescents who adopt the oppositional identity achieve group loyalty by defining certain attitudes and group behavior as White and unacceptable (e.g., speaking standard English, working hard for good grades). They use peer pressure to discourage one another from engaging in these activities. What are manifestations of this discouragement? Students in a high school in Washington, DC, interviewed by Fordham and Ogbu (1986), provide a vivid picture of how they reacted to peer pressures:

> Max, a football player, is from a middle-class home. He is taking advanced courses because his parents make him. Although his parents try to pull him away from his friends, he holds onto them at the expense of his academic progress because they are important to him and his sense of identity. To be accepted, he limits his effort and performance. "You know, I just sacrificed a whole lot out of myself, what I could do, just to make my friends happy, you know. And it never—it just didn't work."
>
> (p. 189)

> Shelvy, an underachieving female, thinks, ideally, that everybody wants to be a brainiac, but fears that if she and her friends perform well in school that would bring some added responsibilities and problems. This began in the sixth grade for Shelvy. "It was me and these two girls, we used to hang together all the time. They used to say we was brainiacs, and no one really liked us . . . it's something you want to be, but you don't want your friends to know. Because once they find out you're a brainiac the first thing they say is, 'she thinks she's cute and she's smart. She thinks she's better than anyone else.' So what do most brainiacs do? They sit back and they know an answer and they won't answer it."
>
> (p. 191)

More recently, Ogbu (2003) conducted research across an affluent suburban district focusing on the academic performance of Black American students. Beginning in elementary school some social pressure was present to keep students from doing homework, but there was more peer pressure in middle and high school that kept students from doing schoolwork. He concluded that student opposition was not directed to making good grades, but to attitudes and behaviors they perceived as acting White.

This opposition or withdrawal is not universal, however. Kao and Tienda (1998) found a high level of aspirations among African Americans and Hispanics that diverged from oppositional identity. A strong, positive identity with one's ethnic group seems to serve as a protective factor. Sanders (1997) found that high-achieving adolescents were keenly aware of racial discrimination and obstacles, but they exerted more effort, resulting in above average grades. These students' attitudes toward effort and achievement are attributed to the positive racial socialization of their homes, communities, and schools. Similarly, Eccles, Wong, and Peck (2006) found that a protective factor for early adolescents is a strong identity with their ethnic group. The negative effect of daily discriminations was reduced for students with a strong, positively connected identity. In contrast, Flores-Gonzales (1999) found that low achievers overwhelmingly had identities that conflicted with their student identity.

What are the strategies of high-achieving students who have learned to compete successfully in the dominant culture, unlike underachieving students such as Max and Shelvy? A primary strategy adopted by high-achieving students is accommodation without assimilation (Mehan et al., 1996; Ogbu, 1992). This happens when students maintain their cultural identities while recognizing the necessity of academic achievement for their future success. Marta and Andrew are two students who exemplify forms of accommodating without assimilating (Mehan et al., 1996):

> Marta, a Latino student, affirms her cultural identity and also achieves academically. In the third grade, Marta pledged to become perfectly bilingual, maintaining her native Spanish while developing acceptable English and academic skills. She fulfilled this goal and entered college in 1992. Her parents respect her bicultural motives and are pleased that she and her friends respect their background.

> Andrew, an African-American student, recognizes that his teachers expect a certain way of talking and acting in school. To accommodate to the school and teachers' expectation for academics, he varies his speech behavior according to different social situations. In the neighborhood Andrew uses the style of his peers, whereas in school he tries to use the standard expected there.

Students like Marta and Andrew maintain dual identities—one in school and one in the neighborhood. Another strategy used by students who want to succeed is to camouflage or disguise their true academic identity by not letting their peers know they study; by acting like the class clown; or by participating in athletics, where it is okay to get an A (Ogbu, 1992). T. Perry (2003) described the type of environment that is likely to promote achievement among African-American students. It is an environment that "extends a culture of achievement to all of its members, and a strong sense of group membership where the expectation that everyone achieve is explicit and regularly communicated in public and group meetings" (p. 107).

The task for schools and teachers is to first recognize the sociocultural influence orientations that students bring to school and then establish a climate that builds a sense of membership, while valuing students' culture and social identity. What classroom characteristics build a sense of membership? The following section provides components of classrooms that support a sense of membership.

A CLASSROOM ENVIRONMENT FOR OPTIMUM MEMBERSHIP AND ENGAGEMENT

A sense of membership and engagement is most likely to be present when student needs for belonging/social connectedness, autonomy/self-direction, and competence are met (Battistich, Solomon, Kim, Watson, & Schaps, 1995; Solomon, Watson, Battistich, Schaps, & Delucchi, 1992). A caring community both conveys a set of values and helps establish the motivation to abide by them. It is characterized by mutual concern and respect among students who care about the welfare of others and give support as needed. Three areas essential for providing such a climate are (a) a classroom structure for autonomy and responsibility, (b) social support through cooperative learning, and (c) teacher support. These areas all fall within the teacher's domain of responsibilities and are areas they can influence.

Classroom Structure for Autonomy and Social Support

A number of studies have documented positive motivational effects when students have opportunities for some degree of autonomy or ownership in classroom learning. Establishing a structure that provides such opportunities requires an understanding of autonomy, classroom structure, and classroom management practices.

Autonomy and Classroom Structure.   Autonomy is viewed as fundamental for enhancement of motivation. Research has consistently demonstrated evidence for importance of autonomy support for student motivation (e.g., Schweinle, Turner, & Meyer, 2006). According to Connell and Wellborn (1991), autonomy is a psychological need for "the experience of choice in initiation, maintenance, and regulation of activity and the experience of connectedness between one's activities and personal goals and values" (p. 51). A sense of autonomy is expressed by the perceived control or the beliefs students have about how effective they can be over the outcomes of their performance (Skinner, Zimmer-Gembeck, & Connell, 1998). For educators, however, the important questions are, what is autonomy or self-direction in a classroom and how can teachers provide the support?

Two ends of a continuum for autonomy—origin and pawn—were described by deCharms (1976, 1984). An *origin* feels like one has the freedom and competence to make choices. A *pawn* feels controlled by external forces in the environment. DeCharms pointed out that we cannot be origins in all situations; students have required courses and teachers have prescribed curriculums. Motivationally, the most important aspect is the extent to which one feels like an origin or pawn. Skinner (1995) stated that, "Although contexts don't 'give' children or adults control, they can provide opportunities for people to exercise control" (p. 54).

Classroom conditions for autonomy occur when teachers communicate choice and allow room for student initiative, with students viewing learning activities as connected to their personal goals and values (Connell & Wellborn, 1991). Although the classroom structure provides opportunities for autonomy, students can and do interpret the same external climate differently (R. M. Ryan & Grolnick, 1986). The establishment of a climate that ensures psychological and physical safety while giving students opportunities for choice with responsibility is a major balancing act for the teacher. Concerns expressed by teachers include the following: Will the classroom environment turn into chaos when I give students choices? How much can students be involved in decision making? What choices are appropriate for students? What capabilities do they have to make choices and take responsibility?

Teachers are rightfully concerned about how much choice to give students. Although it may seem like a paradox, structure is the key to providing opportunity for student choice (Skinner, 1995). Developing student autonomy does not mean that teachers give up their legitimate power and responsibility or what Noblit (1993) termed the *ethical use of power*. A classroom of optimal freedom is not a laissez-faire classroom in which there are no rules, and is not a democratic one; instead, it is one in which students are, in a sense, *grooved* or guided by teachers (deCharms, 1976). Opportunities are provided for students to exercise control, but they are not given control. A teacher's role is to set boundaries for work, social/behavioral expectations, and the transfer of responsibility. Figure 7.1 illustrates a fragile balance. Where does a teacher begin this difficult balancing act?

Viewing students' readiness for choice and self-direction from their zone of proximal development (ZPD) will help teachers decide how much structure students need and what they can do autonomously. The ZPD is the distance between what students can do on their own and what they can do with expert assistance (scaffolding) by more capable peers or adults (Vygotsky, 1978). The task for the teacher is to identify the student's starting level for self-direction, assist or teach them strategies for self-direction at that level, and gradually reduce the amount of monitoring and direction as students take on more responsibility. For example students are likely to need more scaffolded assistance when learning a new concept or skill. The four levels of motivational maturity—ranging from low to high—proposed by R. Ames and C. Ames (1991) serve as a beginning guide for assisting students. Teacher behaviors that provide assistance at each level of motivational maturity are shown in Table 7.1. For students at the low maturity level, the goal is to assist them to move toward high-motivational maturity (see the LINKS model in Chapter 4). Greater direction by the teacher is needed at lower levels of

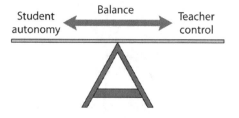

FIG. 7.1. Balance between teacher control and student autonomy.

TABLE 7.1

Teacher Behaviors for Levels of Motivational Maturity

Level of Maturity	Teacher Behavior
Low maturity	Use structure including clear goals and directions with frequent monitoring and positive feedback with corrections.
Low–moderate	Model breaking tasks into subgoals followed by student practice. Continue monitoring but have students begin checking their own work.
High–moderate	Assist students as needed. Encourage student participation in setting goals, defining standards, evaluating their own work and behavior, and devising solutions.
High maturity	Little teacher guidance is needed with students able to judge when they need help. Students set own goals and work through difficulties on their own.

Source. From Ames, R. & Ames, C. (1991) "Motivation and Effective Teaching". In J. L. Idol & B. F. Jones (Eds.), *Educational Values and Cognitive Instruction: Implications for Reformation* (pp. 247–61). Hillsdale, NJ: Lawrence Erlbaum Associates. Adapted by permission.

maturity. As students become more capable of guiding themselves, the teacher gradually removes the level of support.

Although it might be expected that these levels correspond with age, high school teachers (and even college faculty) will find students at lower levels of motivational maturity who need more structure. At the same time, some younger students may be more mature and require less structure.

In summary, autonomy is not just a matter of open-ended choices for students. It is a feeling of ownership by students. The teacher, based on students having the competency to understand and make choices, carefully plans choices. More choices than students can handle can be demotivating (Iyenger & Lepper, 2000). Decisions have to be made about what activities are appropriate and not appropriate for student choices or decision making. Pointers to keep in mind are shown in Strategy 7.1.

REFLECTION. What is your comfort level in providing opportunity for autonomy? Think about your students and their learning tasks. What opportunities for autonomy can you offer students at their level of motivational maturity?

Classroom Management Practices. The establishment of a structure that supports student autonomy is carried out largely

---

Strategy 7.1. Guidelines for Giving Choices

- Once the basic rules and procedures are established at the first of the year, it is possible to give students increased freedom within the limits of the classroom setting.
- Give carefully planned choices and then be sure that students have the competency to understand and make the choices and that you feel comfortable with them. Choices do not have to be given every day.
- Make the choices meaningful and of equal value. Decision making does not mean giving students a choice between an easy or a difficult task, one that requires more effort or less effort. Giving students a choice between essay questions and true–false questions is not a viable choice because these have different purposes in learning and assessment.

---

through the implementation of effective classroom management practices. This is a task that again calls for a balance between structure and autonomy. Freiberg, Stein, & Huang (1995) described such a classroom as one with "a sense of purpose, order, and predictability to the classroom organization allowing for greater creativity and active learning" (p. 3). Ladson-Billings (1994) identified a commonality among successful teachers of African-American children, stating "Psychological safety is a hallmark of each of these classrooms. The students feel comfortable and supported" (p. 73). Again, the issue for teachers is balance between the creation of a classroom that provides opportunity for autonomy and one that is free of behaviors that disrupt learning.

Research on classroom management practices indicates that more effective teachers focus on planning and preparation designed to provide optimum learning time and prevent problems (Emmer & Assiker, 1990). The first few weeks of a school year are the most important because this is a time when norms for academic and social behaviors are established that will extend throughout the year. Once rules are established at the first of the year, it is possible to give students increased freedom within the limits of the classroom setting, gradually "loosening the reins." Students may be involved, to the extent they have the capability, in establishing the rules. Rules common to many classrooms are:

Rule 1.   Be polite and helpful.
Rule 2.   Respect other people's property.
Rule 3.   Listen quietly while others are speaking.
Rule 4.   Respect and be polite to all people.
Rule 5.   Obey all school rules.
          (Evertson, Emmer, & Worsham, 2003, p. 23)

The texts—*Classroom Management for Secondary Teachers* (Emmer, Evertson, & Worsham, 2003) and *Classroom Management for Elementary Teachers* (Evertson, Emmer, & Worsham, 2003)—provide detailed guidance for establishing a positive classroom management system. Strategy 7.2 provides guidelines on establishing norms.

Strategy 7.2.   Establish Norms

Establish norms for:

- Social support system and peer respect. Define respect for your classroom, along with examples of behavior that will not be tolerated. In the classroom described by Noblit (1993), "The worst infraction of all was to laugh if someone did not know the right answer to a question" (p. 30).
- Help seeking. Establish the custom that all students will be helpers and helpees at some point. Students should understand that help seeking when needed is an adaptive strategy, not cheating.
- Academic work. Discuss with students the meaning of student responsibility and the motivational effects of different attributions for success and failure.
- Accountability and monitoring. Explain how work will be monitored, how students can monitor, and the type of feedback students can expect.

McCollum (1995) found evidence for the importance of classroom management for high levels of engagement in high-poverty classrooms. The majority of high-poverty classrooms had high levels of engagement characterized by (a) well-established, but flexible, routines, (b) few disruptions, and (c) ongoing monitoring of student work. The importance of orderly behavior by students for an effective learning environment cannot be underestimated. This was found to be the most critical condition for whether teachers implemented new teaching practices (Newmann, Rutter, & Smith, 1989). Similarly, some teachers in an urban high school did not use instructional practices such as cooperative learning and whole-class discussion because of apprehension about possible student misbehavior (Alderman, 1996).

McCollum (1995) noted two extremes regarding order in classrooms. Classrooms can be a somewhat happy place with few overt discipline problems but have little academic learning, or they can be highly orderly with no real engagement. Structure or order is often thought of as a detriment to student autonomy. However, optimal structure provides support for student autonomy because it offers students consistency in expectations, feedback, and consequences (Connell, 1990). By the same token, inconsistency results in a lack of autonomy support. Management perspectives of two effective teachers are shown in Exhibit 7.1.

Sources of Social Support

Social support involves interaction between teacher and students and between students. What elements of support are found in supportive classrooms? Classrooms characterized by cohesiveness, satisfaction, and goal direction were preferred by students and were associated with positive outcomes (Battistich et al., 1995). These researchers proposed that student social responsibility may contribute directly to student academic competence. They argue that, in the context of school reform for academics, the attainment of the above "'nonacademic' outcomes is as important as the acquisition of academic outcomes" (Battistich et al., 1999). In this section, sources of social support—cooperative learning and teacher support—are described.

Cooperative Learning

Epstein (1988) asserted that students' social and academic peer group relations are critical for developing character, per-

---

Exhibit 7.1. Teacher Examples of Classroom Management Perspectives

I know it seems old fashioned but I believe the students benefit from structure. I look them squarely in the eye at the beginning of the year and tell them you will read, and you will read soon. I tell my entire class we all have to know how to read and it's everybody's responsibility to make sure everyone learns to read well. (Ladson-Billings, 1994, p. 114)

As for order, Stephanie Terry's classroom was one of the most orderly I have ever seen—I never once heard her raise her voice, never saw her shame a child . . . order emerged out of curriculum she had created and the sense it gave students that what they were doing is important. "They've come to know that is the place where they do good work and they won't get much done—they won't get to do science, for example—if they don't get along, if everything is chaotic." The whole approach to classroom management couldn't help having an effect on social relations. One of the first things I noticed was the consideration Stephanie's students had for one another. The work the children did fostered a particular attitude toward self and a kind of cooperative interaction. She encouraged both individual responsibility and respect for others. (Rose, 1995, pp. 110–11)

---

sonal ethics, and social values. The grouping structures used in the classroom are a key factor for this goal. Group structures affect how students interact, become friends, and influence each other in engagement in learning. Cooperative learning is a grouping structure that can be an important factor in building a classroom that supports a sense of membership. Cooperative learning was one of the elements in the Child Development Project (CDP), which had the goal of developing a classroom climate as a caring community (Solomon et al., 1992).

Cooperative, along with competitive and individualistic, learning is one of three types of goal structures that can operate in a classroom. The processes at work for each type of goal structure differentially affect student motivation (Slavin, 1995). Students compete against each other for rewards and grades in a competitive structure. In a norm-based grading system (e.g., some form of grading on a curve), students' grades are determined by how they rank. This form of competition promotes negative motivational outcomes by emphasizing the importance of ability in performance, thus separating winners and losers (C. Ames & R. Ames, 1984). Students who win evaluate their ability as high and those who lose see their ability as low—conditions that foster a performance goal orientation.

The criteria for success in an individualistic goal structure are absolute standards, as is generally the case in standards-based school reform. One student's effort has no effect on others' goal attainment. This structure fosters a learning goal orientation where effort is perceived as valued. The limitation of an individualistic structure is that it does not explicitly foster peer interaction for learning.

Cooperative learning structures are based on the premise that each student's efforts toward a common goal contribute to other students' learning (Johnson, Maruyama, Johnson, Nelson, & Skon, 1981). Students can attain personal goals only by helping their team members to attain the learning objectives. What is the contribution of cooperative learning groups to the sense of school membership and belonging and engagement? Cooperative learning has been found to be beneficial for diverse groups of students: lower achieving, minority, mainstreamed or included, as well as higher achieving students (Slavin, 1995). According to Berndt and Keefe (1992), cooperative learning contributes to a classroom environment that (a) encourages the formation of supportive friendships between classmates, (b) encourages students to act in helpful rather than competitive ways toward classmates, and (c) provides students time and opportunity to interact with each other.

Small-group learning teams were singled out as being particularly useful for strengthening in-school support systems for African-American students (M. L. Clark, 1991). Interracial friendships are enhanced when African-American and White students have the opportunity to work cooperatively on class assignments and to participate together in extracurricular activities.

Motivational Effects of Cooperative Learning. What are the motivational effects of cooperative learning? Research on cooperative methods indicates that they have positive effects on achievement and on student self-esteem and locus of control (Slavin, 1995). Slavin argued that the most important motivational outcome of cooperative learning is the effect on student self-esteem. Two components of self-esteem affected by cooperative learning are (a) a feeling of being liked by peers, and (b) a feeling of academic competence. The motivation of low-achieving students, in particular, can be enhanced or inhibited by the type of goal structure.

If the structure is competitive, low-achieving students will perceive that they lack ability in comparison with their more successful classmates. Low achievers should experience greater success in cooperative classrooms because cooperative group structures tend to minimize the focus on ability (C. Ames & R. Ames, 1984). More important, cooperative goal structures can foster peer norms for higher achievement (Slavin, 1995).

The extent to which the group goal is perceived as learning or performance is related to the engagement of the group members (Blazevski, McKendrick, & Hruda, 2002). *Social loafing*, the tendency to let others do the work in cooperative groups, was more prevalent when the group perceived a performance goal. More engagement or less social loafing was associated with perceived learning goals. The perceived performance goal was more detrimental to the low achievers.

Establishing Effective Groups. There are several types of cooperative learning structures (e.g., STAD, Jigsaw, Group Investigation). The key question for teachers, however, is what makes an effective group regardless of the type of structure? The most important factor is that groups operate effectively. A common thread for all structures is that each student has a responsibility for the attainment of the group goal. Tasks for learning are divided among students; they cooperate to be sure all students can fulfill their responsibility because the group's success depends on efforts of all group members who share the same reward (grade). Slavin contended that effective group learning depends on group rewards and individual accountability. A number of sources are available that provide specific guidelines for establishing effective cooperative learning (e.g., Cohen, 1994; Johnson, Johnson, & Holubec, 1994; Kagen, 1992;

Slavin, 1995). The next section focuses on the composition of groups.

Composition of Groups. Group membership is an important factor in establishing a climate that fosters a sense of membership. As a general rule, cooperative learning groups are organized heterogeneously (mixed according to gender, ability, and ethnicity). The CDP project (Solomon et al., 1992) goes further. A goal of the project was to make sure that, by the end of year, students will have worked in groups with most, if not all, of their classmates. Similarly, N. Miller and Harrington (1992) suggested periodically rotating teams so students can have firsthand experience with as many of their classmates as possible. In the case of elementary classrooms, different teams can be used in different curriculum units. A question arises as to how to form groups when there are only a small number of minority students in the class. When this is the case, Miller and Harrington recommended that, rather than spreading the few minorities across as many teams as possible, it is better to have several heterogeneous groups that are balanced according to cultural diversity, with the remaining groups homogeneous. A cooperative learning group is depicted in Fig. 7.2.

What are potential problems in group composition? Cohen (1994) identified status as a potential motivational problem when groups are heterogeneously grouped according to ability. For example, students known to be high or low achieving may be given higher or lower status by other students based on these ability expectations. In this case, students with low status may have less access to resources, less opportunity for talk, and may

FIG. 7.2. Cooperative teamwork.

be ignored by other group members. N. Miller and Harrington (1992) explained the problems in terms of social identity. If a student focuses on his or her lack of academic skills, these skills may become less valued, resulting in the student seeking to forge a different identity (e.g., tough guy) to restore his or her self-esteem. To reduce dominance by high-status students in the group, Cohen (1994) recommended training students in group participation norms; that is, actually having students practice the norms, not just telling students about these participation norms. Morris (as cited in Cohen, 1994) developed the following group participation norms to train students:

- Say your own ideas.
- Listen to others; give everyone a chance to talk.
- Ask others for their ideas.
- Give reasons for your ideas and discuss many different ideas. (Cohen, 1994, p. 53)

Additional guidelines and cautions in using cooperative groups are shown in Strategy 7.3.

In summary, effective use of cooperative learning, in some form, is a key component in building a climate where peers

---

Strategy 7.3.   Guidelines for Using Cooperative Groups

- Do not assume students will have social skills to work as an effective group. Teachers (to their dismay) occasionally think students such as those in college preparatory classes will automatically have such skills. When these students have been accustomed to performance goal classroom structures, they believe that, if team members learn more, their ability is diminished.
- Foster a learning goal orientation to help address student beliefs described previously.
- Distribute responsibility among group members. Make sure all group members are responsible for a task specific to the group's goal.
- Have groups set team goals as a marker for progress and evaluate their goal accomplishment each session.

support and help each other. In Chapter 2, help seeking was described as an adaptive skill for coping with academic success and related to attributional beliefs. Help seeking should be seen as a normal social interaction in a classroom climate that supports a sense of membership. Nelson-Le Gall (1991, 1992) argued that, although whole class and individualistic structures impede help seeking, cooperative learning promotes it. An important role of the teacher is to establish norms for help seeking as an adaptive strategy. In cooperative learning, there are both help seekers and help givers. A student seeking help may ignore classmates—a readily available source of help—because of explicit or implicit classroom norms that convey a message that cooperative work is a form of cheating. Cooperative learning, when well designed and implemented, helps students see help seeking as an adaptive strategy.

Teacher's Role in Social Support and Student Perspective

One of the learner-centered psychological principles is social influences on learning (American Psychological Association [APA], 1997). This principle underscores the importance of quality personal relationships for providing a positive classroom climate that supports a sense of belonging, self-respect, self-acceptance, and learning. How important is teacher support for establishing such a climate? Personal support from teachers and other students is the third condition listed by Newmann (1992) as setting the stage for social bonding. The teacher's role is especially important in view of the press toward high-stakes testing and meeting standards. V. E. Lee and Smith (1999) conducted research on reform in Chicago schools and found that student learning was associated with schools and classrooms that provided social support combined with academic expectations and support. If either social support or press for standards was missing, the result was lower achievement.

Teachers play a critical role in creating a supportive classroom climate. Beginning with kindergarten, a positive student–teacher relationship is associated with both academic and social competencies (N. E. Perry & R. S. Weinstein, 1998). Academic performance of minority students is enhanced when their teachers and other school personnel are seen as supportive and helpful

(M. L. Clark, 1991). Teacher support is evidenced by (a) showing concern for all students; and (b) being interested in their ideas, experiences, and products (Solomon et al., 1992). Ladson-Billings (1994) described such teachers as believing that "students have to care not only about their own achievement but also about their classmates' achievement" (p. 69).

How do students describe teacher support? A. M. Ryan and Patrick (2001) described *teacher support* as "the extent to which students believe teachers value and establish personal relationships with them" (p. 440). One of the most frequent characteristics mentioned by students is caring. Caring is usually described in such phrases as rapport and concern for students. McLaughlin (1991) described caring in a broader framework: It is carried out through interpersonal relationships, classroom management, curriculum, and teaching approaches. The following are descriptions and examples of teacher support, in the broader sense, gathered through classroom observations and interviews with teachers and students (Dillon, 1989; Ladson-Billings, 1994; Nieto, 1992, 1994; Rose, 1995):

- A low-track, secondary English class in a rural area reported that, because their teacher "cared for them personally and cared about their performance and learning in class," the students cared more about their schoolwork (Dillon, 1989, p. 242).
- "They're all great—All my teachers were wonderful. Its [sic] just a feeling you have. You know they really care for you. You just know it. You can tell. Teachers who don't have you in any of their classes or haven't had you, they still know who you are" (Nieto, 1994, p. 407).
- "In Calexia, caring had as much to do with faith and cognition as with feeling. All children whatever their background had the capacity to learn. And this belief brought with it a responsibility: It was the teacher's intellectual challenge to come to understand what must be done to tap that potential" (Rose, 1995, p. 87).
- "Mr. Lopez . . . the way he taught, made you interested in math. He just made me feel that, not to give up, that you can do it. That's the only way to solv[e] problems" (Walker, 2006).

In these examples, concern and interest are tied to developing academic and social skills of all students. As Page (1991) observed, simply giving students individual attention does not develop a supportive classroom environment. A teacher's attempts to attend to social needs in a low-track ninth-grade classroom through individual attention backfired. This is illustrated by the following incident in a classroom that alternated between order and chaos:

- The teacher moved back and forth assisting four students individually for 15 to 30 sec each. Although this appeared to provide encouragement, as recommended for supportive classrooms, the individual attention to the students was both unsolicited and distracting (refer to Chapter 2 where unsolicited help by the teacher may be viewed as a low-ability cue by the student).

Page concluded that this class lacked cohesiveness. There were no shared norms for social interaction and support. Instead, each person tried to satisfy his or her individual needs, competing for the teacher's attention.

Support in Culturally Diverse Classrooms

It was noted earlier that one detriment to school membership is lack of identification with school by minority students. The social aspects of the classroom environment have been found to be more important to children of color than to mainstream children (Delpit, 1995). How is teacher support demonstrated in a culturally diverse classroom? The first step as a teacher is to have knowledge about students' cultures (Ogbu, 1992; Tucker & Herman, 2002; Villegas, 1991). Relevant knowledge helps teachers to (a) be sensitive to verbal and nonverbal signals from learners, (b) create a classroom climate that encourages students to express themselves, (c) be sensitive to themes of social relevance, and (d) help students recognize and accept that they can participate in two cultural frameworks for different purposes without losing their identity or being disloyal to their group.

In her profiles of successful teachers of African-American children, Ladson-Billings (1994) concluded that teachers worked to ensure each student of his or her individual importance. If students are of different cultural groups than the teacher, it is especially important for the teacher to work to develop commonalities with all students. For example, a White teacher from a different religion, with little in common with lower income African-American students, used the following techniques to draw students out, have them share their interests, and introduce them to new interests:

- She begins the year with an "entry questionnaire" that enables her to discover what students like to do outside of school, leisure-time activities, subjects they like and dislike. "I try to find out as much as I can about the students early in the year so I can plan an instructional program that motivates them and meets their needs . . . is also a great way to learn a little about their reading and writing levels." She also acknowledges their birthdays (Ladson-Billings, 1994, p. 67).
- Following are what students liked about an eighth-grade class: "The teacher listens to us, respects us, lets us express our opinion, looks us in the eye when she talks to us, speaks to us when she sees us in the halls or cafeteria" (Ladson-Billings, 1994, p. 68).

The successful minority students interviewed by Nieto (1994) described supportive teachers in various ways:

- Yolanda felt fortunate to have many teachers she felt understood and supported her in ways such as commenting on her bilingual ability, being a member in a folkloric Mexican dance group, or simply talking with her and other students about their lives. She added, "I really got along with the teachers a lot. They were always calling my mom, like I did a great job. Or they would start talking to me. And they were always congratulating me" (pp. 406–7).
- Vanessa noted, "[Most teachers] are really caring and supportive and are willing to share their lives and are willing to listen to mine. They don't just want to talk about what they're teaching you; they also want to know you" (p. 407).

Foster (1987) reported an African-American student's description of a good teacher as:

> We had fun in her class but she was mean. I can remember she used to say, "Tell me what's in the story, Wayne." She pushed, she used to get on me and push me to know. She made us learn. We had to get in the books. There was this tall guy and he tried to take her on, but she was in charge of the class and she didn't let anyone run her. I still have this book we used in her class.
>
> (p. 68)

Nieto concluded that the most common characteristic expressed by these students was a teacher who had affirmed them in language, culture, or concerns. This type of teacher called on students' linguistic and cultural knowledge, but not in a superficial way, and students were aware of the distinction between these. Tucker et al. (2002) examined the variables that affected engagement of low-income African-American students. The most consistent findings indicated that teacher involvement had a direct effect on student engagement; students who reported a high level of interest and involvement by their teachers had the highest level of engagement.

Villegas (1991) pointed out that it is unrealistic to expect a teacher to have a thorough understanding of all cultural groups. The important factor is to know procedures for gaining information about all students, especially those of different cultures. Other ways to gain information are shown in Strategy 7.4. In the final analysis, Delpit (1995) asserted that teachers have to accept students of diverse cultures and accept the responsibility to teach them.

CONCLUSION

Osterman (2000) concluded that a sense of belonging influences achievement through its effects on engagement. Building a sense of membership so that all students experience a sense of belonging is dependent on the conditions identified by Newmann (1992): (a) agreement on the goals of education, (b) fairness and equal opportunity, (c) personal support from teachers and peers, and (d) valid successful experiences. One constant is that the

---

Strategy 7.4. Learning about Students' Backgrounds

- Have students introduce themselves to you at the beginning of the year. This can be done through an interest questionnaire, as described earlier. Have students tell about what they like to do outside of school, their favorite/least favorite subjects, a successful experience they had in your subject, and their goals.
- Observe students in situations other than the classroom (e.g., the playground, the cafeteria, the gymnasium, informal groups before school).
- Ask students questions about their cultural practices.
- Talk with parents as much as possible.
- Work with children to research various ethnic groups.
- Read about various ethnic groups.

Source. Based on Ogbu (1992).

---

combination of social support and high expectations increases the likelihood of student engagement, which contributes to student success. As Comer (2005) reminded us, "For many children, academic learning is not a primary, natural, or valued task. It is positive relationships and sense of belonging that a good school culture provides that give these children the comfort, confidence, competence, and motivation to learn" (p. 748).

REVIEW OF MAJOR POINTS

1. Social context influences classroom engagement, academic effort, and subsequent school success and failure at all levels of schooling. A sense of school membership is an important foundation for educational engagement because students who experience a sense of belongingness are more likely to adopt goals valued by the school. The basis for a sense of school membership is social bonds that connect students to the school. Four factors that establish social bonds to the school are attachment, commitment, involvement in both academic and nonacademic school

activities, and students' belief that an education is important, along with faith that the school will provide them with an education.

2.   A sense of belonging and engagement in school is affected by social identity—an identity based on group membership. The extent to which a group identifies with goals and values of school and/or devalues academic effort and achievement affects engagement for learning. The peer group plays a major role in the extent to which academic effort and achievement are valued or devalued. Factors that lead to negative views of achievement include stereotypic images such as brain–nerd connection, pressure toward nonacademic activities such as social activities and part-time work, teacher passive acceptance of the peer group structure, favoritism toward athletes, and peer group separation.

3.   A sense of membership and cognitive engagement is affected in important ways by the sociocultural orientations that students bring to school. Ogbu explained the cultural-ecological role of school performance: that some minorities do better in school than others because of their different historical and cultural experiences. Students may develop the strategy of oppositional social identity to protect their cultural identity. A primary strategy adopted by high-achieving students who have learned to compete successfully in the dominant culture is accommodation without assimilation—maintaining their cultural identities, but recognizing the necessity of academic achievement for their future success.

4.   The task for schools and teachers is to establish a climate that builds a sense of membership while valuing students' culture and social identity. Four broad conditions of school that set the stage for a sense of membership are clarity of purpose, fairness, personal support, and success. Three areas essential for establishing a classroom for optimum membership and engagement are classroom structure for autonomy and responsibility, cooperative learning, and teacher support.

5.   Classroom autonomy occurs when teachers allow student initiative and choice and students view learning activities as connected to their personal goals and values. Two ends of a continuum for autonomy are characterized as origin, the perception that one has the freedom and competence to make choices; and pawn, the perception of being controlled by external forces. A

major issue for teachers is to establish a balance between the creation of a classroom that provides opportunity for choice and one that is free of behaviors that disrupt learning. A teacher's role is to set boundaries for work, social/behavioral expectations, and responsibility. Teachers carefully plan choices based on students having the competency to understand and make the choices.

6.   A classroom environment that supports autonomy is built through effective classroom management principles from the beginning of the school year. Classrooms that have high levels of engagement (including high-poverty classrooms) are characterized by well-established, but flexible routines, few disruptions, and ongoing monitoring of student work.

7.   Classrooms that provide social support are characterized by cohesiveness, satisfaction, and goal direction. Sources of social support include cooperative learning and teacher support.

8.   Three types of goal structures operate in a classroom—cooperative, competitive, and individualistic learning—with each type differentially affecting student motivation. Cooperative learning has been found to be beneficial for diverse groups of students including lower-achieving, minority, mainstreamed or included, as well as higher-achieving students. Cooperative goal structures can foster peer norms for higher achievement.

9.   Cooperative learning groups are organized heterogeneously (mixed according to gender, ability, and ethnicity). Effective groups provide social support and foster engagement: Each student has a responsibility for the attainment of the group goal, tasks for learning are divided among students, and group rewards are used with individual accountability. Help seeking should be seen as a normal social interaction in a classroom climate that supports a sense of membership.

10.   Teacher support is evidenced by showing concern for all students and being interested in their ideas, experiences, and products. In a culturally diverse classroom, teacher support is demonstrated by teachers having knowledge about students' culture and working to ensure each student of his or her individual importance. Because it is unrealistic to expect a teacher to have a thorough understanding of all cultural groups, the important factor is to know procedures for gaining information about all students, especially those of different cultures.

Motivational Toolbox

1. Important points to think about and lingering questions

2. Strategies I can use now

3. Strategies I want to develop in the future

CHAPTER 8

Tasks, Recognition, and Evaluation for Optimal Engagement and Motivation

Meaningful cognitive demands of formal education cannot be mastered through passive listening and reading, nor through being entertained; they require an engaged student.

—Newmann (1992, p. 14)

According to C. Ames (1992) the classroom context sets the stage for motivation. A classroom where students are engaged and motivated does not just happen. The previous chapter established the importance of the social context for fostering student engagement. This chapter focuses on the motivational characteristics of three instructional variables that foster student involvement and motivation in learning: (a) learning tasks and activities, (b) incentives and recognition that promote and recognize student engagement, and (c) motivational effects of evaluation (C. Ames, 1992). These three variables form the core of classroom instruction affecting students' beliefs about their own ability, their willingness to apply effort, their goals, and, consequently, their engagement in learning. Educators can influence student goal orientation toward learning by emphasizing these three instructional variables (Urdan, 2001). How these variables are used determine the extent to which the classroom supports a learning or performance orientation or intrinsic or extrinsic motivation.

CLASSROOM TASK MOTIVATION

This section examines the nature of task characteristics as they affect student motivation and engagement. Tasks and activities are the primary instructional variables that engage students in learning. "Tasks influence learners by directing their attention to the particular aspects of content and by specifying ways of processing information" (Doyle, 1983, p. 161). Motivation for instruction demands that teachers not only "bring the task to the students," but also "bring students to the task" (Blumenfeld, Mergendoller, & Puro, 1992, p. 237). This means specific task characteristics will attract student attention and interest. By the same token, teachers need to use strategies to promote student effort and/or the use of higher levels of thinking. This reciprocal relationship is shown in Fig. 8.1.

Task Features and Types

What features or types of tasks are likely to get best efforts and highest engagement from students? Newmann, Wehlage, and Lamborn (1992) described engaging tasks as "meaningful, valuable, significant and worthy of one's effort" (p. 23). Descriptors used to describe tasks that are motivating are authentic work or tasks (e.g., Fredricks, Blumenfeld, & Paris, 2004; Darling-Hammond, Ancess, & Falk, 1995; Newmann, Secada, & Wehlage, 1995), active in-depth learning (Darling-Hammond, 1997), and

FIG. 8.1.   Reciprocal relationship for task motivation.

thoughtful tasks (Blumenfeld, 1992). A common feature of these tasks is the focus on higher order thinking, such as analysis and integration of knowledge, production of solutions or products, and connection to the world beyond school. From a review of the research on engagement, Marks (2000) concluded that authentic work brings about greater student engagement.

An example of a complex task requiring higher order thinking was reported by Newmann et al. (1995). In a social studies lesson, eighth-grade students were asked to consider the impact of workers who were laid off from work on the community. The lesson began with the teacher helping the students to define terms related to the issue (e.g., layoff, unemployment rate, local economy). The teacher then presented information about the economy of their community, and others of similar size but with different types of business and employment. In small groups, the students were asked to use the information they had been given and answer this question: What generalizations can you state about each of the local economies? Groups developed and reported their generalizations. After discussion, the class developed a final generalization. To accomplish the task, students had to use the higher order thinking skills of analysis, development of hypotheses and generalizations, and comparison and contrast. What are the motivational aspects of tasks of this nature?

Task Complexity and Student Cognitive Engagement

One assumption is that high-level, challenging tasks, such as the social studies lesson, will have a positive influence on motivation and lead to greater student engagement. From a social-cognitive perspective, however, the role of task influence on motivation is more complicated because student perception of the task plays a mediating role. Although challenging tasks can increase student motivation, it is not an automatic occurrence (Blumenfeld, 1992). An important element to consider is the interaction between task complexity and the types of information processing required of the student.

Doyle (1983) suggested that classroom tasks vary according to the type of mental operation needed. Some types of learning activities require a low level of cognitive processing, whereas others require a high level. Memory tasks (e.g., spelling) that simply ask students to reproduce information they have learned require only low levels of processing, with low risks for students. Challenging or complex tasks—where students are expected to apply information or draw inferences (e.g., evaluating portfolio entries or solving word problems in math)—require a high level of cognitive processing. When tasks are more open-ended and challenging, they are more risky for the student, and motivation may decrease. Blumenfeld (1992) proposed reasons why high-level challenging tasks, by themselves, may not lead to greater engagement by students:

- As the task becomes more difficult, either in the content or form it is to take, students may be unwilling to expend the effort necessary to accomplish it as intended.
- If students lack background knowledge of the content or an understanding of how to complete the task, cognitive engagement for complex tasks may decrease.
- As the amount of work increases in lengthy tasks, such as long-term projects, students may become discouraged and just concentrate on finishing the task.

To reduce the risks, students may try to negotiate with the teacher to simplify the assignment and/or the evaluation. If students are only held accountable for completing work and not for the content and understanding, a high-level task can be turned into a low-level task, lowering the level of cognitive processing. The dilemma for a teacher is that risk can lower motivation for the student, but lowering the risk for the student can lower the level of learning. It is important that a balance between students' skill and challenge be maintained. Being aware of these points can help teachers better plan challenging tasks with enhanced motivation.

Social Organization and Task Engagement

The social context of the classroom also affects student task engagement. Cooperative learning was introduced in Chapter 7 as a means of fostering students' sense of membership and belonging. Cooperative learning also impacts the proportion of engaged time students spend on academic tasks; cooperative learning groups have a higher proportion of engaged time than do students not in cooperative groups (Slavin, 1995). This was confirmed by Moriarty, Douglas, Punch, and Hattie (1995), who studied the effects of classroom environment on motivation. Students in the cooperative learning environment had a higher degree of purposeful activity and task-related interaction. In the competitive environment, students not only had more off-task behavior but it increased over time.

In summary, successful groups promote student interactions that increase cognitive processing, higher order thinking, and integration of information (Blumenfeld, Marx, Soloway, & Krajcik, 1996). If groups do not work well together, however, student engagement declines (Blumenfeld, 1992). As emphasized in Chapter 7, it is not just the use of cooperative learning, but how effectively the groups work that positively contributes to student engagement. For group work to foster cognitive engagement, students have to learn to share ideas, disagree, and resolve differences in perspectives (Blumenfeld et al., 1996).

What teaching practices increase student engagement in tasks? The following section provides direction in this area.

Teacher Practices that Increase Student Task Engagement

"Tasks do not exist independently from teachers. In order for high-level tasks to work, teachers need to ensure that students engage cognitively with them" (Blumenfeld, 1992, p. 97). Instructional practices related to student engagement were observed in several studies (Blumenfeld, 1992; Blumenfeld et al., 1992; Meece, 1991; Meece, Blumenfeld, & Puro, 1989). Although higher engagement was more likely in classrooms rated as having a high-learning goal orientation by students, this was not sufficient (see Chapter 3 for learning orientation). These studies provided insight into practices that differentiated between teachers who were able to sustain high-level tasks and those who were less effective in the high-learning classrooms. Practices that made a difference were evident in whole-class, small-group, and hands-on tasks (Blumenfeld, 1992). Blumenfeld summarized teacher practices in classrooms related to high levels of student engagement:

- *Opportunities to learn.* Teachers offered their students opportunities to learn by their choice of topics, activities, and type of task product. They provided meaningful topics and problems.
- *Instruction.* Teachers used a variety of high-quality instructional techniques, including using concrete illustrations and analogies, connecting new concepts to students' prior knowledge, and requiring student application of the concepts.
- *Press.* Teachers pressed (pushed) students to think by requiring them to explain and justify answers; teachers reframed questions and broke tasks into smaller parts when students failed to comprehend. They monitored for comprehension rather than for correctness of procedures, encouraging answers from all students with techniques like asking for votes or asking students to compare responses.
- *Support.* Teachers used scaffolding to lead students gradually toward comprehension by providing samples for students to use, modeling the thinking processes and strategies needed instead of giving answers, breaking the task into manageable steps, and encouraging collaboration among students and independence from the teacher.
- *Evaluation.* Teachers emphasized comprehension and mastery of content, showing less concern with just finishing tasks or having the right response. They allowed students who had not achieved a satisfactory level to rework assignments or retake a quiz.

What do such strategies look like in a classroom? Two teachers were selected by Blumenfeld (1992) to contrast how the use of the strategies made a difference in student engagement in their classes. The teachers, A and B, were similar in a number of areas: Both assigned tasks that required thought, problem solving, and complex procedures; both integrated previous lessons; and both required a product that involved developing a design from a variety of materials. Although students in both classes reported a high learning goal motivation orientation, students in Teacher B's class reported lower levels of active learning or engagement. One key difference was less press and support for thought by Teacher B. Although the students in this class were attentive, Teacher B did not require widespread responding, which is necessary for cognitive engagement. Exhibit 8.1 shows a contrast of the practices of the two teachers, and Strategy 8.1 provides guidelines for increasing task motivation.

Exhibit 8.1. Contrast between Teachers A and B

Teacher B often makes connections among key concepts himself rather than asking students to do so. During discussion and recitation, he probes or asks students to elaborate less often than does Teacher A and frequently expands on students' answers himself rather than asking them to think through the issue. He does not break down the problem or actually hold students accountable for planning and explaining their plans. His monitoring more often focuses on procedural rather than conceptual issues, and he does not often engage in extended dialogue with the students to help them problem solve or clarify their thinking. Instead he often just says, "Try again." Finally, students are not held accountable for understanding by having to write down or share conclusions with the group. Essentially, students in Teacher B's class could be highly involved in the task and quite motivated to learn, but would not necessarily have to think in depth about what happened. One way to characterize the difference is that Teacher A "brings the lesson to the students" via the opportunities for thought her practices afford, and she "brings the students to the lessons" via her practices that press for and support active learning. Teacher B brings the "lesson to the students," but he less effectively "brings students to the lesson" (Blumenfeld, 1992, p. 97).

Strategy 8.1. Increasing Task Motivation

1. Establish a mastery or learning climate and structure for the classroom by including the following components (Meece, 1991):

   • opportunities for students to develop an increased sense of competence by using concrete examples as needed and relating these to students' personal experience;
   • some opportunity for self-directed learning;

Strategy 8.1. *Contd.*

- peer cooperation and collaboration with guidance for effective cooperative work; and
- emphasis on the intrinsic value of learning by showing students its relevance outside of school.

2. Break a long-term project into steps or phases. Be sure students see the goal of the final product and the steps for completion.

3. Use a variety of types of tasks and task structures that are appropriate for the particular goal. These include whole-class, small-group, or cooperative learning, demonstrations, simulations, technology, and projects. Variation in types of tasks will help convey to students that there are many types of ability and intelligences.

4. Make sure that students have the capabilities needed to complete a task. For long-term projects, students need the capabilities of long-term and proximal goal setting and self-monitoring. For group work, they need social skills to work together. To use information from the Internet, students need capabilities to organize and integrate large amounts of information.

5. Support students through the use of scaffolding by providing examples as needed and modeling thinking. At the same time, press students to explain and justify answers and elicit responses from all students.

Task Interest

A widely accepted premise by educators and students is that interest enhances motivation. Interest—whether text material or task activity—is important motivationally because it influences attention and persistence and, in the long run, acquisition of knowledge by students. Thus, making the task interesting is often seen as the panacea for lack of engagement. As in other aspects of motivation, the nature and role of interest is more complex. What do we know about interest and its influence?

Situational and Individual Interest. Two types of interest—situational and individual (personal)—may be evident in classrooms (Hidi, 1990, 2000; Hidi & Renninger, 2006; Renninger, 2000). Situational interest results from some instructional activity or text material such as interesting text, a science experiment, a computer simulation, or a learning activity relevant to students' lives that triggers an interest. It may or may not have long-term effects on learning. In contrast, individual interest is a personal interest, such as space exploration, based on a deep level of knowledge that a student brings to the classroom. As such, it develops slowly over time, is relatively stable, and has a powerful effect on student learning and performance. Although the two types of interest are triggered by a different source, each influences the other.

Situational interest has been described as having two phases, first as a trigger for the student's interest in a topic or activity, second as maintaining the interest. If this interest is maintained over time, it may develop into an individual interest. More recently, Hidi and Renninger (2006) proposed a four-phase model of interest development. The first phase begins with triggering of interest by an environmental factor followed by maintained interest. At the next phase, the student may generate further interest through questions and experimentation and by the help or support of others. In the final phase, the student has a well-developed individual interest.

An example of moving from a triggered or situational interest to a sustained individual interest is that of Homer Hickham (1999). At age 14, he saw Sputnik pass over Coalwood, West Virginia. As stated in Chapter 5, his possible self as a rocket scientist was formed. External resources supported this triggered situational interest. These included: his science teacher, peers he solicited to form a team, including one who had scientific knowledge, and members in the community. His teacher helped him find a way to develop expertise in Calculus that was not offered by the school. This interest in rockets was maintained and Homer Hickham became a rocket scientist. This example illustrates to some extent the four phases of interest development (Hidi & Renninger, 2006).

Situational interest is asserted to be more important for the classroom because teachers have more control over this than on the individual interests students bring with them (Bergin, 1999; Hidi, 1990; Mitchell, 1993). The reliance on individual interest would require individualization for each and every student, which is too time-consuming for teachers (Hidi, 1990). Furthermore, some individual interests may not contribute to goals of learning. For example, drugs may be of high interest to a student who is into the drug culture, but this neither contributes to engagement in classroom tasks nor enhances decision making about drugs.

An important aspect of situational interest for teachers is whether it is short term (catches student attention) or continues over time (holds student attention: Mitchell, 1993). Some features of lessons catch or trigger student interest but may not hold interest in the long run, whereas others hold or ensure the continuation of interest over time. Mitchell (1993) differentiated between activities that caught or activities that held the interest of secondary mathematics students by having students list aspects of their classrooms that were interesting or boring and explain why. Students indicated that computers, groups, and puzzles stimulated (caught) their interest but did not hold it over time. The following held their interest: learning activities in math that were meaningful (e.g., when math content was related to their real-life problems), and activities in which they felt they were active participants in learning (e.g., laboratory activities and projects in math where students actually did something).

Interest and Comprehension of Text. Much of the research on interest focused on its relationship to reading comprehension. When reading, children and adults understand and remember information better from topics of high interest than from topics of low interest (Garner, Alexander, Gillingham, Kulikowich, & Brown, 1991). However, a distinction is made between making it interesting and finding an interest. What is the significance of this distinction for text comprehension?

Making it interesting refers to the use of highly interesting but unimportant details placed in the text or added to a lecture to make it more interesting (Garner et al., 1991). *Finding an interest* refers to identifying topics that are of interest to students and then finding text and other materials on these topics. Garner et al. reminded us that, although John Dewey (1913) strongly believed in the role of interest for learning, he cautioned against artificial means to induce interest (e.g., interesting facts that are irrelevant to the topic). Wade (1992) stated, "Vivid, personalized anecdotes and seductive details will usually be considered interesting. However, this is not a viable strategy for creating interest" (p. 272). In fact, research has confirmed that when seductive details are placed in text, students recall these details, but they do not recall important generalizations (Garner et al., 1991; Wade, 1992).

Interest and Cultural Relevance. In Chapter 7, teachers' knowledge of students' culture was identified as important for building a supportive social climate. Knowledge of cultural factors also contributes to task interest and engagement. Rueda and Moll (1994) saw the motivational role of culture as similar to a bridge between the student and classroom tasks and activities. They described a classroom literacy project with junior high school students in predominantly working class, Latino neighborhoods. Teachers were concerned about the quantity and quality of student writing. During the project, writing assignments shifted from low-level activities, where students responded to worksheets and teacher questions, to activities that emphasized writing for communication. The assignments involved students writing about issues of significance to them in their community (e.g., immigration, gang life, bilingualism). According to the researchers, the shift to culturally relevant topics had immediate effects on student writing production. The amount of text written by students increased, as did their coherence and organization. Embedding the writing in the cultural context would be an example of situational interest (Bergin, 1999).

The connection of instruction to students' background was also found to be associated with student engagement in high-poverty classrooms (Shields, 1995). In math, reading, and writing, teachers who connected these subjects to the student backgrounds had more students actively engaged in learning. Shields (1995) equated meaning in learning to having a sense of connection between home and school.

Task Enrichment and Engagement. Will situational factors such as enrichment or embellishment of tasks lead to increased student interest and engagement in more traditional learning activities? Bergin (1999) pointed out that research on interest has not provided a list of interesting activities. Embellishments asserted to make tasks more attractive and enjoyable for students include student control, curiosity, and personalization (Brophy, 1987; Lepper & Cardova, 1992; Malone & Lepper, 1987).

- *Choice or control.* Higher engagement is more likely when students feel a sense of ownership or some control in their learning educationally sound choices (Malone & Lepper, 1987). Types of choice include elementary students choosing the books they read for pleasure (Gambrell & Morrow, 1996), students evaluating their work (Turner & Meyer, 1995), students in cooperative learning groups dividing tasks among themselves for a major assignment, and a student deciding how much practice will be needed to learn the words missed on a spelling test. In all cases, students must have the competencies to make the choices and assume responsibility for the choices (deCharms, 1976).
- *Curiosity.* Activities that appeal to students' curiosity are likely to attract students' interest (Lepper & Hodell, 1989). Providing students with information that is surprising or inconsistent with their prior knowledge can provoke curiosity (Brophy, 1987). An example is found in Kay Toliver's (1993) math classes. Toliver often used literature to introduce mathematical topics to gain students' interest. In one example, she used a Dr. Seuss story about a mysterious substance—oobleck—to introduce a lesson on complex fractions. "After reading a short excerpt from the story with my students, I introduce the idea of a complex substance; from there, I introduce the concept of complex fractions as it relates to the story line" (p. 42).
- *Contextualization and personalization.* Tasks are likely to be appealing to students when they are more personal or presented in a naturalistic context (Cardova & Lepper, 1996). This also makes abstract concepts more concrete for learners. For example, when Ms. Hudson, a high school English teacher, begins the study of *Romeo and Juliet* by showing the movie before reading the play, the play is less abstract and more meaningful for students.

Although embellishments can trigger task interest and attractiveness, they are not a panacea for student engagement. Lepper and Cardova (1992) expressed concern that "A number of the activities we observed children using in schools appeared to have purchased motivation at the expense of learning. These were activities that children found interesting and exciting, but from which they seemed to learn little, except how to 'win' the game" (p. 192).

With the advent of technological enhancements, it is important to know how they affect student motivation and learning. A research study was designed to determine if the embellishment of computer-based learning to make it more fun would increase the motivation and learning of students (Cardova & Lepper, 1996). Learning activities were embellished by contextualization, personalization, and choice. In the embellishment conditions, students rated initial motivation higher than did students in the control group; they reported being more willing to spend extra time in the learning activity, experiencing greater enjoyment, and using complex cognitive operations. However, there was no difference between the groups in long-term intrinsic motivation.

Based on findings from research on embellishing tasks, the researchers concluded that embellishments have beneficial effects on motivation when certain principles are followed (Cardova & Lepper, 1996; Lepper & Cardova, 1992).

- Embellishments do not automatically enhance intrinsic motivation. They must be carefully planned to ensure that they support learning, not undermine it.
- Embed the embellishments in the learning activities so as not to distract students from the important objectives.
- The most important principle is a match between the actions required for learning and the actions required for enjoyment. For example, the goals of winning the game and the goals of learning the material should be congruent.
- As a final caution, the novelty of the embellishments may wear off and eventually lose their impact on developing individual interest and motivation.

Implications for Teachers.   Teachers are often criticized for not making learning more interesting, but there are other considerations for motivating students (Hidi, 2000). Learning tasks change as students grow older, with the likelihood of increasing demands; thus the "play" type of interest that students had as children no longer holds. For example, learning to speak a second language requires hard work and drills that are not necessarily interesting. In these situations, the use of self-regulatory strategies by students to make tasks more interesting is often overlooked (Hidi & Harackiewicz, 2000). For example, they might choose to work with another person. Strategies for increasing interest are described in Strategy 8.2.

Strategy 8.2. Strategies for Increasing Task Interest

- Interest does not develop in isolation, it needs the teacher's support (Hidi & Renninger, 2006).
- Identify topics that are of interest to students and then provide material on high-interest topics. Caution: It is difficult, if not impossible, for teachers to cater to the personal interest of every child.
- Develop questions to stimulate curiosity (Hidi & Renninger, 2006).
- Design tasks that create bridges between classroom activities and the culture of students and their concerns outside of school.
- Help students with attention and metacognition (see Chapter 5) so they can selectively read for main ideas as well as for interesting details (Garner, Brown, Sanders, & Menke, 1992).
- Stimulate task interest or appreciation by telling students how important the skills and information are for everyday life and for being a successful student.
- Make abstract content more personal, concrete, or familiar to students. Use pictures, demonstrations, and hands-on activities as needed to make abstract concepts concrete.

Task Value Beliefs

The value or meaning of a task for a student is influential for task engagement and is related to task interest (Jacobs & Eccles,

2000; Renninger, 2000). Task value is a component of expectancy value theory (Eccles, Adler, et al., 1983; Wigfield & Eccles, 1992). This theory suggests that the strength of motivation in a particular situation is determined both by our expectation to succeed (see Chapter 3) and the value the success has for the individual.

The value component is concerned with the question, "Do I want to do this task and why?" (Eccles, Wigfield, & Schiefele, 1998, p. 1028). Potentially, a task might have three types of value (Eccles & Wigfield, 1995). *Attainment value* is the importance of doing well on a task or demonstrating competence such as mastering a skill, showing that we are liked, or showing that we are smart. *Intrinsic or interest value* is the enjoyment or the satisfaction one gets from the task. A student might enjoy problem solving or using graphic programs on the computer. *Utility value* refers to the usefulness of the task, especially as it relates to future goals. One might not have an interest in learning to use a keyboard, but it might have a high utility value in terms of future job opportunities. Utility value is more extrinsic in nature (a discussion of extrinsic and less intrinsic value appears in the following section). A student can have more than one type of value for a task.

What is the influence of these task value beliefs on student engagement and performance? A longitudinal study was conducted to determine the extent grade 4 task values and ability beliefs predicted high school literacy choices (Durik, Vida, & Eccles, 2006). Self-concept of ability at the fourth grade predicted all three measures—leisure reading, course choices, and career aspirations—at the tenth grade. Intrinsic value predicted only leisure reading and course choices. The results of the study highlight the importance of teachers helping students early on to develop perceptions of competency and intrinsic value for literacy.

Sansone and Smith (2000) concluded that an important part of self-regulation is the belief that an activity is valuable. Wigfield (1994) saw a role for teachers and students. Teachers can attempt to make learning more relevant to student lives, and students need to develop self-regulated learning strategies. As students develop more strategies and become more successful, "their valuing of those tasks will increase as well" (Wigfield, 1994, p. 120).

INTRINSIC AND EXTRINSIC MOTIVATION
AND ACADEMIC ENGAGEMENT

From self-determination theory, Ryan and Deci (2000) described three types of motivation. *Intrinsic motivation* is typically defined as students engaging in actions for their own sake and without coercion such as satisfaction, as sense of competence, interest, learning, and challenge. *Extrinsic motivation* occurs when students engage in activities for external reasons (outside of themselves) such as praise, grades, special privileges, and certificates or material rewards. Pressure from someone and coercion are also forms of extrinsic motivation. Another type of motivation is *amotivation*, a lack of motivation or students not seeing a connection between their actions and the outcome (similar to learned helplessness; see Chapter 2).

Should teachers expect that their students are intrinsically motivated for all learning or that all students are intrinsically motivated? Intrinsic motivation is important for academic engagement, but numerous studies found that academic intrinsic motivation decreases from upper elementary to high school years (see Eccles et al., 1998; Gottfried, Fleming, & Gottfried, 2001).

Teachers may highly desire students who are intrinsically motivated for academic work, but many tasks required in school are not intrinsically motivating to students (Brophy, 1983; Ryan & Deci, 2000). To counteract this, many teachers rely heavily on extrinsic incentives including praise, tokens, smiley faces, and special recognition, such as "student of the month."

This section begins by explaining the continuum from extrinsic to intrinsic motivation and is followed by the relationship between intrinsic and extrinsic motivation. Next, guidelines for using extrinsic rewards effectively are given. This section concludes with a discussion regarding strategies for enhancing intrinsic motivation and the limitations.

Extrinsic to Intrinsic Motivation: A Continuum

Traditionally, intrinsic and extrinsic have been viewed as polar opposite types of motivation. A current view of motivation acknowledges that these two types of motivation are not incompatible and can coexist (Covington & Mueller, 2001; Lepper, Corpus, & Iyenger, 2005). According to the self-determination view, the relationship is a continuum from most extrinsic to least extrinsic, not opposing forms of motivation (Deci & Ryan, 1991; Rigby, Deci, Patrick, & Ryan, 1992; Ryan & Deci, 2000). The continuum represents the extent to which students are controlled by the reward or determine their own actions. Based on this four-phase model, the more students determine their actions, the more intrinsic their motivation. The four phases from more controlling to most autonomous are as follows:

1. *External regulation*—Students' behavior is externally controlled by rewards or punishment. For example, a student completes her homework for teacher praise or to avoid staying after school.

2. *Introjected regulation*—Students follow rules because of pressure or to avoid anxiety or for ego enhancement, but they do not accept the rule internally. For example, a student does her homework because that is what good students are supposed to do, not because it helps her learn.

3. *Identified regulation*—Students accept a regulation because it is personally important for goal attainment. For example, a student works hard to improve her GPA enough to be accepted to the college she aspires to.

4. *Integrated regulation*—Students integrate and internalize different values and roles and are self-determined. For example, an adolescent values being a good athlete and a good student, and these values could conflict. But one can be a student and an athlete, and this is compatible with the student's self-identity and long-term goals.

The shift from extrinsic to intrinsic motivation is illustrated by an answer written by a high school senior in response to an essay question (see Exhibit 8.2). As this student illustrates, individuals may pursue tasks for both intrinsic and extrinsic reasons. A runner may run for the challenge and satisfaction experienced and also to compete and attain a scholarship for college. Both types of motivation can be present at any given time, and their strengths may vary from situation to situation. According to Lepper et al. (2005), the critical issue is not whether one is intrinsically or extrinsically motivated but how much of each one displays.

Exhibit 8.2.   Shift from Extrinsic to More Intrinsic

The shift from extrinsic to intrinsic motivation is illustrated in the following answer written by a high school senior in response to an essay question:

When I came to [high school] I started jogging for several reasons: 1) I was told to; 2) it was a challenge; 3) I figured I needed the exercise. For these reasons, I jogged periodically in my sophomore and junior years and I'm sure that the activity benefited me to some extent. My jogging this year, however, has been quite different in the source of motivation and the end rewards. Because of the research I did on aerobics I began to see jogging & fitness not as just activity but as a whole philosophy. I now feel that fitness is a necessary part of my life. As you once said, jogging can be more than pure physical activity; it can also be a source of aesthetic pleasure and accomplishment. For me jogging has been the latter.

The Relationship between Extrinsic and Intrinsic Motivation

A primary concern for educators is how to balance the use of extrinsic incentives as needed to promote student task engagement while establishing a climate that fosters intrinsic motivation. Stipek (1996) concluded that the elimination of extrinsic incentives is neither desirable nor realistic in today's classrooms. One drawback to the use of rewards is that, often, only a few students get all the rewards. Honor rolls by default are based on grades that may reflect the achievement level of the students when they entered the school, not improvement (Maehr, Midgley, & Urdan, 1992). However, Corno and Rohrkemper (1985) asserted that intrinsic motivation to learn is a necessary but insufficient component for academic achievement. If rewards are used appropriately, intrinsic and extrinsic motivation will be complementary components (Covington & Mueller, 2001). As Ryan and Deci (2000) suggested, an essential strategy for successful teaching is knowing how to use extrinsic forms of motivation to promote more autonomous motivation.

Effects of Extrinsic Rewards on Intrinsic Motivation. The effect of extrinsic rewards on intrinsic motivation has been the subject of many research studies. The prototype for this research was a study that identified an intrinsically motivating activity, established different reward conditions for the activity, and assessed the extent of the activity following the reward (Lepper, Greene, & Nisbitt, 1973). Drawing with felt pens was identified as an intrinsic activity for some children in a preschool classroom. These children were placed in one of three conditions: (a) the children were told they would be rewarded with a "Good Player" certificate for playing with felt pens, (b) children were given an unexpected reward after they completed the activity, and (c) children neither expected nor received a reward for participation. Two weeks later, the children were observed during free play to determine the amount of drawing activity with the felt pens. The group in the expected reward condition spent less time in drawing activities than did either of the other two groups. These findings were interpreted to indicate that the more conspicuous the reward is, the more likely the person will attribute his or her actions to the reward, thus becoming more dependent on the extrinsic incentive.

Although such early research findings were interpreted to mean that extrinsic rewards given for an already intrinsically motivating activity had an undermining effect on intrinsic motivation in ages ranging from preschool to college students (e.g., Lepper & Greene, 1975), the effects of rewards on intrinsic motivation have been found to be much more complex. In some circumstances rewards enhance intrinsic activity, whereas in others they have negative effects (Cameron & Pierce, 1994). The effects of rewards under different conditions are discussed in the following sections.

Controlling and Informational Aspects of Rewards. According to Deci and Ryan (1985), rewards affect motivation through controlling or informational aspects. When students' participation in an activity becomes a means to receive a reward, the effect of the reward is explained as controlling, diminishing the sense of autonomy. The controlling effect is more likely to occur when students are rewarded with no accompanying information about developing competence in the activity or when the teacher highlights the connection between performing the activity and receiving the reward (e.g., "Remember, if you don't do your homework, you won't get your homework points"). Rewards can have a positive effect when students are given information that the reward signifies their developing competence (e.g., "You earned the honor of being class leader next week for accomplishing Level 2 of the rubric, your best work yet"). This is similar to attributional feedback with information that might lead to more autonomous extrinsic motivation.

Rewards, Task Contingencies, and Goals. The effects of rewards on student motivation and performance will have differential effects according to the type of contingency or condition established for receiving the reward (Deci & Ryan, 1985). For classroom learning, students might be rewarded for either completing the task or the quality of the task outcome. Which do you think will have a more positive effect on student motivation and performance? Schunk (1983b) found that rewards contingent on the quality of the task outcome had positive effects on the level of task performance, self-efficacy judgments, and skill development of children. The positive effects were not found when children were rewarded only for task participation or task completion. Schunk explained that the differences in the effects of the two types of rewards occurred because task-contingent children were rewarded for progress, conveying the message that a sense of efficacy can be developed through effort. When rewards are given only for student participation, the importance of progress or improvement is not emphasized (Fig. 8.2).

The combination of task-outcome rewards and proximal goals was also found to have a positive effect on student self-efficacy (Schunk, 1984a). In this situation, rewards were thought to influence student goal commitment. According to Ford (1995), a desired reward undermines intrinsic motivation only if it creates an unintended goal conflict; that is, when the reward is more conspicuous than the original goal. The conspicuous reward distracts the person's attention from the original goal to the reward

FIG. 8.2.   Certificate to recognize improvement.

(e.g., "I get points for good grades, which I can use to buy something at the school store, so I want to get more points"). The reward system overshadows the student's satisfaction in their learning accomplishments or progress. However, rewards can facilitate motivation when a person has no goals or is avoiding a goal.

Verbal Praise.   Intrinsic interest can be enhanced by the use of verbal praise and positive feedback (Cameron & Pierce, 1994). Brophy (1981) concluded that, on the whole, teachers do not rely on praise for specific motivation and consequently do not systematically use it. In addition, praise is not distributed evenly, with outgoing, confident students receiving the most praise. Student reactions to praise tend to change as they grow older. Miller and Hom (1997) compared the reactions of students in Grades 4, 6, and 8 to vignettes where students received varying amounts of praise, blame, and rewards. A notable finding was that the eighth graders valued rewards and praise less than younger students. The authors concluded that praise may be interpreted as low ability by these older students.

What characteristics contribute to the effectiveness of praise? O'Leary and O'Leary (1977) identified three qualities that contribute to the effectiveness of praise:

1.   *Contingency.* As with other types of rewards, praise must be given contingent on the performance of the student. Brophy (1981) concluded that the majority of praise given in classrooms

does not function well because it is not contingent on performance.

2. *Specificity.* Praise should indicate the specific performance that is being recognized. This corresponds closely with guidelines for attributional feedback: specify the actions of the student (ability, effort, or strategies) that led to the performance.

3. *Sincerity / variety / credibility.* The praise should sound sincere to the individual receiving it. This is not likely to occur if a teacher makes a comment like "super job" for all types of performance. Using the same phrase repeatedly for any performance will, over time, erode the impact of praise and leave it meaningless for students.

In addition, praise can be overused by nonselectively praising all student work and responses, so that praise becomes meaningless in terms of influencing student motivation (Brophy, 1981). Lists such as "86 Words of Encouragement" are frequently circulated among teachers. Few of the phrases meet the criteria for effective praise (e.g., "that's great," "outstanding"). Differences in effective and ineffective praise are presented in Table 8.1 (Brophy, 1981).

Which is more positive for continuing motivation, praising students for being smart or for effort? Research conducted by Mueller and Dweck (1998) indicated that praise for intelligence can backfire by undermining motivation and performance. Dweck (2000) concluded that, when children are praised for their intelligence after a success, this could foster an entity view of intelligence and a performance goal that leaves them vulnerable in conditions of failure. The children are set up for internal attributions to lack of ability for failure.

Guidelines for Using Incentives

The undermining effects of extrinsic rewards do not mean that extrinsic rewards should never be used (Ford, 1992). A summary of the effects of extrinsic rewards on intrinsic motivation follows (Cameron & Pierce, 1994; Ford, 1995; Ryan & Deci, 2000):

- Verbal praise and positive feedback, when used appropriately, enhance students' intrinsic interest.

TABLE 8.1

Guidelines for Effective Praise

Effective Praise	*Ineffective Praise*
1. Is delivered contingently	1. Is delivered randomly or unsystematically
2. Specifies the particulars of the accomplishments	2. Is restricted to global positive reactions
3. Shows spontaneity, variety, and other signs of credibility; suggests clear attention to the student's accomplishment	3. Shows bland uniformity, which suggests a conditioned response made with minimal attention
4. Rewards attainment of specified performance criteria (which can include effort criteria)	4. Rewards mere participation, without consideration of performance processes or outcomes
5. Provides information to students about their competence or the value of their accomplishments	5. Provides no information at all or gives students information about their status
6. Orients students toward better appreciation of their own task-related behavior and thinking about problem solving	6. Orients students toward comparing themselves with others and thinking about competing
7. Uses students' own prior accomplishments as the context for describing present accomplishments	7. Uses accomplishments of peers as the context for describing students' present accomplishments
8. Is given in recognition of noteworthy effort or success at difficult (for *this* student) tasks	8. Is given without regard to the effort expended or the meaning of the accomplishment (for *this* student)
9. Attributes success to effort and ability, implying that similar successes can be expected in the future	9. Attributes success to ability alone or to external factors such as luck or easy task
10. Fosters endogenous attributions (students believe that they expend effort on the task because they enjoy the task and/or want to develop task-relevant skills)	10. Fosters exogenous attributions (students believe that they expend effort on the task for external reasons—to please the teacher, win a competition or reward, etc.)
11. Focuses students' attention on their own task-relevant behavior	11. Focuses students' attention on the teacher as an external authority figure who is manipulating them
12. Fosters appreciation of and desirable attributions about task-relevant behavior after the process is completed	12. Intrudes into the ongoing process, distracting attention from task-relevant behavior

Source. From Brophy, J. (1981). "Teacher Praise: A Functional Analysis". *Review of Educational Research, 51*, 5–32. Reprinted by permission.

- Rewards have a negative impact on intrinsic motivation when they are given simply for engaging in a task or in an attempt to control the behavior of the person without consideration of any standard of performance.
- When the reward received is greater than initially expected, a person is more likely to view him or herself as performing for the reward.
- When students attribute the task outcome to their improving competency, a reward is more likely to enhance intrinsic motivation rather than undermine it.
- When high intrinsic motivation is already present, be cautious about introducing extrinsic rewards because they may dampen the intrinsic motivation.

Hennessey (1995) found that rewards did not have an undermining effect on intrinsic motivation when extrinsic factors were present if children are immunized or trained to focus on intrinsic factors. An implication for teachers is to build on intrinsic motivation factors in discussions with students as a means of immunizing them from the detrimental effects of rewards.

The preceding discussion reveals that the use of extrinsic rewards is a complicated issue that can have unexpected or undesirable results if the possible consequences are not understood. Because rewards are used so extensively in many schools, the findings about the detrimental effects of rewards must appear confusing to teachers and parents. Further guidelines for extrinsic rewards are shown in Strategy 8.3.

REFLECTION.   Examine the use of rewards in your classroom. Is there opportunity for all students to achieve legitimate recognition in some way? Does your reward system recognize developing competence and skills?

Fostering Intrinsic Motivation

According to Ryan and Deci (2000), intrinsic motivation is based on the three psychological needs: competence, autonomy, and relatedness. Given that intrinsic motivation to learn is a necessary but insufficient component for academic achievement in

Strategy 8.3. Guidelines for Extrinsic Rewards

Sufficient Rewards. Avoid "scarcity of rewards" where only a few students get all of the rewards, recognition, or approval (Covington, 1992, p. 135). Do the same students continue to receive recognition in award assemblies, and are rewards virtually nonexistent for students who are low achievers? Awards such as "student of the month" or "teacher of the month" may place individuals in competition or may turn into "whose turn is it now?" The next guideline offers one solution.

Rewards for Improvement. Rewards should recognize development of student competencies and progress. When giving rewards, keep the focus on improvement rather than on ability. For example, rather than always giving awards only to those who make the honor roll or the highest grade (as is frequently the case), establish a reward system whereby students are routinely recognized for a "personal best" or individual improvement.

Getting Started. Extrinsic rewards can be used to get children started in an activity where there may not be much initial interest. If extrinsic rewards can be used to start children reading or playing an instrument, they may begin to experience new sources of motivation and enjoyment from the activity itself (Lepper, 1988). For example, a high school physical education department focused on fitness in which the primary activity was jogging. The teachers decided on ribbons to recognize accomplishments: a one-mile ribbon and then cumulative awards for 5, 15, and 25 miles. After the minimum (floor level) was attained, the additional awards were dependent on students' goals and effort. Student comments on their accomplishments included, "I'm so proud of myself." This is a clear example of an award that signified accomplishment. Some students continued to exceed the minimum but never came for additional ribbons.

Fade Out Extrinsic Rewards. When extrinsic rewards are used, gradually diminish them, shifting the focus to a more intrinsic one when possible. This often happens when students gain competence in an area, and this increased ability becomes more satisfying than the reward (Lepper, 1988; see Exhibit 8.1).

Public Rewards. One must be careful when using public recognition as a reward. The widespread use of charts reporting student accomplishments was noted by R. Ames and C. Ames (1991) in elementary classrooms. A teacher reported placing a chart that listed all students' names in the back of the room. Stars were placed by the names each time they got a perfect score. The teachers reported, however, that only the two students with the most stars checked the charts. The chart was likely a demotivator for the other students. All students who meet the desired criteria, such as passing a state-required proficiency test, could be given recognition.

Combine Rewards with Other Motivational Strategies. Rewards have been combined with other motivational strategies such as goal setting. Ruth (1996) combined contingency contracts with goal setting for students with behavioral and emotional difficulties. The combination of rewards and goals provided maximum success for the students.

classrooms, what can educators and parents do to support and cultivate it? One recent approach for teachers and parents is to frame students' learning activities as intrinsic (Vansteenkiste, Lens, & Deci, 2006). For example, tell students that, by learning new strategies for studying, they will develop more competence as a student. In contrast telling them the strategies will help them receive higher grades is an extrinsic frame.

The following suggestions are drawn from motivational perspectives presented in this and previous chapters:

- *Classroom social context.* Establish a classroom context that supports sense of membership and opportunity for developing autonomy (see Chapter 7).
- *Task motivation.* To increase interest, embellish tasks to make them more attractive by including student control, curiosity, and personalization (see Strategy 8.2). At the same time, emphasize meaningful learning with tasks that provide authentic work (see Strategy 8.1).
- *Extrinsic rewards.* Use rewards appropriately to enhance intrinsic motivation (see Strategy 8.3).

- *Social-cognitive factors contribute to intrinsic motivation.* These include:
  o *Attributions for success.* Dev (1998) concluded that if students attribute their success to factors they can control, such as effort and effective use of strategies, they are likely to be intrinsically motivated.
  o *Self-efficacy.* A high sense of self-efficacy supports intrinsic motivation by increasing self-perceived competence, increasing perceived control over one's actions, and promoting intrinsic interest (Bandura, 1997; Zimmerman & Kitsantas, 1997). When challenges match perceived capabilities, almost any activity can be made intrinsically interesting (Csikszentmihalyi, 1990).
  o *Learning goal orientation.* Establish a classroom structure that focuses on the tasks, authority, recognition, and evaluation components of a learning goal. Focus on the intrinsic value of learning (C. Ames, 1992; Meece, 1991; see Table 3.2).
  o *Goal setting.* Personal standards through goal setting can contribute to intrinsic interest through satisfaction from goal accomplishment (Bandura, 1997) (e.g., the student who derived satisfaction from jogging).

A research intervention designed to influence students' intrinsic reading motivation was conducted by Guthrie, Wigfield, and VonSecker (2000). The intervention, Concept Oriented Reading Instruction (CORI), integrated the following variables: autonomy support, collaboration support, competence support through strategy instruction, learning goals, and real world interactions. The results indicated that, compared to the control group, students who received the CORI training reported higher curiosity and strategy use. The authors concluded that it is likely that all five variables contributed to an increase in intrinsic motivation and that classroom contexts can be designed to influence motivation positively.

Limitations of Intrinsic Motivation.   Is intrinsic motivation the solution for increasing student engagement? One perspective is that intrinsic motivation to learn is a necessary but insufficient component for academic achievement in classrooms; that is, one can enjoy learning or have an interest in a subject but lack the strategies necessary for continuing motivation (Corno & Rohrkemper, 1985). Damon (1995) went further in expressing a concern that the benefits of intrinsic motivation have been oversold. One concern is that many learning activities required by the curriculum and viewed as necessary by the teacher may not be seen as interesting or necessary by students (Bandura, 1986; Brophy, 1983). It was noted previously that challenging, thoughtful tasks, which should be intrinsically motivating in and of themselves, may not lead to engagement (Blumenfeld, 1992). Nisen (1992) asserted that, just as students can come to rely on extrinsic rewards for motivation, they may also rely on immediate interest or personal desire. This handicaps learners when they are learning material that is necessary but of no personal interest to them. In this situation, it was found that rewards helped students persist when they were assigned boring, difficult tasks. This finding is in contrast to students who had an intrinsic interest in a topic but quit as soon as they lost interest.

Sustained effort and success in school, athletics, or work may require the use of both intrinsic and extrinsic sources (Lepper & Henderlong, 2000; Wehlage et al., 1989). Thus, it is important to understand the complex relationship between intrinsic motivation and extrinsic rewards.

EVALUATION, GRADING PRACTICES, AND OPTIMAL MOTIVATION

Classroom assessment is important motivationally because students use the information to form beliefs about learning and achievement in their subjects (Brookhart, Walsh, & Zientarski, 2006). School and classroom assessment practices can have both positive and negative effects on student motivation and engagement. One of the learner-centered principles, standards and assessment (American Psychological Association [APA], 1997), stresses the role of assessments in the learning process with the potential to enhance motivation. Crooks (1988) reviewed research on the influence of evaluation practices on students and concluded that evaluation influences motivation in the following areas:

- monitoring progress and developing skills of self-evaluation;
- students' motivation to study the subject and their perceptions of their capabilities in the subject;
- students' choice of (and development of) learning strategies;
- students' continuing motivation; and
- students' self-perceptions, such as their self-efficacy as learners.

Given that motivation is affected by evaluation, the first question is, how do different types of assessment systems affect motivation?

Criterion- and Norm-Referenced Assessments

Criterion- and norm-referenced assessments use different comparative standards. In criterion-referenced assessment, criteria for the grades are established in advance. The grades are then determined on the basis of students' attainment of the specific skills regardless of other students' performance. A norm-referenced assessment system assigns grades to students based on how their performance stands in relation to that of their classmates (Airasian, 1996). Grading systems that rank students in some way are using norm-referenced assessment. Such a system has no clearly defined standard; the most extreme example is grading on the curve. In other words, a criterion-referenced system shows real achievement, whereas a norm-referenced system does not indicate any specific knowledge or skill attainment (Wiggins, 1993). When a teacher reports, "Regina made the highest grade on the test," this does not indicate how much she learned; it only suggests how her performance compares to others.

Which system is most likely to yield the greatest motivation—competing against an accepted standard or competing against others? Guskey (2001) stated, "In standards-based systems, grading and reporting must be criterion-referenced" (p. 20). A grading system that makes a student's grade dependent on the performance of others places the emphasis on an ability or performance goal focus rather than on a mastery or learning goal focus (Mac Iver, 1993). In contrast, competing against a defined standard allows students to monitor their progress toward achieving the standard, which should shift their emphasis to improving their previous performance, not scoring higher than classmates.

Level of Standards

What level of standards has the most positive influence on student motivation? "Clear and worthy standards, combined with the measuring of incremental progress always provide incentives to the learner, even when the gap between present performance and the standard is great" (Wiggins, 1993, p. 153). The effect of evaluation standards on student effort was part of a large-scale study by Natriello and Dornbush (1984). Not surprisingly, the findings indicate that higher standards led to greater student effort and the likelihood of their attending class (similarly, difficult goals lead to greater productivity than easy goals; see Chapter 4). However, if students believed that the standards were unattainable, they were more likely to become disengaged from learning. Furthermore, students' effort was affected by the extent to which they believed the evaluation of their work accurately reflected the level of their performance. If students believed the evaluation was faulty in some way, they were less likely to think the task deserved their effort.

More recently, Brookhart and colleagues (Brookhart, 1998; Brookhart & DeVoge, 1999) extended research to relationships among perceptions of task difficulty, self-efficacy, effort, and achievement in Grade 3 classrooms. One noteworthy finding was that student self-efficacy judgments were based on their previous assessment experiences with similar assignments. In addition, the teacher's initial presentation of the assignments as having a performance or learning goal orientation affected how students approached them. For example, when a teacher presents an assignment and says "work hard to get an A," an implicit message for a performance goal is conveyed, whereas "work hard to understand this" conveys a learning goal. This finding underscores the influence of teacher feedback and the need to be aware of how students may perceive the feedback.

Similarly, Butler (2006) hypothesized that if students were told in advance whether they would be evaluated by comparisons to others or as a way of monitoring their progress, this would serve as a cue about the purpose of the activity. The subsequent research findings, in fact, did influence whether student achievement goals were performance or mastery.

Motivational Variables Considered by Teachers in Grading

Which motivational variables do teachers consider when arriving at grades and on what criteria are these judgments made? In one study, teachers responded to classroom grading scenarios by indicating how they would evaluate the student and why they made the decision (Brookhart, 1993). Brookhart concluded that the meaning of a grade for teachers was closely related to the idea of student work. Guskey (2001) characterized the use of work habits or effort as process criteria. When describing grades or grading, teachers frequently used phrases or terms like the "work (s)he did" and "perform" or "performance," denoting something students did or accomplished. Teachers reported that they considered effort as well as achievement when assigning grades.

Which student behaviors do teachers consider as effort? Among the behaviors noted in the Natriello and Dornbush (1984) study were (a) the number of assignments completed, (b) the number of assignments turned in on time, (c) the extra amount of time spent to master particular tasks, and, to some degree, (d) the extent to which a student strived to be an overachiever.

How do teachers use other variables such as student ability levels, effort, and attitude to adjust student achievement scores? A case study of the grading practices of 15 high school teachers found that 13 of the 15 teachers gave significant weight to effort and motivation as grading variables, although they stated that they strived not to use student attitudes in grades (Stiggins, Frisbie, & Griswold, 1989). The teachers were divided in terms of how they included ability into the grading decisions. Half of the teachers stated they used different grading procedures for high- and low-ability students. For example, teachers graded high-ability students solely on achievement, whereas they graded low-ability students on achievement and effort.

There are no easy answers to the use of factors such as effort and ability. From this evidence, consider the following when using effort as a criterion for grading:

- There is not a right way to use effort as part of the grading criteria. It is important to understand effort as a motivational factor and how the evaluation system can recognize and cultivate it.
- Operationalize effort; that is, specify what effort is and how it is taken into account in evaluation (see Strategy 2.7).
- When students have an opportunity to improve a project or paper, effort is built into the task.

REFLECTION. Think about how you include or will include effort in your grading system. Do you include effort and do you think it is effective for promoting student motivation and learning?

Evaluation and Feedback

When evaluating student performance, what type of feedback to the student is most likely to foster motivation? Feedback is an outcome of evaluation, but it can act as an incentive as well, depending on the type. Brookhart and DeVoge (1999) concluded that it is important for teachers to help students interpret feedback. When evaluating a paper, for example, the best feedback is a comment to help a student understand why the paper worked or why a mistake is a mistake. Wiggins (1993) asserted that feedback should provide user-friendly information about how students are doing and how they might improve, not just comments of praise and blame. This is similar to attributional feedback (see Chapter 2) and informational feedback (as discussed in this chapter).

Involving students more in the assessment process can affect motivation positively (Chappius & Stiggins, 2002; Shepard, 2000; Stiggins, 1999). Scoring rubrics provide explicit criteria for assessment. The increasing use of rubrics as part of assessment provides explicit criteria. This satisfies a fairness principle, according to Shepard (2000), by allowing students to be more involved in the learning process through self-assessment. Self-regulatory strategies, record keeping and self-monitoring are part of student assessment. This is one area where attribution, self-efficacy, incentive, and evaluation intersect.

Implications for Assessment Practices

With the current emphasis on accountability, it is important that teachers provide a positive motivational climate for assessment. Harlen and Crick (2003) conducted a review of research on testing and motivation for learning. The following are recommendations:

- Emphasize learning goals and interests, not performance goals.
- Help students understand the goals they are learning and the criteria (rubrics).
- Avoid social comparison of student tests and other forms of assessment.
- Help students develop self-assessment capabilities.
- Use feedback as an indication of developing competence, similar to attributional feedback.

An Evaluation System Based on Motivation Principles: Incentives-Based Improvement Program

What would an evaluation program be like that is based on specific motivational principles? Mac Iver (1993) developed such a program based on goal-setting theory (Locke & Latham, 1984: see Chapter 4) and achievement goal theory (C. Ames, 1992: see Chapter 3). Mac Iver argued that these principles can be used to diagnose major weaknesses in traditional evaluation and recognition practices and provide a basis for an improvement system. A traditional norm-referenced system has the following characteristics that influence motivation:

- Success is defined in competition with others, making the goals unreachable for many students.
- When students' best efforts go unnoticed and unrewarded, their commitment to the goal of academic success is likely to be lessened.
- Focusing on ability by rewarding comparative achievements rather than individual improvement highlights ability differences among pupils, does not reward strategic effort, and

does not encourage students to see beginning mistakes as a normal part of learning new skills.

To overcome these detriments to motivation, Mac Iver designed a system where goals would be specific and challenging but reachable. This encourages a mastery-focused orientation because it deemphasizes the importance of normative standards. It also creates a classroom environment where students of differing abilities have fairly equal opportunities for success. Equally important is creating a climate where no students (including high-ability students) are likely to consistently experience success without strategic effort. An improvement point-scoring system devised for cooperative learning (Slavin, 1990) was modified as the basis for an individual evaluation and recognition program.

The Incentives for Improvement Program was implemented by volunteer teachers in 23 middle school classrooms in inner city Baltimore schools (Mac Iver, 1993). Three major components were involved:

- *Rounds of quizzes.* Students were given a base score that was the average percentage correct on recent quizzes. The specific goal for students on a quiz was to increase their own base scores by more than nine points. Each round consisted of three quizzes.
- *Improvement points.* Improvement points were awarded according to the extent that students met their specific goal. This meant students also received clear feedback concerning their goal attainment. Scoring is shown in Table 8.2.
- *Recognition.* Official recognition was provided for all students who raised their performance level throughout the year in the form of "Rising Star" or "Milestone" rewards. The types of recognition included certificates and other small rewards to provide variety (e.g., a pencil with a "milestone award" imprint or an "I am a rising star" button).

There were positive effects for students in the Incentives for Improvement Program in several areas. Compared with students not in the program, they (a) had significantly higher

TABLE 8.2
How to Earn Improvement Points

If You ...	Then You Earn
Beat your base score by more than 9 points	30 improvement points
Beat your base score by 5 to 9 points	20 improvement points
Score within 4 points of your base score	10 improvement points
Get a perfect paper	30 improvement points
Score within 5 points of a perfect paper	20 improvement points

Source. From Mac Iver, D. J. & Reuman, D. A. (1993/94) "Giving Their Best: Grading and Recognition Practices that Motivate Students to Work Hard". *American Educator,* *17*(4), 24–31. Reprinted by permission.

fourth-quarter grades in target courses, (b) earned higher final grades than students in matched nonparticipating classes, and (c) were more likely to pass. Those students who were most at risk (those with low general averages from the previous year) especially benefited: 12 percent more of the students who were in experimental classes passed than did students in control classes. These students reported expending more effort (e.g., studying harder for quizzes and tests and working closer to their potential) than did students in control classes.

Mac Iver concluded that, by giving students a proximal, concrete goal to strive for on every graded assignment, project, test, or quiz, the program may motivate more students to perform up to their potential with beneficial effects on their grades. The program also affects teacher practices. When teachers closely monitor student progress in a regular and systematic way, they are more aware of the accomplishments of low-performing students, which can in turn lead to increased teacher efficacy and motivation.

In the context of the high-stakes testing and accountability that exists today, the motivation of students is a critical factor. If the testing and accountability is to increase learning and achievement, students must come to believe that it is about their own success. "Teachers must understand and be able to describe the achievement expectations they believe are important for their students" (Ramirez, 1999, p. 207).

CONCLUSION

Dimensions of classroom instruction—tasks, incentives, evaluation, and autonomy (see Chapter 7)—are asserted by C. Ames (1992) to be essential for a classroom structure that supports a learning goal orientation for students. This chapter explored these dimensions as they affect motivation and engagement of students. Taken altogether, these components place the emphasis on effort instead of ability. Then, within the structure, the crucial role of the teacher is to teach the personal qualities of self-regulation. The key component in building a classroom structure for optimal student motivation and engagement is, in the long run, the teacher's own instructional efficacy. The integration of these components is shown in Fig. 8.3. This will be a major step in building a classroom for motivational equality.

FIG. 8.3. Components for motivational equality.

REVIEW OF MAJOR POINTS

1. Tasks and activities that engage students in learning are described as meaningful, authentic, challenging, and thoughtful, all of which require higher level thinking. The interaction

between task complexity and information processing is required of students. More challenging tasks may not lead to greater engagement by students by themselves. The dilemma for a teacher is that risk can lower motivation for the student, but lowering the risk for the student can lower the level of learning.

2. Teaching practices that increase student task engagement are increasing opportunities to learn, using a variety of high-quality instructional techniques, pressing (pushing) students for thinking that requires them to explain and justify answers, scaffolding to lead students gradually toward comprehension, and using evaluations that emphasize comprehension and mastery of content. Effective group work fosters cognitive engagement when students learn to share ideas, disagree, and resolve differences in perspectives.

3. Task interest is important motivationally because it influences attention and persistence and also the acquisition of knowledge by students. There are two types of interest. Individual interest is the personal interest that a student brings to the classroom and situational interest results from some instructional activity or text material used in the classroom. Situational interest is more important for the classroom and may be short term (catch student attention) or continue over time (hold student attention). Seductive details added to text to make it interesting are more often recalled by students than important generalizations. Identify topics that are of interest to students, then find text and other materials on these topics.

4. Tasks can be enriched to increase student interest and engagement by opportunity for student sense of choice and ownership—activities that provoke curiosity and personalization of learning. Cultural knowledge acts as a bridge between the student and interest in classroom tasks and activities. Teachers' knowledge of students' culture is important for contributing to task interest and engagement. Related to task interest is task value. Three types of task value are attainment, intrinsic, and utility.

5. Extrinsic and intrinsic motivation represent a continuum from most extrinsic to least extrinsic, not two different types of motivation. In some circumstances, extrinsic rewards undermine or reduce intrinsic motivation; in other circumstances, they enhance intrinsic motivation. Rewards affect motivation through

informational or controlling aspects. Rewards contingent on the quality of the task outcome rather than task completion are more likely to have positive effects on the level of task performance and motivational factors. Rewards have a negative impact on intrinsic motivation when they are given simply for engaging in a task without consideration of any standard of performance.

6. Verbal praise and positive feedback can enhance students' intrinsic interest under certain conditions. Praise is more effective when it is contingent on performance, indicates the specific performance that is being recognized, and is sincere to the individual receiving it.

7. Guidelines for use of extrinsic rewards include recognizing a variety of competencies; avoiding the scarcity of rewards problem where only a few students get all of the recognition; focusing the rewards on improvement rather than on ability; and using this to get individuals started in an activity, then gradually diminish usage, which shifts the focus to a more intrinsic one where possible.

8. Intrinsic motivation can be cultivated by establishing a classroom context that supports sense of autonomy and a learning goal orientation, increasing task interest, encouraging attributions for success effort, helping students to strengthen self-efficacy, and setting goals.

9. Intrinsic motivation is also viewed as a necessary but insufficient component for academic engagement. Learning activities that are viewed as necessary by the teacher and required by the curriculum may not be seen as interesting or necessary by students. Similar to relying on extrinsic rewards for motivation, students may also rely on immediate interest or personal desire for motivation, and are handicapped when learning material that is necessary but of no personal interest to them. Sustained effort and success in school, athletics, or work may require the use of both intrinsic and extrinsic sources.

10. Evaluation influences motivation by helping students monitor progress, influencing students' motivation to study and the choice of learning strategies, and influencing students' continuing motivation and self-efficacy as learners.

11. The criteria for evaluation influence student motivation. A criterion-referenced assessment is determined on the basis of students' attainment of preset criteria. A norm-referenced

assessment system assigns grades to students based on how their performance compares to that of their classmates. Criterion-referenced assessment is more likely to promote learning goals. In standards-based assessment, grading and reporting must be criterion-referenced. The level of standards for evaluation influences student motivation: higher standards are more likely to be associated with greater effort by students. Effort is often used by teachers to determine student grades.

12. Depending on how it is given, feedback is both an outcome of evaluation and an incentive. Motivational feedback should provide user-friendly information about how students are doing and how they might improve, not just comments of praise and blame. Scoring rubrics provide explicit criteria for assessment. The increasing use of rubrics as a part of standards provides explicit criteria.

13. Recommendations for a positive motivational climate for assessment in the context of high-stakes testing include: emphasize learning goals, self-referenced comparisons, and help students develop self-evaluation capabilities.

14. An evaluation program that focused on goals, effort, and improvement was devised by Mac Iver (1993) to increase student motivation. The program based on these components resulted in improved grades and more students passing their work.

Motivational Toolbox

1. Important points to think about and lingering questions

2. Strategies I can use now

3. Strategies I want to develop in the future

CHAPTER 9

Possibilities for Motivational Equality and Student Achievement

A major goal of formal education should be to equip students with the intellectual tools, self-beliefs, and self-regulatory capabilities to educate themselves throughout their lifetime.

—Bandura (1993, p. 136)

The problem of motivational inequality and challenges was introduced in Chapter 1. To reiterate, *motivational equality* means students have optimum motivation for intellectual development. In the climate of educational reform with higher standards and high-stakes testing, it is especially important to provide instructional and motivational resources to support motivational equality for all students. An extensive knowledge base exists that provides possibilities for motivation. A primary assertion is that motivation has to be explicitly addressed as part of classroom instruction, not just to meet academic content standards, but also to help students develop their potential.

This chapter begins with a discussion of concerns and issues that are often expressed by preservice and practicing teachers about the implementation of motivation strategies. This is followed by description of comprehensive programs and a classroom intervention that included motivation as a component. A problem-solving model for planning motivation strategies and opportunities for using motivation is offered in the final section.

POSSIBLE CONCERNS AND ISSUES

There are general issues that must be thought about and resolved or they may become barriers to implementation of motivation strategies in the classroom. What barriers do you envision when thinking about the implementation of a motivational plan of action? Think about the following issues.

How much do you really want to improve motivation? You may think this question is unnecessary. As teachers, although we value student motivational qualities such as effort and self-control, we may think it is not our job to teach these. We often focus on these qualities only from a negative viewpoint (e.g., "Students don't try, they don't have goals": Sockett, 1988). The flip side is, "What am I going to do to help these students develop adaptive motivational beliefs and strategies?" This aspect is often neglected or it is assumed that these qualities are unteachable. Murphy and Alexander (2000) examined motivational terminology in the current literature and concluded "the most compelling perception is the number of motivational constructs significantly linked to students' academic growth and development" (p. 44). The important point is the extent to which teachers see these constructs as susceptible to instructional intervention. In previous chapters, we have seen that teachers can influence many factors that affect motivation.

The students in my classroom come from many different cultures. I'm afraid of imposing motivational qualities because they might be contradictory to their culture. Motivational qualities such as beliefs about the value of formal education, school achievement, good behavior, and parent involvement are neutral or similar and are valued across different cultures (Goldenberg & Gallimore, 1995; Sockett, 1988). For example, Goldenberg and Gallimore found that immigrant Latino parents were similar to U.S. residents regarding the importance of education as a ladder of social and occupational mobility. Similarly, the family patterns of high-achieving African-American students valued academic pursuits and established achievement norms for their children (R. Clark, 1983).

If these common goals among different cultures are not acknowledged, disparities between home values and school practice are more likely (Goldenberg, 1994). For example, Goldenberg reported that a parent complained about teachers who perceived that children from immigrant Latino backgrounds were deprived. To compensate for this perception, teachers let students play all day instead of teaching them. This was contrary to the achievement goals that parents had for their children.

The most important factor for motivation with diverse student populations is to learn about their families' cultural values. Do not assume that all within the culture share the same values. Teachers can then build on commonalities between school and families while acknowledging and honoring the cultural differences. As Bempechat (1998) stated, "Cultural sensitivity—ever more necessary in our schools—is realized through a healthy balance between respecting the ways in which culture and ethnicity guide the academic and motivational support that parents provide for their children and maintaining high academic goals for all children" (p. 115).

In today's climate of emphasizing standards with high-stakes testing, can teachers emphasize passing the test and maintain a focus on learning? Reform movements have devoted little attention to the importance of student motivation (Meece & McColskey, 1997; R. S. Weinstein, 2002). Weinstein argued that motivation is important if students are to rise to the expectations of higher standards, and as an educational outcome in its own right. In the short term, it may seem that valuable time would be taken from content needed to pass the test. However, if the absence of qualities such as effort, goals, and study strategies interferes with students' academic progress, then our option is to teach students the tools they need. As R. S. Weinstein (2002) stated, "to cope successfully in a changing world, one must *want* to learn and know *how* to learn" (p. 76). When teachers help students learn self-regulation in the context of achieving standards, it will foster academic learning (Comer, 2005). Roderick and Engel (2001) conducted a study in Chicago schools that provides insight into the role of student effort in high-stakes testing and the influence of teachers. See Exhibit 9.1.

Exhibit 9.1.   Student Effort, High-Stakes Testing, and Teachers' Role

- *Effort.*   Student effort was an important predictor of outcomes on the test. As the researchers cautioned, if the responsibility for achievement and goals of the reform are placed solely on students, the students with lowest skills are particularly placed in jeopardy.

- *Social context.*   The mechanism through which motivation translated into substantive work effort was dependent on the degree of collective responsibility for learning that teachers were able to create in their classrooms and convey to students.

- *Role of teachers.*   Teachers influenced students' perception of the task and their motivation in other ways.

  —*Expectations.* They helped students understand the purpose of the standards and did not assume that low-achieving students will necessarily respond negatively to a strong emphasis on achievement.

  —*Efficacy and support.* They helped students feel supported with a sense of efficacy for achieving their goals.

  —*Structure of activities.* They structured learning activities so that they are meaningful and all seemed to be essential components for success.

MOTIVATION INTERVENTIONS

This section describes interventions that had success in enhancing motivation and achievement. The interventions include two comprehensive programs that confronted barriers to achievement and provided possibilities for motivational equality and an intervention by teachers designed to incorporate motivation in the context of school reform.

Comprehensive Programs

The comprehensive programs addressed a number of barriers and issues that might detract from student achievement. Two such programs are:

- The Benchmark program for poor readers.
- Advancement Via Individual Determination (AVID), a program that places previously low-achieving students in college preparatory classes and provides the support for them to succeed.

These two programs were selected because they are comprehensive, include motivational components, and show evidence of success in challenging educational situations.

Benchmark.   Benchmark, a school for poor readers, has the premise that every student is teachable (Gaskins, 1994; Gaskins & Elliot, 1991). Students enter the program at ages 7 to 10, essentially as nonreaders. Twenty years of research-based curriculum development has gone into the program, designed to guide students to be goal-oriented, planful, strategic, and self-assessing. Faculty selected 17 core cognitive strategies that were needed by all students. The self-regulatory strategies include learning and metacognitive strategies, as well as organization, effort, and self-control.

The strategies are taught within each content area. A mini-course, Psych 101: A Course for Learning About Learning, is embedded in each content course. The first topic in the mini-course is belief about intelligence, with the emphasis on intelligence as incremental. Students are taught that they have control over how smart they are (see Chapter 3 for an incremental-entity view of intelligence in motivation). After 4 days, this topic is followed by the study of effort, focusing on the meaning and types of effort. Students are then taught metacognitive control strategies in four categories: control of person, control of task, control of environment, and control of strategies. Note the similarity to the volitional control strategies described in Chapter 5.

Ongoing evaluation of the program at Benchmark revealed that middle school students made progress during the 3-year project as measured by academic assessment measures and teacher reports (Gaskins, 1994). Teacher anecdotal reports indicate that students used a variety of awareness and control strategies. The curriculum and teaching strategies of this program continue to undergo revision. Detailed descriptions of the curriculum and lessons can be found in *Implementing Cognitive Strategy Instruction across the School* (Gaskins & Elliot, 1991).

AVID.   A student from the AVID program, Lilia, was introduced in Chapter 5. AVID is an *untracking* program that places previously low-achieving students (primarily from low-income, minority backgrounds) in the same college preparatory programs as high-achieving students (Mehan et al., 1996). The program began with one teacher, Mary Catherine Swanson, who was determined that students would not automatically be placed in a remedial track based on their background (Ruenzel, 1997). She believed that "rigor without support is a prescription for failure and that support without rigor is a tragic waste of potential" (Swanson, cited in Swanson, Marcus, & Elliott, 2000, p. 1). The students were typically passive learners who did not know what serious study entailed. Although they had goals to attend college, they had no idea of the type of preparation and steps needed to be ready.

AVID developed a set of essentials founded on a philosophy that effort can create ability (Resnick, 1997, 1999). AVID students receive explicit instruction in the informal curriculum of school (Mehan et al., 1996). The instructional features include the following:

- *Beliefs about individual effort, motivation and opportunity.* At the beginning students were told that the program believed in them and that they would be prepared to go to college if they studied hard and were motivated.
- *Study and test-taking skills.* The centerpiece of the program is a special method of notetaking for compiling main ideas, abstracting key concepts, and identifying questions that guide analysis. Test taking—including preparation for the SAT—organization, and time management, are taught in all classes.
- *Step-by-step planning and preparation for college entry.*

Students are coached about the complicated process of entering college. They learn how to write their statement of purpose, fill out applications, and apply for financial aid. This is similar to the PLAN program described in Chapter 5.

• *Work effectively in groups.*
• *Conflict resolution for interacting with teachers.* Students are taught social skills such as how to talk to teachers and ask for help.
• *Teacher advocates.* The teachers in AVID act as advocates on behalf of students in both academic and personal matters.

Mehan et al. (1996) found that the number of AVID graduates who attend college is greater than the national average. For example, 55 percent of the African-American students who participated in the program for at least 3 years attend college, compared with 33 percent nationally. Forty-three percent of the Hispanic students attend college, compared with 20 percent nationally. Texas schools that implemented AVID showed improvement in advanced course enrollment, Advanced Placement testing, accountability rates, and high school graduation rates (Watt, Powell, Mendiola, & Cossio, 2006).

These two programs provide possibilities for students to develop their potential. They also provided possibilities for how schools and teachers can make a difference. Both programs developed explicit curriculums for their target population. The development of personal competencies, such as study skills, that can help students be academically successful was not left to chance or as an implicit by-product of schooling. The programs also required investment in the professional preparation of teachers.

A Classroom Motivational Intervention in the Context of Educational Reform

Numerous strategies for assisting students in developing adaptive attitudes and strategies have been presented in prior chapters. A promising motivational intervention in the context of mathematics reform is described next.

As previously noted, motivation was usually left out as a component of reform movements (Meece & McColskey, 1997). A research study designed to assist teachers with implementation of a reform in mathematics included a brief motivational component (Stipek, Givvin, Salmon, & Macgyvers, 1998).

The reform mathematics intervention devoted one day of a one-week workshop and 10 hours of biweekly meetings on motivation. The motivational components that were introduced included information about student beliefs, beliefs about ability, self-efficacy in mathematics, interest and enjoyment of math activities, and emotions associated with math. The teachers were helped with strategies to seek additional motivational information and to interpret the student responses. The results indicated modest positive effects on the group that received the motivational training. Teachers placed more focus on learning goals, less on performance, and placed more emphasis on effort and encouragement of student autonomy. An important finding was that students in these classrooms reported higher self-confidence in their ability to do mathematics.

Although the training was brief and the outcomes are modest, the results suggest that a motivation component should be integrated into the context of reform interventions. If this brief intervention has these positive effects, we might speculate about what the outcome would be if the motivation component were extended.

PLANNING AND IMPLEMENTING MOTIVATIONAL STRATEGIES OR PROGRAMS

As stated in Chapter 1, it is important for teachers to actively plan for optimal motivation and engagement, not just react to problems. With a plan based on applicable knowledge, teachers are in a position to plan and implement motivation strategies, revise and refine it as needed.

A Problem-Solving Model for Planning

Planning and implementing a motivational plan requires decision making. A problem-solving model is a useful process for reflecting on your practice, and devising and implementing a motivational plan. One such model for planning is the IDEAL problem-solving model. The model is composed of the following phases: (a) *I*dentifying a problem, (b) *D*efining a problem, (c) *E*valuating alternatives, *A*nd (d) *L*ooking back or evaluating the plan (Bransford & Stein, 1994).

Identifying a problem.   Identifying and defining the motivational problems or challenges is the first step. Examining your current practice does this. What motivational problems exist in your school or classroom? What are positive practices? What do you want to improve? What do you want and expect students to accomplish? Information about student motivation comes from both formal and informal discussions and written assignments. Strategy 9.1 presents ideas for gathering information about student perceptions of motivation and their strategies.

Strategy 9.1.   Gathering Motivational Information by Verbal Reports

- Ms. Hudson began the school year by having students write about one achievement they had experienced. She then typed up the stories without names and passed them back to the students for discussion. An activity like this not only gives information, but also gets students thinking about their achievement motivation and goals.
- Conduct group discussions on how students define success and how they know they are successful. This will provide insight about the extent to which students have performance and learning goal orientations. Discussion of success will also give indications whether students define success in comparison to others or to their own accomplishments.
- Have students predict their performance on exams and tell how they studied. Then, they can compare their prediction with their actual grade and explain how they will study next time (see Exhibit 2.1).
- At the beginning of the year, ask students to write about "What makes you feel successful, in math, writing, etc." and "Describe one successful experience in science or art."

An obvious starting point is to gather information about students' attributional beliefs. The results may surprise you. For example, third-grade teachers inaccurately judged high-ability students to have more positive attributions than low-ability students (Carr & Kurtz-Costes, 1994). Ability level can be misleading. Some lower achievers may possess a positive but inaccurate view of their abilities, whereas some higher achievers may attribute their performance primarily to external factors. Strategy 2.1 suggested ways to gather information about students' attributions for success and failure.

Defining a problem. The definition includes the characteristic, causes, the overall goal, and sets the stage for exploring possible strategies. At the beginning, your goals may be both long and short term, group and individual. A long-term goal for the class might be, "I want to develop a classroom climate to support and foster self-regulation so that my students can become independent learners and develop a core of resiliency." A short-term goal for an individual may simply be, "I want to get Tyrone to complete his assignments."

Evaluating alternatives. This phase involves brainstorming possible strategies to address the problem then choosing the most appropriate. Teacher efficacy is important because a major consideration is the extent you can or will change a basic teaching approach. Implementation of strategies such as attributional feedback does not require changes in your basic instructional approaches. For instance, strategies to get Tyrone to complete his assignments are not likely to require changes in a basic approach to teaching. The goal to establish a climate to support and foster self-regulation will require more comprehensive changes in your classroom. One guideline for beginning intervention strategies is to take a "small but beautiful" approach (Pressley, Johnson, et al., 1989). This means trying the plan or strategies on a small scale and then monitoring the effects. For example, the LINKS model (Chapter 4) might be the best choice for a student like Tyrone who is not completing his assignments.

Looking back or evaluating the plan. The next step (and a very important one) is monitoring and evaluating the effects of the action plan. Possible sources of feedback are:

- *Student data.* What student data are important? For example, did Tyrone's assignment-completion record increase after you used the LINKS model to help him complete assignments? What is Tyrone's assessment of his progress?
- *Observation.* Who can observe your classroom and provide useful feedback about what you are doing? Possible sources are a peer teacher or an administrator.
- *Self-evaluation.* Keep a journal or log describing the effects of the intervention and your own reactions to the strategy or plan. This can also be a source of self-efficacy as you note progress.
- *Revise as needed.* The sources will provide you with information for revising as needed.

Motivation Strategies in the Classroom

The successful implementation of motivation strategies depends a great deal on the teacher's motivation. The motivational characteristics of efficacy, effort, goal setting, risk taking, volition, and persistence are especially important for putting plans into action.

Where do I begin? The beginning of the school year is the time to establish the classroom climate for optimal motivation, and engagement for all students. This includes expectations, beliefs about ability and effort, a climate where students feel a sense of belonging. This is the time to discuss adaptive motivation processes with students, attributions for success and failure, the meaning of effort in your class, views of intelligence, and the importance of learning strategies. Exhibit 9.2 presents a template for a STEPS manual for success that I developed for my classes to convey expectations and support.

Opportunities for Motivation in the Classroom

McCaslin (2006) argued that "student motivation—learning and motivation to learn—needs to be integrated into the concept of achievement" (p. 487). That is, students need to understand that achievement is more than test scores. Motivation strategies can be integrated whenever appropriate during the course of instruction and some strategies may need to be explicitly taught. For

Exhibit 9.2. Template for a Student Motivation Manual

Overview of Expectations	Expectations for the course and the importance of becoming an effective student and why we want students to excel.
Need for Strategy Instruction	Our awareness of student need for motivation and learning strategies and our commitment to help students to learn and/or refine learning strategies.
Profiles of Successful and Unsuccessful Students	Learning strategy and motivational profiles (based on composites) of successful and unsuccessful students.
Motivation Strategies	Attitudes, motivation, and strategies that will enhance students' chances of success in the course (e.g., high expectations, goals, effort learning goal focus, seeking help when needed, time management and volitional strategies).
Learning Strategies	A beginning list of strategies includes use of text aids, elaboration, organization (such as graphic organizers), metacognitive strategies.
Supplements Included	Guidelines for attention and concentration, notetaking, and effective participation in small groups. Forms for goal setting, a time management log, and record keeping.

The content depends on courses and age of students. Posters can be used for younger students.

Source. From Alderman (unpublished).

example, attribution was taught to college students and integrated into the course assignments (Masui & De Corte, 2005). There are a number of classroom situations that can be anticipated where teachers would have opportunities to draw upon the motivation knowledge and strategies in communicating messages and addressing problems. These include:

1. communicating expectations to your students;
2. communicating messages about "possible selves";
3. communicating with parents about your expectations, their child's progress, and needs;
4. giving feedback that focuses on developing competence;
5. helping student(s) cope with failure;
6. explaining to students:

   a. why education is important for their future,
   b. why they have to work hard in your class; how effort helps them to "get smarter";

7. teach goal-setting strategies and self-monitoring when students begin a long-term project;
8. create classroom conditions for a sense of belonging for all students.

The classroom climate sets the tone for positive motivation. As Battistich et al. (1999) proposed, the emphasis might be to cultivate student "identities as capable, responsible, self-directed learners" (p. 416).

POSSIBILITIES AND HOPE

We began this exploration into motivation by delineating problems and challenges. It was asserted that the knowledge base offers possibilities for teachers to help students reach their potential. Yes, there are motivational problems and challenges in schools. However, there are also many possibilities for addressing the problems. The important question is one posed by Asa Hilliard (1991): "Do we have the will to educate all students?" (p. 31). If we do not take the challenge now, when will we? We cannot solve problems overnight, but teachers and students together can begin the journey toward a future with hope. The expectation for this journey is *progress, not miracles.*

Glossary

Academic press: The extent to which a school pursues high standards, or a teacher pushes students to excel.

Attribution: The perceived causes of success and failure.

Autonomy: The need to see one's actions as internally initiated; students' opportunity for choice, independence, and responsibility.

Ceiling expectation: The assumption that student background sets an upper limit of attainment.

Distal goals: Long-term goals that are far removed in time.

Ego-involvement: Evaluate ability in comparison with others.

Engagement: Students' active involvement, commitment, and willingness to work to succeed in school.

Entity view of intelligence: Belief that intelligence is global and fixed.

Extrinsic motivation: Motivation from sources outside an individual.

Failure-avoiding strategies: Strategies used to protect self-worth from view that one is not smart.

Floor expectation: The minimum level that all students are expected to achieve.

General teaching efficacy: Belief about the extent to which teachers in general can be effective with different students.

Goal-setting: A specific outcome an individual aims to achieve.

Incremental view of intelligence: Belief that intelligence is malleable; as one learns more, intelligence is increased.

Individual interest: The personal interest a student brings to the classroom.

Instrumental activity: Explicit activity to attain a goal.

Intrinsic motivation: The source of motivation is internal to the person.

Learned helplessness: In a response to failure, the belief that one is powerless to change the circumstances.

Learner-centered principles: A set of 14 principles drawn from research in psychology and applied to education. The principles are divided into cognitive and metacognitive, motivational and affective, developmental and social, and individual difference.

Learning goal: Focus on learning and increasing competence, use of self-referenced comparisons; see also *task involvement* and *mastery goal*.

Level of aspiration: The goals to which one aspires with reference to the level of difficulty.

Maladaptive motivation patterns: Self-defeating behaviors and beliefs, such as negative attributions.

Mastery goal: See *learning goal*.

Metacognition: Awareness of one's knowledge, strategy use, and the use of self-corrective activities.

Oppositional social identity: Rejection of values of the dominant culture for fear of losing identity.

Origin: Tendency to be the cause of one's actions; related to autonomy.

Pawn: Feeling of powerlessness or being controlled by external sources.

Performance approach goal: Focus on attaining positive judgments of one's competence in comparison to others.

Performance avoidance goal: Focus on avoiding the perception of incompetence in comparison to others.

Performance goal: Focus on demonstrating high ability.

Personal teaching efficacy: Teachers' beliefs about how much they personally can effect learning.

Possible selves: One's vision of the future that includes positive and negative selves.

Proximal goal: A nearby or short-term goal.

Resiliency: Ability to bounce back in adverse circumstances.

Scaffold: Assistance provided by an expert peer or an adult in the zone of proximal development.

Self-efficacy: Belief about one's capabilities to perform the actions necessary to accomplish a task.

Self-fulfilling prophecy effects: When a teacher forms different expectations and uses different instructional practices, resulting in different effects on students.

Self-handicapping: Creating an obstacle as a reason for one's performance to maintain a positive self-image.

Self-instruction: Verbal or covert instruction to control one's actions.

Self-monitoring: Observation and evaluation of one's progress.

Self-reference: Comparison of one's performance to previous performances.

Self-regulated learning: Students' active participation in their own learning: including regulation of cognitive, motivational, and metacognitive components.

Self-worth: Motive to maintain a positive image of one's ability or competence.

Situational interest: Interest evoked by classroom activities or content.

Social comparison: Using performance of others as the standard for comparison of one's achievement or ability.

Stereotypic threat: Vulnerability to racial stereotypes that leads to disidentification with school.

Sustaining expectation effect: Teachers respond to students in the same way although their behavior is changing, resulting in maintaining the behavior.

Task involvement: Goal orientation for increasing learning or understanding (see *learning goal*).

Volition: Using strength of will and strategies to persist despite obstacles.

References

Abi-Nader, J. (1987). "A house for my mother": An ethnography of motivational strategies in a successful college preparatory program for Hispanic high school students. Unpublished Ph.D. Dissertation, Georgia State University.

—— (1990). "A house for my mother": Motivating Hispanic high school students. *Anthropology & Education Quarterly, 21*, 41–58.

—— (1991). Creating a vision of the future. *Phi Delta Kappan, 72*, 546–49.

Airasian, P. W. (1996). *Assessment in the classroom*. New York: McGraw-Hill.

Alderman, M. K. (1985). Achievement motivation and the preservice teacher. In M. K. Alderman & M. W. Cohen (Eds.), *Motivation theory and practice for preservice teachers* (pp. 37–57). Washington, DC: ERIC Clearinghouse on Teacher Education.

—— (1990). Motivation for at-risk students. *Educational Leadership, 48*, 27–30.

—— (1994). *STEPS for success*. Unpublished Manuscript.

—— (1996, April). *Two sides of the coin, motivation problems and needs in an urban high school and the knowledge base from research: Does it match?* Paper presented at the Annual Meeting of American Educational Research Association, New York.

Alderman, M. K., Klein, R., Seeley, S., & Sanders, M. (1993). Preservice teachers as learners in formation: Metacognitive self-portraits. *Reading Research and Instruction, 32*, 38–54.

Allinder, R. M. (1995). An examination of the relationship between teacher efficacy and curriculum-based measurement and student achievement. *Remedial and Special Education, 16*(4), 247–54.

Allington, R. (1980). Teacher interruption behaviors during primary grade oral reading. *Journal of Educational Psychology, 72*, 371–77.

Alloy, L. B., Abramson, L. Y., Peterson, C., & Seligman, M. E. (1984). Attributional style and the generality of learned helplessness. *Journal of Personality and Social Psychology, 46*(3), 681–87.

293

Alvidrez, J. & Weinstein, R. S. (1999). Early teacher perceptions and later student academic achievement. *Journal of Educational Psychology, 91*(4), 731–46.

American Psychological Association (1997). *Learner Centered Principles*: American Psychological Association.

Ames, C. (1992). Classrooms: Goals, structures, and student motivation. *Journal of Educational Psychology, 84*(3), 261–71.

Ames, C. & Ames, R. (1984). Goals, structure, and motivation. *The Elementary School Journal, 85*(1), 39–52.

Ames, C. & Archer, J. (1988). Achievement goals in the classroom: Students' learning strategies and motivational processes. *Journal of Educational Psychology, 80*, 260–67.

Ames, R. (1983). Help-seeking and achievement orientation: Perspectives from attribution theory. In B. M. DePaulo, A. Nadler, & J. D. Fisher (Eds.), *New directions in helping: Vol. 2. Help-seeking* (pp. 165–86). New York: Academic Press.

Ames, R. & Ames, C. (1991). Motivation and effective teaching. In J. L. Idol & B. F. Jones (Eds.), *Educational values and cognitive instruction: Implications for reformation* (pp. 247–61). Hillsdale, NJ: Lawrence Erlbaum Associates.

Ames, R. & Lau, S. (1982). An attributional analysis of student help seeking in academic settings. *Journal of Educational Psychology, 74*, 414–23.

Anderman, E. & Midgley, C. (2004). Changes in self-reported academic cheating across the transition from middle school to high school. *Contemporary Educational Psychology, 29*, 499–517.

Anderman, E. M., Austin, C. C., & Johnson, D. M. (2001). The development of goal orientations. In A. Wigfield & J. S. Eccles (Eds.), *Development of achievement motivation* (pp. 197–220). San Diego: Academic Press.

Anderman, E. M., Griesinger, T., & Westerfield, G. (1998). Motivation and cheating in early adolescence. *Journal of Educational Psychology, 90*, 84–93.

Anderman, E. M. & Wolters, C. W. (2006). Goals, values, and affect: Influences on student motivation. In P. A. Alexander & P. H. Winne (Eds.), *Handbook of educational psychology, 2nd ed.* (pp. 369–89). Mahwah, NJ: Lawrence Erlbaum Associates.

Anderman, L. H. (2003). Academic and social perceptions as predictors of change in middle school students' sense of school belonging. *The Journal of Educational Research, 72*(1), 5–22.

Anderman, L. H. & Freeman, K. E. (2004). Students' sense of belonging in school. In P. R. Pintrich & M. L. Maehr (Eds.), *Motivating students, improving schools: The legacy of Carol Midgley* (Vol. 13, pp. 27–63). New York: Elsevier.

Andrews, G. R. & Debus, R. (1978). Persistence and the causal perception of failure: Modifying cognitive attributions. *Journal of Educational Psychology, 70*(2), 154–66.

Argyris, C. & Schon, D. (1974). *Theory in practice: Increasing professional effectiveness*. San Francisco: Jossey-Bass.

Armour, D., Conry-Oseguera, P., Cox, P., King, N., McDonnell, L., Pascal, A., et al. (1976). *Analysis of the school preferred reading program in selected Los Angeles minority schools* (Report No, R-2007-LAUSD): The Rand Corporation.

Ashton, P. (1984). Teacher efficacy: A motivational paradigm for effective teacher education. *Journal of Teacher Education, 35*(5), 28–32.

Ashton, P. T. & Webb, R. B. (1986). *Making a difference: Teachers' sense of efficacy and student achievement*. New York: Longman.

Baird, J. R. (2002, April). *Volitional control and learning: A focus on "homework."* Paper presented at the Annual Meeting of The American Educational Research Association.

Bandura, A. (1986). *Social foundations of thought and action*. Englewood Cliffs, NJ: Prentice-Hall.

—— (1993). Perceived self-efficacy in cognitive development and functioning. *Educational Psychologist, 28*(2), 117–48.

—— (1997). *Self-efficacy: The exercise of control.* New York: Freeman.

Bandura, A., Barbaranelli, C., Caprara, V., & Pastorelli, C. (1996). Multifacted impact of self-efficacy beliefs on academic functioning. *Child Development, 67,* 1206–22.

Bandura, A. & Cervone, D. (1983). Self-evaluative and self-efficacy mechanisms governing the motivational effects of goal systems. *Journal of Personality and Social Psychology, 45,* 1017–28.

—— (1986). Differential engagement of self-reactive influences in cognitive motivation. *Organizational Behavior and Human Decision Processes, 38,* 92–113.

Bandura, A. & Schunk, D. H. (1981). Cultivating competence, self-efficacy, and intrinsic interest through proximal motivation. *Journal of Personality and Social Psychology, 41,* 586–98.

Baron, R. M., Tom, D. Y. H., & Cooper, H. M. (1985). Social class, race, and teacher expectations. In J. B. Dusek (Ed.), *Teacher expectations* (pp. 215–69). Hillsdale, NJ: Lawrence Erlbaum Associates.

Battistich, V., Solomon, D., Kim, D.-i., Watson, M., & Schaps, E. (1995). Schools as communities, poverty levels of student populations, and student attitudes, motives, and performances: A multilevel analysis. *American Educational Research Journal, 32*(2), 627–58.

Battistich, V., Watson, M., Solomon, D., Lewis, C., & Schaps, E. (1999). Beyond the three R's: A broader agenda for school reform. *The Elementary School Journal, 99*(5), 415–32.

Bell, C. M. & Kanevsky, L. (1996, April). *Promoting positive achievement motivation in a regular grade 2 classroom.* Paper presented at the Annual Meeting of the American Educational Research Association, New York City.

Bempechat, J. (1998). *Against all odds.* San Francisco: Jossey-Bass.

Bempechat, J., Graham, S. E., & Jimenez, N. V. (1999). The socialization of achievement in poor and minority students. *Journal of Cross-Cultural Psychology, 30*(2), 139–58.

Bempechat, J., Nakkula, M. J., Wu, J. T., & Ginsberg, H. P. (1996). Attributions as predictors of mathematics achievement: A comparative study. *Journal of Research and Development, 29*(2), 53–59.

Benard, B. (1993). Fostering resiliency in kids. *Educational Leadership, 49*(3), 44–47.

—— (2004). *Resiliency: What have we learned?* San Francisco: WestEd.

Benson, R. (1988). Helping pupils overcome homework distractions. *The Clearing House, 61,* 370–72.

Benz, C., Bradley, L., Alderman, M., & Flowers, M. (1992). Personal teaching efficacy: Developmental relationships in education. *Journal of Educational Research, 85*(5), 274–86.

Bereby-Meyer, Y. & Kaplan, A. (2005). Motivational influences on transfer of problem solving. *Contemporary Educational Psychology, 30,* 1–22.

Bergin, D. (1989). Student goals for out-of-school learning activities. *Journal of Adolescent Research, 4,* 92–109.

—— (1999). Influences on classroom interest. *Educational Psychologist, 34*(2), 87–98.

Berman, P., McLaughlin, M. W., Bass, G., Pauly, E., & Zellman, G. (1977). *Federal programs supporting educational change. Vol. VII: Factors affecting implementation and continuation.* Santa Monica, CA: The Rand Corporation.

Berndt, T. J. & Keefe, K. (1992). Friends' influence on adolescents' perceptions of themselves at school. In D. H. Schunk & J. L. Meece (Eds.), *Student perceptions in the classroom* (pp. 51–68). Hillsdale, NJ: Lawrence Erlbaum Associates.

Blazevski, J. L., McKendrick, R., & Hruda, L. Z. (2002). *The interplay of personal and group achievement goals in collaborative learning groups: Implications for student engagement.* Paper presented at the American Educational Research Association, New Orleans.

Blumenfeld, P. C. (1992). The task and the teacher: Enhancing student thoughtfulness in science. In J. Brophy (Ed.), *Advance in research on teaching* (Vol. 3, pp. 81–114). Greenwich, CT: JAI Press.

Blumenfeld, P. C., Marx, R. W., Soloway, E., & Krajcik, J. (1996). Learning with peers: From small group cooperation to collaborative communities. *Educational Researcher, 25*(8), 37–40.

Blumenfeld, P. C., Mergendoller, J. R., & Puro, P. (1992). Translating motivation into thoughtfulness. In H. H. Marshall (Ed.), *Redefining school learning* (pp. 207–39). Norwood, NJ: Ablex.

Boekaerts, M. & Niemivirta. (2000). Self-regulated learning: Finding a balance between learning goals and ego-protective goals. In M. Boekaerts, P. R. Pintrich, & M. Zeidner (Eds.), *Handbook of self-regulation* (pp. 417–50). San Diego: Academic Press.

Bong, M. (2002). Between- and within-domain relations of academic motivation among middle and high school students: Self-efficacy, task-value, and achievement goals. *Journal of Educational Psychology, 93*(1), 23–34.

Bong, M. & Clark, R. E. (1999). Comparison between self-concept and self-efficacy in academic motivation research. *Educational Psychologist, 34*, 139–54.

Borkowski, J. G. (1988). Understanding inefficient learning: Attributional beliefs and the training of memory and comprehension strategies. In P. M. M. Gruneberg & R. Symonds (Eds.), *Practical aspects of memory* (pp. 287–93). New York: Wiley.

Borkowski, J. G. & Muthukrishna, N. (1992). Moving metacognition into the classroom: "Working models" and effective strategy teaching. In M. F. Pressley, K. R. Harris, & J. T. Gutherie (Eds.), *Promoting academic literacy: Cognitive research and instructional innovation* (pp. 477–501). Orlando, FL: Academic Press.

Borkowski, J. G. & Thorpe, P. K. (1994). Self-regulation and motivation: A lifetime perspective on underachievement. In B. J. Zimmerman & D. H. Schunk (Eds.), *Self-regulation of learning and performance* (pp. 45–74). Hillsdale, NJ: Lawrence Erlbaum Associates.

Borkowski, J. G., Weyhing, R. S., & Carr, M. (1988). Effects of attributional retraining on strategy-based reading comprehension in learning-disabled students. *Journal of Educational Psychology, 80*(1), 46–53.

Bouffard-Bouchard, T., Parent, S., & Larivee, S. (1991). Influence of self-efficacy on self-regulation and performance among junior and senior high-school age students. *International Journal of Behavioral Development, 14*(2), 155–64.

Bransford, J. & Stein, B. S. (1994). *The ideal problem solver: A guide for improving thinking, learning, and creativity* (2nd ed.). New York: W. H. Freeman.

Braun, C. (1976). Teacher expectations: Sociopsychological dynamics. *Review of Educational Research, 46*, 185–213.

Britton, B. K. & Tessor, A. (1991). Effects of time management practices on college grades. *Journal of Educational Psychology, 83*, 405–10.

Brookhart, S. M. (1993). Teacher grading practices: Meaning and value. *Journal of Educational Measurement, 30*(2), 123–42.

—— (1998). Determinants of student effort on schoolwork and school-based achievement. *The Journal of Educational Research, 91*, 201–08.

Brookhart, S. M. & DeVoge, J. G. (1999). Testing a theory about the role of classroom assessment in student motivation and achievement. *Applied Measurement in Education, 12*(4), 409–25.

Brookhart, S. M., Walsh, J. M., & Zientarski, W. A. (2006). The dynamics of motivation and effort for classroom assessments in middle school science and social studies. *Applied Measurement in Education, 19*(2), 151–84.

Brookover, W., Beady, C., Flood, P., Schweitzer, J., & Wisenbaker, J. (1979). *School social systems and student achievement: Schools can make a difference*. New York: Bergin.

Brophy, J. E. (1981). Teacher praise: A functional analysis. *Review of Educational Research, 51*, 5–32.

—— (1983). Conceptualizing student motivation. *Educational Psychologist, 18*, 200–15.

—— (1985). Teacher–student interaction. In J. B. Dusek (Ed.), *Teacher expectancies* (pp. 303–28). Hillsdale, NJ: Lawrence Erlbaum Associates.

—— (1987). Socializing student motivation to learn. In M. L. Maehr & D. Klieber (Eds.), *Advances in motivation and achievement: Enhancing motivation* (Vol. 5, pp. 181–210). Greenwich, CT: JAI Press.

—— (1999). Research on motivation in education: Past, present, and future. In T. C. Urdan (Ed.), *The role of context* (Vol. 11, pp. 1–44). Stanford, CT: JAI Press.

—— (2005). Goal theorists should move on from performance goals. *Educational Psychologist, 40*(3), 167–76.

Brophy, J. E. & Kher, N. (1986). Teacher or social cues as a mechanism for developing student motivation to learn. In R. Feldman (Ed.), *Social psychology applied to education* (pp. 257–88). New York: Cambridge University Press.

Brown, B. B. (1993). School culture, social politics, and the academic motivation of U.S. students. In T. M. Tomlinson (Ed.), *Motivating students to learn* (pp. 63–98). Berkeley, CA: McCutchan.

Brown, J. & Weiner, B. (1984). Affective consequences of ability versus effort ascriptions: controversies, resolutions, and quandaries. *Journal of Educational Psychology, 76*(1), 146–58.

Brownell, M. T. & Pajares, F. (1999). Teacher efficacy and perceived success in mainstreaming students with learning and behavior problems. *Teacher Education and Special Education, 22*(3), 154–64.

Burris, C. C., Heubert, J. P., & Levin, H. M. (2006). Accelerating mathematics achievement using heterogeneous grouping. *American Educational Research Journal, 43*(1), 105–36.

Butkowsky, I. S. & Willows, D. M. (1980). Cognitive-motivational characteristics of children varying in reading ability: Evidence for learned helplessness in poor readers. *Journal of Educational Psychology, 72*(3), 408–22.

Butler, R. (2006). Are mastery and ability goals both adaptive? Evaluation, initial goal construction and the quality of task engagement. *British Journal of Educational Psychology, 76*, 595–611.

Butler, R. & Neuman, O. (1995). Effects of task and ego achievement goals on help-seeking behaviors and attitudes. *Journal of Educational Psychology, 87*(2), 261–71.

Butler, R. & Orion, R. (1990). When pupils do not understand the determinants of their success and failure in school: Relations between internal, teacher and unknown perceptions of school achievement. *British Journal of Educational Psychology, 60*, 63–75.

Cameron, J. & Pierce, W. D. (1994). Reinforcement, reward, and intrinsic motivation: A meta-analysis. *Review of Educational Research, 64*, 363–424.

Cannon, J. R. & Scharmann, L. C. (1996). Influence of a cooperative early field experience on preservice elementary teachers' science self-efficacy. *Science Education, 80*(4), 419–36.

Cardova, D. I. & Lepper, M. R. (1996). Intrinsic motivation and the process of learning: Beneficial effects of contextualization, personalization, and choice. *Journal of Educational Psychology, 88*(4), 715–30.

Carr, M. & Kurtz-Costes, B. E. (1994). Is being smart everything? The influence of student achievement on teachers' perceptions. *British Journal of Educational Psychology, 64*, 263–76.

Carroll, L. (1963). *Alice's great adventure*. New York: Macmillan.

Chappius, S. & Stiggins, R. J. (2002). Classroom assessment for learning. *Educational Leadership, 60*(1), 40–43.

Chemers, M. M., Hu, L., & Garcia, B. F. (2001). Academic self-efficacy and first year college students' performance and adjustment. *Journal of Educational Psychology, 93*(1), 55–64.

Cheong, Y. F., Pajares, F., & Oberman, P. S. (2004). Motivation and academic help-seeking in high school computer science. *Computer Science Education, 14*(1), 3–19.

Chester, M. D. & Beaudin, B. Q. (1996). Efficacy beliefs of newly hired teachers in urban schools. *American Educational Research Journal, 33*(1), 233–57.

Claiborn, W. (1969). Expectancy effects in the classroom: A failure to replicate. *Journal of Educational Psychology, 60*, 377–83.

Clark, E. W., Wehby, J., Hughes, C., Johnson, S. M., Plank, D. R., Barton-Atwood, S. M., et al. (2005). Preparing adolescents with high-incidence disabilities for high-stakes testing with strategy instruction. *Preventing School Failure, 49*(2), 55–62.

Clark, M. D. (1997). Teacher response to learning disability: A test of attributional principles. *Journal of Learning Disabilities, 30*(1), 69–79.

Clark, M. D. & Artiles, A. J. (2000). A cross-national study of teachers' attributional patterns. *The Journal of Special Education, 34*(2), 77–89.

Clark, M. L. (1991). Social identity, peer relations, and academic competence of African-American adolescents. *Education and Urban Society, 24*(1), 41–52.

Clark, R. (1983). *Family life and school achievement*. Chicago: University of Chicago Press.

Clifford, M. M. (1986). The effects of ability, strategy, and effort attributions for educational, business, and athletic failure. *British Journal of Educational Psychology, 56*, 169–79.

Cohen, E. G. (1994). *Designing groupwork* (2nd ed.). New York: Teachers College Press.

Collier, G. (1994). *Social origins of mental ability*. New York: Wiley.

Comer, J. P. (2005). Child and adolescent development: The critical missing element in school reform. *Phi Delta Kappan, 86*(10), 757–63.

Connell, J. P. (1990). Context, self, and action: A motivational analysis of self-system processes across the life span. In D. Cicchetti & M. Beechly (Eds.), *The self in transition: Infancy and childhood*. Chicago: University of Chicago Press.

Connell, J. P. & Wellborn, J. G. (1991). Competence, autonomy, and relatedness: A motivational analysis of self-system processes. In M. R. Gunnar & L. A. Roufe (Eds.), *Self processes and development* (pp. 43–72). Hillsdale, NJ: Lawrence Erlbaum Associates.

Cooper, H. & Good, T. L. (1983). *Pygmalion grows up: Studies in expectation communication process*. New York: Longman.

Corbett, D., Wilson, B., & Williams, B. (2002). *Effort and excellence in urban classrooms*. New York: Teachers College Press.

Corno, L. (1993). The best-laid plans: Modern conceptions of volition and educational research. *Educational Researcher, 22*(2), 4–22.

—— (1994). Student volition and education: Outcomes, influences, and practices. In D. H. Schunk & B. J. Zimmerman (Eds.), *Self-regulation of learning and performance* (pp. 229–54). Hillsdale, NJ: Lawrence Erlbaum Associates.

—— (2001). Volitional aspects of self-regulated learning. In B. H. Zimmerman & D. H. Schunk (Eds.), *Self-regulated learning and academic achievement* (pp. 191–226). Mahwah, NJ: Lawrence Erlbaum Associates.

—— (2004). Introduction to the special issue work habits and work styles. *Teachers College Record, 106*(9), 1669–94.

Corno, L. & Kanfer, R. (1993). The role of volition in learning and performance. In

L. Darling-Hammond (Ed.), *Review of research in education* (Vol. 19, pp. 3–43). Washington, DC: American Educational Research Association.

Corno, L. & Randi, J. (1999). A design theory for classroom instruction in self-regulated learning? In C. R. Reigeluth (Ed.), *Instructional design theories and models* (pp. 293–318). Mahwah, NJ: Lawrence Erlbaum Associates.

Corno, L. & Rohrkemper, M. (1985). The intrinsic motivation to learn in classrooms. In C. Ames & R. Ames (Eds.), *Research on motivation in education* (Vol. 2, pp. 53–90). New York: Academic Press.

Covey, S. (1989). *The 7 habits of highly effective people.* New York: Simon & Schuster.

Covington, M. V. (1984). The self-worth theory of achievement motivation: Findings and implications. *The Elementary School Journal, 85*(1), 5–20.

—— (1992). *Making the grade: A self-worth perspective on motivation and school reform.* New York: Cambridge University Press.

—— (1998). *The will to learn: A guide for motivating young people.* Cambridge, UK: Cambridge University Press.

Covington, M. V. & Beery, R. (1976). *Self-worth and school learning.* New York: Holt, Rinehart & Winston.

Covington, M. V. & Mueller, K. J. (2001). Intrinsic versus extrinsic motivation: An approach/avoidance reformulation. *Educational Psychology Review, 13*(2), 157–76.

Covington, M. V. & Omelich, C. L. (1979). Effort: The double-edged sword. *Journal of Educational Psychology, 71*, 169–82.

Covington, M. V. & Omelich, C. L. (1987). "I knew it cold before the exam": A test of the anxiety-blockage hypothesis. *Journal of Educational Psychology, 79*, 393–400.

Crooks, T. J. (1988). The impact of classroom evaluation practices on students. *Review of Education Research, 58*(4), 438–81.

Csikszentmihalyi, M. (1990). *Flow: The psychology of optimal experience.* New York: Harper & Row.

Culler, R. E. & Holahan, C. J. (1980). Test anxiety and academic performance: The effects of study-related behaviors. *Journal of Educational Psychology, 72*, 16–20.

Damon, W. (1995). *Greater expectations.* New York: The Free Press.

Darling-Hammond, L. (1997). *The right to learn: A blueprint for creating schools that work.* San Francisco: Jossey-Bass.

Darling-Hammond, L., Ancess, J., & Falk, B. (1995). *Authentic assessment in action.* New York: Teachers College Press.

Darling-Hammond, L. & Ifill-Lynch, O. (2006). If they'd only do their work. *Educational Leadership, 63*(5), 8–13.

Day, J. D., Borkowski, J. G., Dietmeyer, D. L., Howsepian, B. A., & Saenz, D. S. (1992). Possible selves and academic achievement. In L. T. Winegar & J. Valsinar (Eds.), *Children's development within social context* (pp. 181–201). Hillsdale, NJ: Lawrence Erlbaum Associates.

Day, J. D., Borkowski, J. G., Punzo, D., & Howsepian, B. (1994). Enhancing possible selves in Mexican-American students. *Motivation and Emotion, 18*(1), 79–103.

deCharms, R. (1976). *Enhancing motivation.* New York: Irvington/Wiley.

—— (1984). Motivational enhancement in educational settings. In R. E. Ames & C. Ames (Eds.), *Research on motivation in education* (Vol. 1, pp. 275–310). Orlando, FL: Academic Press.

Deci, E. L. & Ryan, R. M. (1985). *Intrinsic motivation and self-determination in motivation.* New York: Plenum.

—— (1991). A motivational approach to self: Integration in personality. In R. Dienstbier (Ed.), *Nebraska symposium on motivation* (Vol. 38, pp. 237–88). Lincoln, NB: University of Nebraska Press.

Delpit, L. (1995). *Other people's children.* New York: The New Press.

Dembo, M. H. (2004). Don't lose sight of the student. *Principal Leadership, 4*(8), 3742.

Dev, P. C. (1998). Intrinsic motivation and the student with learning disabilities. *Journal of Research and Development in Education, 31*, 98–108.

Dewey, J. (1913). *Interest and effort in education.* New York: Houghton Mifflin Company.

Diener, C. I. & Dweck, C. S. (1978). An analysis of learned helplessness: Continuous changes in performance, strategy, and achievement cognitions following failure. *Journal of Personality and Social Psychology, 36*, 451–62.

Diez, M. E. (2001). Will reform based on standards and assessment make a difference in the 21st century? *Mid-Western Educational Researcher, 14*(1), 22–27.

Dillon, D. R. (1989). Showing them that I want them to learn and that I care about who they are: A microethnography of the social organization of a secondary low-track English-reading class. *American Educational Research Journal, 26*, 227–59.

Doverspike, J. (1973). Group and individual goals: Their development and utilization. *Educational Technology, 13*(2), 24–26.

Doyle, W. (1983). Academic work. *Review of Educational Research, 53*, 159–200.

Dresel, M., Scober, B., & Ziegler, A. (2005). Nothing more than dimensions? Evidence for a surplus meaning of specific attributions. *The Journal of Educational Research, 99*(1), 31–44.

Durik, A. M., Vida, M., & Eccles, J. S. (2006). Task values and ability beliefs as predictors of high school literacy choices: A developmental analysis. *Journal of Educational Psychology, 98*(2), 382–93.

Dweck, C. S. (1975). The role of expectations and attributions in the alleviation of learned helplessness. *Journal of Personality and Social Psychology, 31*, 674–85.

—— (1986). Motivational processes affecting learning. *American Psychologist, 41*(10), 1040–48.

—— (1992). The study of goals in psychology. *Psychological Science* (3), 165–66.

—— (2000). *Self-theories: Their role in motivation, personality, and development.* Philadelphia: Taylor & Francis.

—— (2001). The development of ability conceptions. In A. Wigfield & J. S. Eccles (Eds.), *Development of motivation* (pp. 57–88). San Diego: Academic Press.

Dweck, C. S. & Goetz, T. E. (1978). Attributions and learned helplessness. In J. H. Harvey & W. Ickles (Eds.), *New directions in attribution research* (Vol. 2, pp. 157–59). Hillsdale, NJ: Lawrence Erlbaum Associates.

Dweck, C. S. & Leggett, E. L. (1988). A social-cognitive approach to motivation and personality. *Psychological Review, 95*, 256–73.

Dweck, C. S. & Sorich, L. (1999). Mastery oriented-thinking. In C. R. Snyder (Ed.), *Coping* (pp. 232–51). New York: Oxford University Press.

Eccles, J., Adler, T. F., Futterman, R., Goff, S. B., Kaczala, C. M., Meece, J. L., et al. (1983). Expectancies, values, and academic behaviors. In J. T. Spence (Ed.), *Achievement and achievement motivation* (pp. 75–146). San Francisco: W. H. Freeman.

Eccles, J., Wigfield, A., Harold, R. D., & Blumenfeld, P. (1993). Self and task performance during elementary school. *Child Development, 64*, 830–47.

Eccles, J. S. & Midgley, C. (1989). Stage-environment fit: Developmentally appropriate classrooms for young adolescents. In C. Ames & R. Ames (Eds.), *Research on motivation in education: Goals and cognitions* (Vol. 3, pp. 139–86). San Diego: Academic Press.

Eccles, J. S. & Wigfield, A. (1995). In the mind of the achiever: The structure of adolescents' academic motivation related beliefs and self perceptions. *Personality and Social Psychology Bulletin, 21*, 215–25.

Eccles, J. S., Wigfield, A., & Schiefele, U. (1998). Motivation to succeed. In N. Eisenberg (Ed.), *Handbook of child psychology* (5th ed., Vol. 3, pp. 1017–95). New York: Wiley.

Eccles, J. S., Wong, C. A., & Peck, S. C. (2006). Ethnicity as a social context for the development of African-American adolescents. *Journal of School Psychology, 44,* 407–26.

Elliot, A. J. (1999). Approach and avoidance and achievement goals. *Educational Psychologist, 34,* 169–89.

Elliot, A. J. & Dweck, C. S. (2005). Competence and motivation: Competence as the core of achievement motivation. In A. J. Elliot & C. S. Dweck (Eds.), *Handbook of competence motivation* (pp. 3–12). New York: Guilford Press.

Elliot, A. J. & Harackiewicz, J. M. (1996). Approach and avoidance achievement goals and intrinsic motivation: A mediational analysis. *Journal of Personality and Social Psychology, 70,* 461–75.

Elliot, A. J., McGregor, H. A., & Gable, S. (1999). Achievement goals, study strategies, and exam performance: A mediational analysis. *Journal of Educational Psychology, 91*(3), 549–63.

Elliott, E. S. & Dweck, C. S. (1988). Goals: An approach to motivation and achievement. *Journal of Personality and Social Psychology, 54,* 5–12.

Ellison, L. (1992). Using multiple intelligences to set goals. *Educational Leadership, 50,* 69–72.

Emmer, E. T. & Assiker, A. (1990). School and classroom discipline programs: How well do they work? In O. Moles (Ed.), *Student discipline strategies: Research and practice* (pp. 129–65). Albany, NY: SUNY Press.

Emmer, E. T., Evertson, C., & Worsham, M. E. (2003). *Classroom management for secondary teachers* (6th ed.). Boston: Allyn Bacon.

Epstein, J. L. (1988). Effective schools or effective students: Dealing with diversity. In R. Haskins & D. MacRae (Eds.), *Policies for America's public schools: Teachers, equity, and indicators* (pp. 89–126). Norwood, NJ: Ablex.

Evertson, C. (1982). Differences in instructional activities in higher- and lower-achieving junior high English and math classes. *Elementary School Journal, 82,* 329–50.

Evertson, C., Emmer, E. T., & Worsham, M. E. (2003). *Classroom management for elementary teachers* (6th ed.). Boston: Allyn Bacon.

Eysenck, M. W. (1988). Anxiety and attention. *Anxiety Research, 1,* 9–15.

Faircloth, B. S. & Hamm, J. V. (2005). Sense of belonging among high school students representing 4 ethnic groups. *Journal of Youth and Adolescence, 34*(4), 293–309.

Farrell, E. (1990). *Hanging in and dropping out.* New York: Teachers College Press.

—— (1994). *Self and school success.* New York: Teachers College Press.

Ferguson, R. F. (1998). Teacher perceptions and expectations and the Black–White test score gap. In C. Jencks & M. Phillips (Eds.), *The Black–White test score gap* (pp. 273–317). Washington, DC: The Brookings Institution.

Finn, J. D. (Summer, 1989). Withdrawing from school. *Review of Educational Research, 59*(2), 117–42.

Finn, J. D., Pannozzo, G. M., & Voekle, K. E. (1995). Disruptive and inattentive-withdrawn behavior and achievement among fourth graders. *Elementary School Journal, 95*(5), 421–34.

Flavell, J. H., Miller, P. H., & Miller, S. A. (1993). *Cognitive development* (3rd ed.). Englewood Cliffs, NJ: Prentice-Hall.

Flores-Gonzales, N. (1999). Puerto Rican achievers: An example of ethnic and academic identity compatibility. *Anthropology & Education Quarterly, 30*(3), 343–62.

Foote, C. J. (1999). Attribution feedback in the elementary classroom. *Journal of Research in Childhood Education, 13*(2), 155–66.

Ford, M. E. (1992). *Motivating humans: Goals, emotions, and personal agency beliefs.* Newbury Park, CA: Sage.

—— (1995). Motivation and competence development in special and remedial education. *Intervention in School and Clinic, 31*(2), 70–83.

Fordham, S. & Ogbu, J. U. (1986). Black students' school success: Coping with the "burden of 'acting white.'" *The Urban Review, 18*(3), 176–206.

Foster, M. (1987). *"It's cooking now": An ethnographic study of a successful Black teacher in an urban community college.* Dissertation Abstracts International, 48 (7), University Microfilms No ASA18722682.

Fredricks, J. A., Blumenfeld, P. C., & Paris, A. H. (2004). School engagement: Potential of the concept, state of the evidence. *Review of Educational Research, 74*(1), 59–109.

Freiberg, H. J., Stein, T. A., & Huang, S. (1995). Effects of a classroom management intervention on student achievement in inner-city elementary schools. *Educational Research and Evaluation, 1*(1), 36–66.

Frieze, I. H. (1980). Beliefs about success and failure in the classroom. In J. H. McMillan (Ed.), *The social psychology of school learning* (pp. 39–78). New York: Academic Press.

Frieze, I. H. & Snyder, H. N. (1980). Children's beliefs about the causes of success and failure in school settings. *Journal of Educational Psychology, 72*(2), 186–96.

Fritz, J. J., Miller-Heyl, J., Kreutzer, J. C., & MacPhee, D. (1995). Fostering personal teaching efficacy through staff development and classroom activities. *Journal of Educational Research, 88*(4), 200–08.

Fulk, B. J. & Mastropieri, M. A. (1990). Training positive attitudes: "I tried hard and did well." *Intervention in School and Clinic, 26*(2), 79–83.

Furrer, C. & Skinner, E. (2003). Sense of relatedness as a factor in children's academic engagement and performance. *Journal of Educational Psychology, 95*(1), 148–62.

Gaa, J. P. (1973). Effects of individual goal-setting conferences on achievement, attitudes, and goal-setting behavior. *Journal of Experimental Education, 42*, 22–27.

—— (1979). The effect of individual goal-setting conferences on academic achievement and modification of locus of control orientation. *Psychology in the Schools, 16*, 591–97.

Galloway, D., Rogers, C., Armstrong, D., & Leo, E. (1998). *Motivating the difficult to teach.* New York: Longman.

Gambrell, L. B. & Morrow, L. M. (1996). Creating motivation contexts for literacy learning. In L. Baker, P. Afflerbach, & D. Reinking (Eds.), *Developing engaged readers in home and school communities* (pp. 115–36). Mahwah, NJ: Lawrence Erlbaum Associates.

Garcia, T., McCann, E. J., Turner, J. E., & Roska, L. (1998). Modeling the mediating role of volition in the learning process. *Contemporary Educational Psychology, 23*, 392–418.

Gardner, H. (1983). *Frames of mind: The new theory of multiple intelligences.* New York: Basic Books.

Garibaldi, A. M. (1993). Creating prescriptions for success in urban schools: Turning the corner on pathological explanations for academic failure. In T. M. Tomlinson (Ed.), *Motivating students to learn* (pp. 125–38). Berkeley, CA: McCutchan.

Garner, R., Alexander, P. A., Gillingham, M. G., Kulikowich, J. M., & Brown, R. B. (1991). Interest and learning from text. *American Educational Research Journal, 28*(3), 643–59.

Garner, R., Brown, R. B., Sanders, S., & Menke, D. J. (1992). "Seductive details" and learning from text. In K. A. Renninger, S. Hidi, & A. Krapp (Eds.), *The role of interest in learning and development* (pp. 239–54). Hillsdale, NJ: Lawrence Erlbaum Associates.

Gaskins, I. (1994). Classroom applications of cognitive science: Teaching poor readers how to learn, think, and problem solve. In K. McGilly (Ed.), *Classroom lessons: Interpreting cognitive theory and classroom practices* (pp. 129–54). Cambridge, MA: MIT Press.

Gaskins, I. & Elliot, T. (1991). *Implementing cognitive strategy instruction across the school.* Cambridge, MA: Brookline Books.

Gettinger, M. & Seibert, J. K. (2002). Contributions of study skills to academic competence. *School Psychology Review, 31*(3), 350–65.

Ghaith, G. & Shaaban, K. (1999). The relationship between perceptions of teaching concerns, teacher efficacy, and selected teacher characteristics. *Teaching and Teacher Education, 15,* 487–96.

Ghaith, G. & Yaghi, H. (1997). Relationships among experience, teacher efficacy, and attitudes toward the implementation of instructional innovation. *Teaching and Teacher Education, 13,* 451–58.

Gibson, J. D. (1998). *Enhancing motivation of African-American middle school students.* Unpublished Doctoral Dissertation, The University of Akron.

Gibson, S. & Dembo, M. H. (1984). Teacher efficacy: A construct validation. *Journal of Educational Psychology, 76,* 569–82.

Gipps, C. & Tunstall, P. (1998). Effort, ability, and the teacher. *Oxford Review of Education, 24*(2), 149–65.

Goddard, R. D. & Goddard, Y. L. (2001). A multilevel analysis of the relationship between teacher and collectivity efficacy in urban schools. *Teaching and Teacher Education, 17,* 807–18.

Goddard, R. D., LoGerfo, L., & Hoy, W. K. (2004). High school accountability: The role of perceived collective efficacy. *Educational Policy, 18*(3), 403–25.

Goertz, M. E. (2001). Redefining government roles in an era of standards-based reform. *Phi Delta Kappan, 83*(1), 62.

Goldenberg, C. (1992). The limits of expectations: A case for case knowledge about teacher expectancy effects. *American Educational Research Journal, 29*(3), 517–44.

—— (1994). Promoting early literacy achievement among Spanish-speaking children: Lessons from two studies. In E. Heibert (Ed.), *Getting ready from the start: Effective early literacy interventions* (pp. 171–99). Boston: Allyn & Bacon.

Goldenberg, C. & Gallimore, R. (1995). Immigrant Latino parents' values and beliefs about their children's education: Continuities across cultures and generations. In M. L. Maehr & P. R. Pintrich (Eds.), *Advances in motivation and achievement* (Vol. 9, pp. 183–228). Greenwich, CT: JAI Press.

Goldman, S. (1982). Knowledge systems for realistic goals. *Discourse Processes, 5,* 279–303.

Good, T. L. & Brophy, J. E. (1994). *Looking in classrooms* (6th ed.). New York: Harper & Row.

—— (2003). *Looking in classrooms* (9th ed.). New York: Longman.

Good, T. L. & Marshall, S. (1984). Do students learn more in heterogenous or homogeneous achievement groups? In P. Peterson & L. Cherry-Wilkenson (Eds.), *Student diversity in the organization process.* New York: Academic Press.

Good, T. L. & Weinstein, R. (1986). Teacher expectations: A framework for exploring classrooms. In K. K. Zumwalt (Ed.), *Improving teaching (The 1986 ASCD Yearbook)* (pp. 63–85). Alexandria, VA: Association for Supervision and Curriculum Development.

Goodenow, C. (1992). Strengthening the links between educational psychology and the study of social contexts. *Educational Psychologist, 27*(2), 177–96.

—— (1993). The psychological sense of school membership among adolescents: Scale development and educational correlates. *Psychology in the Schools, 30,* 79–90.

Goodenow, C. & Grady, K. E. (1993). The relationship of school belonging and friends' values of academic motivation among urban adolescent students. *Journal of Experimental Education, 62*(1), 60–71.

Gordon, K., Padilla, A. M., Ford, M., & Thoresen, C. (1994, April). *Resilient students' beliefs about their schooling environment: A possible role in developing goals and motivation.* Paper presented at the American Educational Research Association, New Orleans.

Gottfried, A. E., Fleming, J. S., & Gottfried, A. W. (2001). Continuity of academic intrinsic motivation from childhood through late adolescence: A longitudinal study. *Journal of Educational Psychology, 93*(1), 3–13.

Graham, S. L. (1984). Communicating sympathy and anger to black and white children: The cognitive (attributional) consequences of affective cues. *Journal of Personality and Social Psychology, 47*, 40–54.

—— (1989). Motivation in African Americans. In G. L. Berry & J. K. Asaman (Eds.), *Black students: Psychosocial issues and academic achievement* (pp. 40–68). Newbury Park, CA: Sage.

—— (1991). A review of attribution theory in achievement contexts. *Educational Psychology Review, 3*(1), 5–39.

—— (1994). Motivation in African Americans. *Review of Educational Research, 64*(1), 55–117.

Graham, S. E. & Barker, G. P. (1987). Developmental study of praise and blame. *Journal of Educational Psychology, 79*(1), 62–66.

Graham, S. L. & Barker, G. P. (1990). The down side of help: An attributional-developmental analysis of helping behavior as a low-ability cue. *Journal of Educational Psychology, 82*(1), 7–14.

Graham, S. L. & Golan, S. (1991). Motivational influences on cognition: Task involvement, ego involvement, and depth of information processing. *Journal of Educational Psychology, 83*(2), 187–94.

Graham, S. & Harris, K. R. (1996). *Making the writing process work: Strategies for composition and self-regulation*. Cambridge, MA: Brookline Books.

—— (1994). The role and development of self-regulation in the writing process. In D. H. Schunk & B. J. Zimmerman (Eds.), *Self-regulation of learning and performance* (pp. 203–28). Hillsdale, NJ: Lawrence Erlbaum Associates.

Graham, S., Harris, K. R., & Reid, R. (1992). Developing self-regulated learners. *Focus on Exceptional Children, 24*, 1–16.

Graham, S., Harris, K. R., & Troia, G. A. (1998). Writing and self-regulation: Cases from the self-regulated strategy developmental model. In D. H. Schunk & B. J. Zimmerman (Eds.), *Self-regulated learning: From teaching to self-reflective practice* (pp. 20–41). New York: Guilford Press.

Graham, S., MacArthur, C., Schwartz, S., & Page-Voth, V. (1992). Improving the compositions of students with learning disabilities using a strategy involving product and process goal setting. *Exceptional Children, 58*, 322–34.

Graham, S. L. & Weiner, B. (1996). Theories and principles of motivation. In D. Berliner & R. Calfee (Eds.), *Handbook of educational psychology* (pp. 63–84). New York: Macmillan.

Grant, H. & Dweck, C. S. (2003). Clarifying achievement goals and their impact. *Journal of Personality and Social Psychology, 85*(3), 541–53.

Greenspan, S. & Lodish, R. (1991). School literacy: The real ABCs. *Phi Delta Kappan, 72*, 300–08.

Gresham, F. M. (1984). Social skills and self-efficacy for exceptional children. *Exceptional Children, 51*(3), 253–61.

Gresham, F. M., Evans, S., & Elliott, S. N. (1988). Self-efficacy differences among mildly handicapped, gifted, and nonhandicapped students. *The Journal of Special Education, 22*(2), 231–40.

Guskey, T. R. (2001). Helping standards make the grade. *Educational Leadership, 59*(1), 20–27.

Guthrie, J. T., Van Meter, P., McCann, A. D., Wigfield, A., Bennett, L., & Poundstone, C. C. (1996). Growth of literacy engagement: Changes, motivations and strategies during concept-oriented reading instruction. *Reading Research Quarterly, 31*, 306–32.

Guthrie, J. T., Wigfield, A., & VonSecker, C. (2000). Effects of integrated instruction on motivation and strategy use in reading. *Journal of Educational Psychology, 92*(2), 331–41.

Hampton, N. Z. & Mason, E. (2003). Learning disabilities, gender, sources of efficacy, self-efficacy beliefs, and academic achievement in high school students. *Journal of School Psychology, 41*, 101–12.

Hare, B. (1985). Stability and change in self-perception and achievement among black adolescents: A longitudinal study. *The Journal of Black Psychology, 11*, 29–42.

Harlen, W. & Crick, R. D. (2003). Testing and motivation for learning. *Assessment in Education, 10*(2), 169–207.

Harris, K. R. (1990). Developing self-regulated learners: The role of private speech and self-instructions. *Educational Psychologist, 25*(1), 35–49.

Harris, K. R. & Graham, S. (1985). Improving learning disabled students' composition skills: Self-control strategy training. *Learning Disability Quarterly, 8*, 27–36.

Harter, S. (1982). The perceived competence scale for children. *Child Development, 53*, 87–97.

Haycock, K. (2001). Closing the achievement gap. *Educational Leadership, 58*(6), 6–11.

Heider, F. (1958). *The psychology of interpersonal relationships.* New York: Wiley.

Hennessey, B. A. (1995). Social, environmental, and developmental issues and creativity. *Educational Psychology Review, 7*, 163–83.

Heyman, G. D. & Dweck, C. S. (1992). Achievement goals and intrinsic motivation: Their relation and their role in adaptive motivation. *Motivation and Emotion, 16*(3), 231–47.

Hickham, H. (1999). *October sky.* New York: Dell.

Hidi, S. (1990). Interest and its contribution as a mental resource for learning. *Review of Educational Research, 60*, 549–71.

—— (2000). An interest researcher's perspective: The effects of extrinsic and intrinsic factors on motivation. In C. Sansone & J. M. Harackiewicz (Eds.), *Intrinsic and extrinsic motivation: The search for optimal motivation and performance* (pp. 311–39). San Diego: Academic Press.

Hidi, S. & Harackiewicz, J. M. (2000). Motivating the academically unmotivated: A critical issue for the 21st century. *Review of Educational Research, 70*(2), 151–79.

Hidi, S. & Renninger, K. A. (2006). The four-phase model of interest development. *Educational Psychologist, 41*(2), 111–27.

Hill, K. T. (1984). Debilitating motivation and testing: A major educational problem, possible solutions, and policy applications. In R. E. Ames & C. Ames (Eds.), *Research on motivation in education: Student motivation* (Vol. 1, pp. 245–74). New York: Academic Press.

Hill, K. T. & Wigfield, A. (1984). Test anxiety: A major educational problem and what can be done about it. *Elementary School Journal, 85*(1), 105–26.

Hilliard, A. (1991). Do we have the will to educate all children? *Educational Leadership, 49*, 31–36.

—— (2003). No mystery: Closing the achievement gap between Africans and excellence. In T. Perry, C. Steele, & A. Hilliard (Eds.), *Young, gifted and Black: Promoting high achievement among African-American students* (pp. 131–65). Boston: Beacon Press.

Ho, R. & McMurtrie, J. (1991). Feedback and underachieving children: Differential effects on causal attributions, success expectancies and learning processes. *Australian Journal of Psychology, 43*(2), 93–100.

Hodgkinson, H. (1993). American education: The good, the bad, and the task. *Kappan, 74*(8), 619–23.

Hoover-Dempsey, K. V., Bassler, O. C., & Brissie, J. S. (1987). Parent involvement: Contributions of teacher efficacy, school socioeconomic status, and other school characteristics. *American Educational Research Journal, 24*, 417–35.

Howse, R. B., Lange, G., Farran, D., & Boyles, C. D. (2003). Motivation and self-regulation as predictors of achievement in economically disadvantaged young children. *The Journal of Experimental Education, 71*(2), 151–74.

Hoy, A. W. & Spero, R. B. (2005). Changes in teacher efficacy during the early years of teaching: A comparison of four measures. *Teaching and Teacher Education, 21*(4), 343–46.

Hoy, W. K., Sweetland, S. R., & Smith, P. A. (2002). Toward an organizational model of achievement in high schools: The significance of collective efficacy. *Educational Administration Quarterly, 38*(1), 77–93.

Hoy, W. K. & Woolfolk, A. E. (1990). Socialization of student teachers. *American Educational Research Journal, 27*(2), 279–300.

Hudley, C. & Graham, S. (2001). Stereotypes of achievement striving among early adolescents. *Social Psychology of Education, 5,* 201–24.

Interstate New Teacher Assessment and Support Consortium (INTASC) (1992). *Model standards for beginning teacher licensing, assessment and development: A resource for state dialogue.* Washington, DC: Council of Chief State School Officers.

Irvine, J. (1999). The education of children whose nightmares come both day and night. *Journal of Negro Education, 68*(3), 244–53.

Isennagle, A. (1993). A teacher reflects on his urban classroom. In R. Donmoyer & R. Kos (Eds.), *At-risk students* (pp. 369–80). New York: State University of New York Press.

Iyenger, S. S. & Lepper, M. R. (2000). When choice is demotivating: Can one desire too much of a good thing? *Journal of Personality and Psychology, 72*(6), 995–1006.

Jacobs, J. E. & Eccles, J. (2000). Parents, task values, and real-life achievement-related choices. In C. Sansone & J. M. Harackiewicz (Eds.), *Intrinsic and extrinsic motivation: The search for optimal motivation and performance* (pp. 405–39). San Diego: Academic Press.

Jacobs, W. W. (1979). *The monkey's paw.* Logan, IA: Perfection Form.

Johnson, D. W., Johnson, R. T., & Holubec, E. J. (1994). *Cooperative learning in the classroom.* Alexandria, VA: Association for Supervision and Curriculum Development.

Johnson, D. W., Maruyama, G., Johnson, R. T., Nelson, D., & Skon, L. (1981). Effects of cooperative, competitive, and individualistic goal structures on achievement: A metanalysis. *Psychological Bulletin, 89,* 47–62.

Jones, M. G., Jones, B. D., Hardin, B., Chapman, L., Yarbrough, T., & Davis, M. (1999). The impact of high-stakes testing on teachers and students in North Carolina. *Phi Delta Kappan, 81*(3), 199–203.

Joo, Y., Bong, M., & Choi, H. (2001). Self-efficacy for self-regulated learning, academic self-efficacy, and internet self-efficacy in web-based instruction. *Educational Technology and Research and Development, 48*(2), 5–17.

Jussim, L., Eccles, J., & Madon, S. (1996). Social perception, social stereotypes, and teacher expectations: Accuracy and the self-fulfilling prophecy. In M. P. Zanna (Ed.), *Advances in Experimental and Social Psychology* (Vol. 28, pp. 281–388). San Diego: Academic Press.

Kagen, S. (1992). *Cooperative learning resources for teachers.* San Juan Capistrano, CA: Resources for Teachers.

Kao, G. & Tienda, M. (1998). Educational aspirations of minority youth. *American Journal of Education, 108,* 349–84.

Kaplan, A. & Middleton, M. (2002). Should childhood be a journey or a race? Response to Harackiewicz, et al. (2002). *Journal of Educational Psychology, 94,* 646–48.

Karabenick, S. A. (1998). Help seeking as a strategic resource. In S. A. Karabenick (Ed.), *Strategic help seeking: Implications for learning and teaching* (pp. 1–11). Mahwah, NJ: Lawrence Erlbaum Associates.

Karabenick, S. A. & Knapp, J. R. (1991). Relationship of academic help seeking to the use of learning strategies and other instrumental achievement behavior of college students. *Journal of Educational Psychology, 83*(2), 221–30.

Klein, R. (1996). *Teacher efficacy and developmental math instructors at an urban university: An exploratory analysis of the relationships among personal factors, teacher behaviors, and perceptions of the environment.* Unpublished Doctoral Dissertation, The University of Akron.

Knapp, M. S. & Shields, P. M. (1990). Reconceiving academic instruction for the children of poverty. *Phi Delta Kappan, 71*(10), 752–58.

Kruger, L. J. (1997). Social support and self-efficacy in problem solving among teacher assistance teams and school staff. *Journal of Educational Research, 90*, 164–68.

Kuglinski, M. R. & Weinstein, R. S. (2001). Classroom and developmental differences in a path model of teacher expectancy effects. *Child Development, 72*(5), 1554–78.

Ladson-Billings, G. (1994). *The Dreamkeepers.* San Francisco: Jossey-Bass.

Lakaye, T., Margalit, M., Ziv, Z., & Ziman, T. (2006). Comparisons of self-efficacy, mood, effort, and hope between students with learning disabilities and their non-LD-matched peers. *Learning Disabilities Research and Practice, 21*(2), 111–21.

Lee, G. H. (2002). The development of teacher efficacy beliefs: A case study of an African American middle school teacher. In J. J. Irvine (Ed.), *In Search of Wholeness* (pp. 67–85). New York: Palgrave.

Lee, V. E. & Smith, J. B. (1996). Collective responsibility for learning and its effects on gains in achievement for early secondary school students. *American Journal of Education, 104*, 103–45.

—— (1999). Social support and achievement for young adolescents in Chicago: The role of school academic press. *American Educational Research Journal, 36*(4), 907–45.

—— (2001). *Restructuring high schools for equity and excellence: What works.* New York: Teachers College Press.

Leggette, R. M. (1998). Causal beliefs of public school students about success and failure in music. *Journal of Research in Music Education, 46*(1), 102–11.

Lepper, M. R. (1988). Motivational considerations in instruction. *Cognition and Instruction, 5*(4), 289–309.

Lepper, M. R. & Cardova, D. I. (1992). A desire to be taught: Instructional consequences of intrinsic motivation. *Motivation and Emotion, 16*(2), 187–208.

Lepper, M. R., Corpus, J. H., & Iyenger, S. S. (2005). Intrinsic and extrinsic motivational orientations in the classroom: Age differences and academic correlates. *Journal of Educational Psychology, 97*(2), 184–96.

Lepper, M. R. & Greene, D. (1975). Turning work into play: Effects of adult surveillance and extrinsic rewards on children's intrinsic motivation. *Journal of Personality and Social Psychology, 31*, 479–86.

Lepper, M. R., Greene, D., & Nisbitt, R. E. (1973). Undermining children's intrinsic interest with extrinsic rewards: A test of the overjustification hypothesis. *Journal of Personality and Social Psychology, 28*, 129–37.

Lepper, M. R. & Henderlong, J. (2000). Turning "play" into "work" and "work" into "play": 25 years of research on intrinsic versus extrinsic motivation. In C. Sansone & J. M. Harackiewicz (Eds.), *Intrinsic and extrinsic motivation: The search for optimal motivation and performance* (pp. 257–307). San Diego: Academic Press.

Lepper, M. R. & Hodell, M. (1989). Intrinsic motivation in the classroom. In C. Ames & R. Ames (Eds.), *Research on motivation in education* (Vol. 3, pp. 73–105). San Diego: Academic Press.

Lewis, M. & Sullivan, M. W. (2005). The development of self-conscious emotions. In A. J. Elliot & C. S. Dweck (Eds.), *Handbook of competence motivation* (pp. 185–201). New York: The Guilford Press.

Ley, K. & Young, D. B. (1998). Self-regulation behaviors in underprepared (developmental) and regular admission college students. *Contemporary Educational Psychology, 23*, 42–64.

Licht, B. G. (1983). Cognitive-motivational factors that contribute to the achievement of learning-disabled children. *Journal of Learning Disabilities, 16*, 483–90.

Licht, B. G. & Dweck, C. S. (1984). Determinants of academic achievement: The interaction of children's achievement orientation with skill area. *Developmental Psychology, 20*, 628–36.

Licht, B. G., Strader, S., & Swenson, C. (1989). Children's achievement related beliefs: Effects of academic area, sex, and achievement level. *Journal of Educational Research, 82*, 82.

Linnenbrink, E. A. (2005). The dilemma of performance-approach goals: The use of multiple goal contexts to promote students' motivation and learning. *Journal of Educational Psychology, 97*(2), 197–213.

Linnenbrink, E. A. & Pintrich, P. R. (2002). Motivation as an enabler for academic success. *Review of Educational Research, 31*(3), 313–27.

Lloyd, J. E. V., Walsh, J., & Yailagh, M. S. (2005). Sex differences in performance attributions, self-efficacy, and achievement mathematics: If I'm so smart, why don't I know it? *Canadian Journal of Education, 28*(3), 384–408.

Locke, E. A. (2000). Motivation, cognition, action: An analysis of studies of task goals and knowledge. *Applied Psychology: An International Review, 49*, 408–30.

Locke, E. A. & Latham, G. P. (1984). *Goal setting: A motivational technique that works.* Englewood Cliffs, NJ: Prentice-Hall.

—— (1990). *A theory of goal setting and task performance.* Englewood Cliffs, NJ: Prentice-Hall.

—— (2002). Building a practically useful theory of goal setting and task motivation. *American Psychologist, 57*(9), 705–17.

Locke, E. A., Shaw, K. N., Saari, L. M., & Latham, G. P. (1981). Goal setting and task performance: 1969–80. *Psychological Bulletin, 90*, 125–52.

Mac Iver, D. J. (1993). Effects of improvement-focused student recognition on young adolescents' performance in the classroom. In M. L. Maehr & P. R. Pintrich (Eds.), *Advances in motivation and achievement* (Vol. 8, pp. 191–216). Greenwich, CT: JAI Press.

Mac Iver, D. J. & Reuman, D. A. (1993/94). Giving their best: Grading and recognition practices that motivate students to work hard. *American Educator, 17*(4), 24–31.

Mac Iver, D. J., Stipek, D. J., & Daniels, D. H. (1991). Explaining within-semester changes in student effort in junior high school and senior high school courses. *Journal of Educational Psychology, 83*(2), 201–11.

Maehr, M. L., Midgley, C., & Urdan, T. C. (1992). School leader as motivator. *Educational Administration Quarterly, 28*, 410–29.

Maeroff, G. J. (1988). Withered hopes, stillborn dreams: The dismal panorama of urban schools. *Phi Delta Kappan, 69*(9), 632–38.

Malone, T. W. & Lepper, M. R. (1987). Making learning fun: A taxonomy of intrinsic motivation for learning. In R. E. Snow & M. J. Farr (Eds.), *Aptitude, learning, and instruction: III. Conative and affective process analyses* (pp. 223–53). Hillsdale, NJ: Lawrence Erlbaum Associates.

Manning, B. (1988). Application of cognitive behavior modification: First and third graders' self-management of classroom behaviors. *American Educational Research Journal, 25*(2), 193–212.

—— (1991). *Cognitive self-instruction for classroom processes.* Albany, NY: State University of New York Press.

Marcus, H. & Nurius, P. (1986). Possible selves. *American Psychologist, 41*(9), 954–69.

Marks, H. M. (2000). Student engagement in instructional activity: Patterns in the elementary, middle, and high school years. *American Educational Research Journal, 37*(1), 153–84.

Marsh, H. W., Byrne, B. M., & Shavelson, R. (1988). A multifaceted academic self-concept: Its hierarchical structure and its relation to academic achievement. *Journal of Educational Psychology, 80*, 866–80.

Mason, D. A., Schroeder, D. D., Combs, R. K., & Washington, K. (1992). Assigning average-achieving eighth grades to advance mathematics classes in an urban junior high school. *The Elementary School Journal, 92*(5), 387–99.

Masui, C. & De Corte, E. (2005). Learning to reflect and to attribute constructively as basic components of self-regulated learning. *British Journal of Educational Psychology, 75*, 351–72.

Mathews, J. (1988). *Escalante the best teacher in America.* New York: Henry Holt and Company.

McCaslin, M. (2006). Student motivational dynamics in the era of school reform. *Elementary School Journal, 106*(5), 479–90.

McCollum, H. (1995). Managing academic learning environments. In M. Knapp (Ed.), *Teaching for meaning in high poverty classrooms* (pp. 11–32). New York: Teachers College Press.

McCready, L. (1996). *Possible selves of African American adolescents.* Paper presented at the American Educational Research Association, New York, NY.

McDaniel, E. A. & Dibella-McCarthy, H. (1989). Enhancing teacher efficacy in special education. *Teaching Exceptional Children, 21*(4), 34–40.

McDonough, M. L., Meyer, D. K., Stone, G. V. M., & Hamman, D. (1991). *Goal-setting and monitoring among first grade readers during seatwork: Process and differences in process among reading ability groups.* Paper presented at the annual meeting of the National Association of School Psychologists, Dallas, Texas.

McInerney, D. M., Roche, L. A., McInerney, V., & Marsh, H. W. (1997). Cultural perspectives on school motivation: The relevance of goal theory. *American Educational Research Journal, 34*(1), 207–36.

McInerney, D. M. & Van Etten, S. (2001). Introduction. In D. M. McInerney & S. Van Etten (Eds.), *Research on sociocultural influences on motivation and learning* (Vol. 1, pp. ix–xxvi). Greenwich, CT: Information Age Publishing.

McLaughlin, H. J. (1991). Reconciling care and control: Authority in classroom relationships. *Journal of Teacher Education, 42*(3), 182–95.

Medway, F. J. (1979). Causal perception for school-related problems: Teacher perceptions and teacher feedback. *Journal of Educational Psychology, 71*(6), 809–18.

Meece, J. L. (1991). The classroom context and students' motivational goals. In M. L. Maehr & P. R. Pintrich (Eds.), *Advances in motivation and achievement* (Vol. 7, pp. 261–85). Greenwich, CT: JAI Press.

Meece, J. L., Blumenfeld, P. C., & Hoyle, R. H. (1988). Students' goal orientations and cognitive engagement in classroom activities. *Journal of Educational Psychology, 80*(4), 514–23.

Meece, J. L., Blumenfeld, P. C., & Puro, P. (1989). A motivational analysis of elementary science learning environments. In M. Matyas, K. Tobin, & B. Fraser (Eds.), *Looking into windows: Qualitative research in science education* (pp. 13–23). Washington, DC: American Association for the Advancement of Science.

Meece, J. L. & Courtney, D. P. (1992). Gender differences in student perceptions. In D. L. Schunk & J. L. Meece (Eds.), *Student perceptions in the classroom* (pp. 209–28). Hillsdale, NJ: Lawrence Erlbaum Associates.

Meece, J. L., Eccles, J. S., & Wigfield, A. (1990). Predictors of math anxiety and its influences on young adolescents' course enrollment intentions and performance in mathematics. *Journal of Educational Psychology, 82*(1), 60–70.

Meece, J. L. & McColsky, W. (1997). *Improving student motivation: A guide for teachers and school improvement teams* (No. EDD00036). Tallahassee, FL: Southeastern Regional Vision for Education.

Mehan, H., Villanueva, I., Hubbard, L., & Lintz, A. (1996). *Constructing School Success.* New York: Cambridge University Press.

Meichenbaum, D. (1977). *Cognitive Behavior Modification.* New York: Plenum Press.

Mickelson, R. (1990). The attitude-achievement paradox among black adolescents. *Sociology of Education, 63*, 44–61.

Midgley, C., Feldlaufer, H., & Eccles, J. S. (1989). Changes in teacher efficacy and students' self- and task-related beliefs in mathematics during the transition to junior high school. *Journal of Educational Psychology, 81*, 247–58.

Midgley, C., Kaplan, A., & Middleton, M. (2001). Performance-approach goals: Good for what, for whom, under what circumstances, and at what cost? *Journal of Educational Psychology, 93*(1), 77–86.

Midgley, C. & Urdan, T. C. (2001). Academic self-handicapping and achievement goals: A further examination. *Contemporary Educational Psychology, 26*, 61–75.

Miller, A. T. & Hom, H. L. (1997). Conceptions of ability and the interpretation of praise and blame. *The Journal of Experimental Education, 65*, 163–77.

Miller, J. G. (1996). Culture as a source of social motivation. *Psychological Inquiry, 7*(3), 240–43.

Miller, N. & Harrington, H. H. (1992). Social categorization and intergroup acceptance: Principles for the design and development of cooperative learning teams. In R. Hertz-Lazarowitz (Ed.), *Interaction in cooperative groups* (pp. 203–27). New York: Cambridge University Press.

Miller, S. E., Leinhardt, G., & Zigmond, N. (1988). Influencing engagement through accommodation: An ethnographic study. *American Educational Research Journal, 25*(4), 465–87.

Miranda, A., Villaescusa, M. I., & Vidal-Abarca, E. (1997). Is attribution retraining necessary? Use of self-regulation procedures for enhancing the reading comprehension strategies of children with learning disabilities. *Journal of Learning Disabilities, 30*, 503–12.

Miserandino, M. (1996). Children who do well in school: Individual differences in perceived competence and autonomy in above-average children. *Journal of Educational Psychology, 88*(2), 203–14.

Mitchell, M. (1993). Situational interest: Its multifaceted structure in the secondary school mathematics classroom. *Journal of Educational Psychology, 85*, 424–36.

Molden, D. C. & Dweck, C. S. (2000). Meaning and motivation. In C. Sansone & J. M. Harackiewicz (Eds.), *Intrinsic and extrinsic motivation: The search for optimal motivation and performance* (pp. 131–59). San Diego: Academic Press.

Morgan, M. (1985). Self-monitoring of attained subgoals in private study. *Journal of Educational Psychology, 77*, 623–30.

—— (1987). Self-monitoring and goal setting in private study. *Contemporary Educational Psychology, 12*, 1–6.

Moriarty, B., Douglas, G., Punch, K., & Hattie, J. (1995). Importance of self-efficacy as a mediating variable between learning environments and achievement. *British Journal of Educational Psychology, 65*, 73–84.

Mueller, C. M. & Dweck, C. S. (1998). Intelligence praise can undermine motivation and performance. *Journal of Personality and Social Psychology, 75*, 33–52.

Murphy, P. K. & Alexander, P. (2000). A motivated exploration of motivational terminology. *Contemporary Educational Psychology, 25,* 3–53.

National Board for Professional Teaching Standards (NBPTS) (1990). *Toward high and rigorous standards for the teaching profession: Initial policies and perspectives of the National Board for Professional Teaching Standards.* Washington, DC: National Board for Professional Teaching Standards.

National Center for Children in Poverty (2006). *Low-income children in the United States: A brief demographic profile.* New York: The Joseph L. Mailman School of Public Health of Columbia University.

National Center for Educational Statistics (2005). *The condition of education.* Washington, DC: US Department of Education, Office of Educational Research and Improvement.

Natriello, G. & Dornbush, S. M. (1984). *Teacher evaluative standards and student effort.* New York: Longman.

Nelson-Le Gall, S. (1985). Help-seeking in learning. In E. Gordon (Ed.), *Review of research in education* (Vol. 12, pp. 55–90). Washington, DC: American Educational Research Association.

—— (1991). Classroom help-seeking. *Education and Urban Society, 24*(1), 27–40.

—— (1992). Children's instrumental help-seeking: Its role in the social acquisition and the construction of knowledge. In R. Hertz-Lazarowitz & N. Miller (Eds.), *Interaction in cooperative groups* (pp. 49–68). New York: Cambridge University Press.

Nelson-Le Gall, S. & Jones, E. (1990). Cognitive-motivational influences on the task-related help-seeking behavior of black children. *Child Development, 61,* 581–89.

Newman, R. S. (1990). Children's help-seeking in the classroom: The role of motivation factors and attributions. *Journal of Educational Psychology, 82,* 71–80.

—— (1991). Goals and self-regulated learning: What motivates children to seek academic help? In M. L. Maehr & P. R. Pintrich (Eds.), *Advances in motivation and achievement* (Vol. 7, pp. 151–83). Greenwich, CT: JAI Press.

—— (1998). Students' help seeking during problem solving: Influences of personal and contextual achievement goals. *Journal of Educational Psychology, 90*(4), 664–658.

Newman, F. M. (1992). *Student engagement and achievement in American secondary schools.* New York: Teachers College Press.

Newmann, F. M., Rutter, R. A., & Smith, M. S. (1989). Organizational factors that affect school sense of efficacy, community, and expectations. *Sociology of Education, 62*(October), 221–38.

Newmann, F. M., Secada, W. G., & Wehlage, G. G. (1995). *A guide to authentic assessment: Vision, standards and scoring.* Madison, WI: Wisconsin Center for Educational Research.

Newmann, F. M., Wehlage, G. G., & Lamborn, S. D. (1992). The significance and sources of student engagement. In F. M. Newmann (Ed.), *Student engagement and achievement in American secondary schools* (pp. 11–39). New York: Teachers College Press.

Nicholls, J. G. (1978). The development of the concepts of effort and ability, perception of academic attainment, and the understanding that difficult tasks require more ability. *Child Development, 49,* 800–14.

—— (1979). Quality and inequality in intellectual development. *American Psychologist, 34*(11), 1071–84.

—— (1983). Conceptions of ability and achievement motivation: A theory and its implications for education. In M. O. Stevenson, H. W. Stevenson, & S. G. Paris (Eds.), *Learning and motivation in the classroom* (pp. 211–37). Hillsdale, NJ: Lawrence Erlbaum Associates.

—— (1989). *The competitive ethos and democratic education.* Cambridge, MA: Harvard University Press.

—— (1990). What is ability and why are we mindful of it? A developmental perspective. In R. J. Sternberg & J. Kolligian (Eds.), *Competence considered* (pp. 11–40). New Haven, CT: Yale University Press.

Nicholls, J. G. & Miller, A. T. (1984). Development and its discontents: The differentiation of the concept of ability. In J. G. Nicholls (Ed.), *The development of achievement motivation* (pp. 185–218). Greenwich, CT: JAI Press.

Nieto, S. (1992). *Affirming diversity*. New York: Longman.

—— (1994). Lessons from students on creating a chance to dream. *Harvard Educational Review, 64*(4), 38–496.

Nisen, M. (1992). Beyond intrinsic motivation: Cultivating a "sense of the desirable." In F. K. Oser, A. Dick, & J. Patry (Eds.), *Effective and responsible teaching* (pp. 126–38). San Francisco: Jossey-Bass.

Noblit, G. W. (1993). Power and caring. *American Education Research Journal, 30*(1), 23–38.

Noddings, N. (1992). *The challenge to care in schools*. New York: Teachers College Press.

Nolen, S. & Haladyna, T. (1990). Motivation and studying in high school science. *Journal of Research on Science Teaching, 27*, 115–26.

O'Leary, K. & O'Leary, S. (1977). *Classroom management: The successful use of behavior modification*. New York: Pergamon.

Oakes, J. (1985). *Keeping track: How schools structure inequality*. New Haven, CT: Yale University Press.

—— (2005). *Keeping track: How schools structure inequality* (2nd ed.) New Haven, CT: Yale University Press.

Oettingen, G., Honig, G., & Gollwitzer, P. M. (2000). Effective goal regulation of goal attainment. *International Journal of Educational Research, 33*, 705–32.

Ogbu, J. U. (1992). Understanding cultural diversity and learning. *Educational Researcher, 21*(8), 5–14.

—— (2003). *Black American students in an affluent suburb*. Mahwah, NJ: Lawrence Erlbaum Associates.

Ogbu, J. U. & Simons, H. D. (1998). Voluntary and involuntary minorities: A cultural-ecological theory of school performance with some implications for education. *Anthropology & Education Quarterly, 29*(2), 155.

Osterman, K. F. (2000). Students' need for belonging in the school community. *Review of Educational Research, 70*(3), 323–67.

Page, R. N. (1991). *Lower-track classrooms*. New York: Teachers College Press.

Page-Voth, V. & Graham, S. (1999). Effects of goal setting and strategy use on the writing performance of students with writing and learning problems. *Journal of Educational Psychology, 91*(2), 230–40.

Pajares, F. (1996). Self-efficacy beliefs in academic settings. *Review of Educational Research, 66*(4), 543–78.

—— (2006). Self-efficacy during childhood and adolescence: Implications for parents and teachers. In F. Pajares & T. Urdan (Eds.), *Self-efficacy beliefs of adolescents* (pp. 339–67). Greenwich, CT: Information Age Publishing.

Pajares, F., Britner, S. L., & Valiante, G. (2000). Relation between achievement goals and self-beliefs of middle school students in writing and science. *Contemporary Educational Psychology, 25*, 406–22.

Pajares, F. & Johnson, M. J. (1994). Confidence and competence in writing: The role of self-efficacy, outcome expectancy, and apprehension. *Research in the Teaching of English, 28*(3), 313–31.

Pajares, F. & Miller, M. D. (1994). Role of self-efficacy and self-concept beliefs in mathematical problem solving: A path analysis. *Journal of Educational Psychology, 86*(2), 193–203.

Pajares, F. & Schunk, D. H. (2002). Self and self-belief in psychology and education: A historical overview. In J. Aronson (Ed.), *Improving academic achievement* (pp. 5–21). New York: Academic Press.

Palmer, D. J. (1983). An attributional perspective on labeling. *Exceptional Children, 49,* 423–29.

Pang, V. O. & Sablan, V. (1998). Teacher efficacy: Do teachers believe they can be successful with African American students? In M. Dilworth (Ed.), *Being responsive to cultural differences: How teachers learn* (pp. 39–60). Thousand Oaks, CA: Corwin Press.

Paris, S. G., Byrnes, J. P., & Paris, A. H. (2001). Constructing theories, identities, and actions of self-regulated learners. In B. J. Zimmerman & D. H. Schunk (Eds.), *Self-regulated learning and academic achievement* (pp. 253–87). Mahwah, NJ: Lawrence Erlbaum Associates.

Paulsen, G. (1999). *Hatchet.* New York: Simon Pulse.

Peak, L. (1993). Academic effort in international perspective. In T. M. Tomlinson (Ed.), *Motivating students to learn* (pp. 41–62). Berkeley, CA: McCutchan.

Pekrun, R., Goetz, T., Titz, W., & Perry, R. P. (2002). Academic emotions in students' self-regulated learning and achievement: A program of qualitative and quantitative research. *Educational Psychologist, 37*(2), 91–105.

Perry, N. E. (1998). Young children's self-regulated learning and contexts that support it. *Journal of Educational Psychology, 90*(4), 715–29.

Perry, N. E. & VandeKamp, J. O. (2000). Creating classroom contexts that support young children's development of self-regulated learning. *International Journal of Educational Research, 33,* 821–43.

Perry, N. E. & Weinstein, R. S. (1998). The social context of early schooling and children's school adjustment. *Educational Psychologist, 33*(4), 177–94.

Perry, T. (2003). Up from parched earth: Toward a theory of African-American achievement. In T. Perry, C. Steele, & A. Hilliard (Eds.), *Young, gifted and Black: Promoting high achievement among African-American students* (pp. 1–108). Boston: Beacon Press.

Pintrich, P. (1995). Understanding self-regulated learning. In P. Pintrich (Ed.), *Understanding self-regulated learning* (Vol. 63, pp. 3–12). San Francisco: Jossey-Bass.

—— (2000a). An achievement goal theory perspective in issues in motivation terminology, theory, and research. *Contemporary Educational Psychology, 25,* 92–104.

—— (2000b). Multiple goals, multiple pathways: The role of goal orientation in learning and achievement. *Journal of Educational Psychology, 92*(3), 544–55.

Pintrich, P. R. (2003). A motivational science perspective on the role of student motivation in learning and teaching contexts. *Journal of Educational Psychology, 95*(4), 667–86.

Pintrich, P. R. & De Groot, E. V. (1990). Motivational and self-regulated learning components of classroom academic performance. *Journal of Educational Psychology, 82,* 32–40.

Pintrich, P. R. & Schrauben, B. (1992). Students' motivational beliefs and their cognitive engagement in classroom academic tasks. In D. H. Schunk & J. L. Meece (Eds.), *Student perceptions in the classroom* (pp. 149–83). Hillsdale, NJ: Lawrence Erlbaum Associates.

Pintrich, P. R. & Schunk, D. H. (2002). *Motivation in education* (2nd ed.). Upper Saddle River, NJ: Merrill Prentice Hall.

Pintrich, P. R., Zusho, A., Schiefele, U., & Pekrun, R. (2001). Goal orientation and self-regulated learning in the college classroom: A cross-sectional comparison. In F. Salili, C. Chiu, & Y. Hong (Eds.), *Student motivation: The culture and context of learning* (pp. 149–69). New York: Kluwer.

Podell, D. & Soodak, L. (1993). Teacher efficacy and bias in special education referrals. *Journal of Educational Research, 86*(4), 247–53.

Pressley, M. F., Johnson, C. J., Symons, S., McGoldrick, J. A., & Kurita, J. (1989). Strategies that improve children's memory and comprehension of text. *The Elementary School Journal, 90*(1), 3–32.

Pressley, M. F., Woloshyn, V., & Associates (1995). *Cognitive strategy instruction* (Vol. 2). Cambridge, MA: Brookline Books.

Pressley, M. F. & Levin, J. (1987). Elaborative learning strategies for the inefficient learner. In S. J. Ceci (Ed.), *Handbook of cognitive, social, and neuropsychological aspects of learning disabilities* (pp. 175–212). Hillsdale, NJ: Lawrence Erlbaum Associates.

Ramey-Gassert, L. & Shroyer, M. G. (1992). Enhancing science teaching self-efficacy in preservice elementary teachers. *Journal of Elementary Science Education, 4*(1), 26–34.

Ramey-Gassert, L., Shroyer, M. G., & Staver, J. R. (1996). A qualitative study of factors influencing science teaching self-efficacy of elementary teachers. *Science Education, 80*(3), 283–315.

Ramirez, A. (1999). Assessment-driven reform: The emperor still has no clothes. *Phi Delta Kappan, 81*(3), 204–08.

Randhawa, B. S., Beamer, J. E., & Lundberg, I. (1993). Role of mathematics self-efficacy in the structural model of mathematics achievement. *Journal of Educational Psychology, 85*(1), 41–48.

Randi, J. (2004). Teachers as self-regulated learners. *Teachers College Record, 106*(9), 1825–53.

Randi, J. & Corno, L. (2000). A design theory for classroom instruction in self-regulated learning? In C. R. Reigulith (Ed.), *Instructional design theories and models*. Mahwah, NJ: Lawrence Erlbaum Associates.

Raudenbush, S. W., Rowan, B., & Cheong, Y. F. (1992). Contextual effects on the self-perceived efficacy of high school teachers. *Sociology of Education, 65*, 150–67.

Reid, M. K. & Borkowski, J. G. (1987). Causal attributions of hyperactive children: Implications for training strategies and self-control. *Journal of Educational Psychology, 79*, 296–307.

Reiher, R. H. & Dembo, M. H. (1984). Changing academic task persistence through a self-instructional attribution training program. *Contemporary Educational Psychology, 9*, 84–94.

Renninger, K. A. (2000). Individual interest and its implication for understanding intrinsic motivation. In C. Sansone & J. M. Harackiewicz (Eds.), *Intrinsic and extrinsic motivation: The search for optimal motivation and performance* (pp. 373–404). San Diego: Academic Press.

Resnick, L. (1997). *Education and learning to think*. Washington, DC: National Academy Press.

Resnick, L. B. (1999, June 16). Making America smarter: A century's assumptions about innate ability give way to a belief in the power of effort. *Education Week*, pp. 38–41.

Reyna, C. (2000). Lazy, dumb, or industrious: When stereotypes convey attribution information in the classroom. *Educational Psychology Review, 12*(1), 85–110.

Reynolds, M. C. (1994). Special education as a resilience-related venture. In M. C. Wang & E. W. Gordon (Eds.), *Educational resilience in inner-city America* (pp. 131–40). Hillsdale, NJ: Lawrence Erlbaum Associates.

Rigby, C. S., Deci, E. L., Patrick, B. C., & Ryan, R. M. (1992). Beyond the intrinsic-extrinsic dichotomy: Self-determination in motivation and learning. *Motivation and Emotion, 16*(3), 165–85.

Robertson, J. S. (2000). Is attributional training a worthwhile classroom intervention for

K-12 students with learning difficulties? *Educational Psychology Review, 12*(1), 111–34.

Roderick, M. & Camburn, R. (1999). Risk and recovery from course failure in the early years of high school. *American Educational Research Journal, 36*(2), 303–43.

Roderick, M. & Engel, M. (2001). The grasshopper and the ant: Motivational responses of low-achieving students to high-stakes testing. *Educational Evaluation and Policy Analysis, 23*(3), 197–227.

Rogers, D. & Swan, K. (2004). Self-regulated learning and internet searching. *Teachers College Record, 106*(9), 1904–1824.

Rohrkemper, M. (1985). Motivational coursework in teacher education. In M. K. Alderman & M. W. Cohen (Eds.), *Motivational theory and practice for preservice teachers (Teacher Education Monograph No. 4)* (pp. 52–64). Washington, DC: ERIC Clearinghouse in Teacher Education.

Rohrkemper, M. & Corno, L. (1988). Success and failure on classroom tasks: Adaptive learning and classroom teaching. *Elementary School Journal, 88*, 297–312.

Rohrkemper, M. M. (1989). Self-regulated learning and academic achievement: A Vygotskian view. In B. J. Zimmerman & D. H. Schunk (Eds.), *Self-regulated learning and academic achievement: Theory, research, and practice* (pp. 143–67). New York: Springer-Verlag.

Rolison, M. A. & Medway, F. J. (1985). Teachers' expectations and attributions for student achievement: Effects of label, performance pattern, and special education intervention. *American Educational Research Journal, 22*(4), 561–73.

Rose, M. (1989). *Lives on the boundary*. New York: Penguin Books.

—— (1995). *Possible lives*. Boston: Houghton-Mifflin.

Rosenholtz, S. J. (1989). *Teachers' workplace: The social organization of schools*. New York: Longman.

Rosenthal, R. & Jacobson, L. (1968). *Pygmalion in the classroom: Teacher expectation and pupils' intellectual development*. New York: Holt, Rinehart and Winston.

Ross, J. A. (1995). Strategies for enhancing teachers' beliefs in their effectiveness: Research on a school improvement hypothesis. *Teachers College Record, 97*, 227–51.

—— (1998). The antecedents and consequences of teacher efficacy. In J. Brophy (Ed.), *Research on teaching* (Vol. 7, pp. 49–74). Greenwich, CT: JAI Press.

Ross, J. A., Hogaboam-Gray, A., & Hannay, L. (2001). Effects of teacher efficacy on computer skills and computer cognitions of Canadian students in grades K-3. *The Elementary School Journal, 102*(2), 141–56.

Rueda, R. & Moll, L. C. (1994). A sociocultural perspective on motivation. In H. F. O'Neil & M. Drillings (Eds.), *Motivation: Theory and Research* (pp. 117–40). Hillsdale, NJ: Lawrence Erlbaum Associates.

Ruenzel, D. (1997, February 5). AVID learners. *Education Week*, pp. 28–33.

Rust, C. (1992, January 26). Miss Bailey's lessons for life. *Houston Chronicle*, pp. 1G–6G.

Ruth, W. J. (1996). Goal setting and behavior contracting for students with emotional and behavioral difficulties: Analysis of daily, weekly, and goal attainment. *Psychology in the Schools, 23*(April), 153–58.

Ryan, A. M., Gheen, M. H., & Midgley, C. (1998). Why do some students avoid asking for help? An examination of the interplay among students' academic efficacy, teachers' social-emotional role, and the classroom goal structure. *Journal of Educational Psychology, 90*(3), 528–35.

Ryan, A. M. & Patrick, H. (2001). The classroom social environment and changes in adolescents' motivation and engagement in middle school. *American Educational Research Association, 38*(2), 437–60.

Ryan, R. M. & Deci, E. L. (2000). Intrinsic and extrinsic motivation: Classic definitions and new directions. *Contemporary Educational Psychology, 25*, 54–67.

Ryan, R. M. & Grolnick, W. S. (1986). Origins and pawns in the classroom: Self-report and projective assessments of individual differences in children's perceptions. *Journal of Personality and Social Psychology, 50*(3), 550–58.

Ryan, R. M. & Stiller, J. (1991). The social context of internalization: Parent influences on autonomy, motivation, and learning. In M. L. Maehr & P. L. Pintrich (Eds.), *Advances in motivation and achievement* (pp. 115–49). Greenwich, CT: JAI Press.

Sagotsky, G., Patterson, C. J., & Lepper, M. R. (1978). Training children's self-control: A field experiment in self-monitoring and goal-setting in the classroom. *Journal of Experimental Child Psychology, 25,* 242–53.

Sanchez, B., Colon, Y., & Esparza, P. (2005). The role of sense of school belonging and gender in the academic adjustment of Latino adolescents. *Journal of Youth and Adolescence, 34*(6), 619–28.

Sanders, M. G. (1997). Overcoming obstacles: Academic achievement as a response to racism and discrimination. *The Journal of Negro Education, 66*(1), 83–93.

Sansone, C. & Smith, J. L. (2000). Interest and self-regulation: The relation between having to and wanting to. In C. Sansone & J. Harackiewicz (Eds.), *Intrinsic and extrinsic motivation* (pp. 343–72). San Diego: Academic Press.

Schiefele, U. (1991). Interest and learning in motivation. *Educational Psychologist, 26,* 299–233.

Schunk, D. H. (1982). Effects of effort attributional feedback on children's perceived self-efficacy and achievement. *Journal of Educational Psychology, 74,* 548–56.

—— (1983a). Goal difficulty and attainment information: Effects on children's achievement behaviors. *Human Learning, 2,* 107–17.

—— (1983b). Reward contingencies and the development of children's skills and self efficacy. *Journal of Educational Psychology, 75,* 511–18.

—— (1984a). Enhancing self-efficacy and achievement through rewards and goals: Motivational and informational effects. *Journal of Educational Research, 78*(1), 29–34.

—— (1984b). Sequential attributional feedback and children's achievement behavior. *Journal of Educational Psychology, 76,* 1159–69.

—— (1985). Participation in goal setting: Effects on self-efficacy and skills of learning-disabled children. *The Journal of Special Education, 19*(3), 307–17.

—— (1989). Self-efficacy and cognitive skill learning. In C. Ames & R. Ames (Eds.), *Research on motivation in education* (Vol. 3, pp. 13–44). San Diego: Academic Press.

—— (1991). Self-efficacy and academic motivation. *Educational Psychologist, 26,* 207–31.

—— (2001). Social cognitive theory and self-regulated learning. In B. J. Zimmerman & D. H. Schunk (Eds.), *Self-regulated learning and academic achievement* (pp. 125–51). Mahwah, NJ: Lawrence Erlbaum Associates.

Schunk, D. H. & Cox, P. D. (1986). Strategy training and attributional feedback with learning disabled students. *Journal of Educational Psychology, 78*(3), 201–09.

Schunk, D. H. & Hanson, A. R. (1985). Peer models: Influence on children. *Journal of Educational Psychology, 77,* 313–22.

Schunk, D. H., Hanson, A. R., & Cox, P. D. (1987). Peer model attributes and children's achievement behaviors. *Journal of Educational Psychology, 79,* 54–61.

Schunk, D. H. & Pajares, F. (2002). The development of academic self-efficacy. In A. Wigfield & J. Eccles (Eds.), *Development of achievement motivation* (pp. 16–31). San Diego: Academic Press.

Schutz, P. A. (1989). *An interactive process ontology for the self-regulating aspects of knowing, learning and emoting: The relationship between goals and feedback in learning.* Unpublished Dissertation, the University of Texas at Austin.

—— (1991). Goals in self-directed behavior. *Educational Psychologist, 2*(1), 55–67.

—— (1994). Goals as the transactive point between motivation and cognition. In P. R. Pintrich, D. R. Brown, & C. E. Weinstein (Eds.), *Student motivation, cognition, and learning*. Hillsdale, NJ: Lawrence Erlbaum Associates.

Schutz, P. A., Crowder, K. C., & White, V. C. (2001). The development of a goal to become a teacher. *Journal of Educational Psychology, 93*(2), 299–308.

Schweinle, A., Turner, J. C., & Meyer, D. K. (2006). Striking the right balance: Students' motivation and affect in elementary mathematics. *The Journal of Educational Research, 99*(5), 271–93.

Seligman, M. E. P. & Maier, S. F. (1967). Failure to escape traumatic shock. *Journal of Experimental Psychology, 74*, 1–9.

Shachar, H. & Shmuelevitz, H. (1997). Implementing cooperative learning, teacher collaboration and teachers' sense of efficacy in heterogeneous junior high schools. *Contemporary Educational Psychology, 22*, 53–72.

Shelton, T. L., Anastopoulos, A. D., & Linden, J. D. (1985). An attribution training program with learning disabled children. *Journal of Learning Disabilities, 18*, 261–65.

Shepard, L. A. (2000). The role of assessment in a learning culture. *Educational Researcher, 29*(7), 4–14.

Shields, P. M. (1995). Engaging children of diverse backgrounds. In M. Knapp (Ed.), *Teaching for meaning in high-poverty classrooms* (pp. 33–46). New York: Teachers College Press.

Shih, S. & Alexander, J. M. (2000). Interacting effects of goal setting and self- or other-referenced feedback on children's development of self-efficacy and cognitive skill within the Taiwanese classroom. *Journal of Educational Psychology, 92*(3), 536–43.

Simmons, W. & Grady, M. (1990). *Black male achievement: From peril to promise. Report of the Superintendent's Advisory Committee on black male achievement*. Prince Georges County, MD: Prince Georges County Schools.

Singham, M. (1998). The canary in the mine: The achievement gap between Black and White students. *Phi Delta Kappan, 80*(1), 8–15.

Skinner, E. A. (1995). *Perceived control, motivation, & coping*. Thousand Oaks, CA: Sage.

Skinner, E. A., Zimmer-Gembeck, M. J., & Connell, J. P. (1998). Individual differences and the development of perceived control. *Monographs of the Society for Research in Child Development, 63*(2–3).

Slavin, R. E. (1990). *Cooperative learning: Theory, research, and practice*. Englewood Cliffs, NJ: Prentice-Hall.

—— (1995). *Cooperative learning* (2nd ed.). Boston: Allyn & Bacon.

Sloane, F. C. & Kelly, A. E. (2003). Issues in high-sakes testing programs. *Theory into Practice, 42*(1), 12–17.

Smith, S. M. (2001). The four sources of influences on computer self-efficacy. *Delta Pi Epsilon, 43*(1), 27–39.

Smolen, L., Newman, C., Walthen, T., & Lee, D. (1995). Developing student self-assessment strategies. *TESOL Journal, 5*(1), 22–26.

Sockett, H. (1988). Education and will: Aspects of personal capability. *American Journal of Education, 96*, 95–214.

Solomon, D., Watson, M., Battistich, V., Schaps, E., & Delucchi, K. (1992). Creating a caring community: Educational practices that promote children's social development. In F. K. Oser, A. Dick, & J. Luc-Patry (Eds.), *Effective and responsible teaching* (pp. 383–96). San Francisco: Jossey-Bass.

Soodak, L. & Podell, D. (1998). Teacher efficacy and the vulnerability of the difficult-to-teach student. In J. Brophy (Ed.), *Expectations in the Classroom* (Vol. 7, pp. 75–109). Greenwich, CT: JAI Press.

Sparks, G. (1988). Teachers' attitudes toward change and subsequent improvements in classroom teaching. *Journal of Educational Psychology, 80*(1), 111–17.

Steele, C. M. (1992, April). Race and the schooling of black Americans. *The Atlantic Monthly, 269*, 68–78.

—— (1997). A threat in the air: How stereotypes shape intellectual identity and performance. *American Psychologist, 52*(6), 613–29.

Steiner, R., Wiener, M., & Cromer, W. (1971). Comprehensive training and identification for peer and good readers. *Journal of Educational Psychology, 62*, 506–13.

Stevenson, H. & Lee, S. (1990). Contexts of achievement: A study of American, Chinese, and Japanese children. *Monographs of the Society for Research in Child Development, 55*(1–2), 1–119.

Stiggins, R. J. (1999). Assessment, student confidence, and school success. *Phi Delta Kappan, 81*(3), 191–203.

Stiggins, R. J., Frisbie, D. A., & Griswold, P. A. (1989). Inside high school grading practices: Building a research agenda. *Educational Measurement: Issues and Practice, 9*, 5–14.

Stipek, D. (1996). Motivation and instruction. In D. C. Berliner & R. C. Calfee (Eds.), *Handbook of educational psychology* (pp. 85–113). New York: Macmillan.

Stipek, D., Givvin, K. B., Salmon, J. M., & Macgyvers, V. L. (1998). Can a teacher intervention improve classroom practices and student motivation in mathematics? *The Journal of Experimental Education, 66*(4), 319–37.

Stipek, D. & Gralinski, H. (1996). Children's theories of intelligence and school performance. *Journal of Educational Psychology, 88*, 397–407.

Stipek, D. & Mac Iver, D. (1989). Developmental change in children's assessment of intellectual competence. *Child Development, 60*, 521–38.

Stipek, D. & Ryan, R. H. (1997). Economically disadvantaged preschoolers: Ready to learn but further to go. *Journal of Educational Psychology, 89*, 711–23.

Stodolsky, S. (1988). *The subject matters*. Chicago: University of Chicago Press.

Suarez-Orozco, M. M. (1989). *Central American refugees and U. S. high schools: A psychological study of motivation and achievement*. Palo Alto, CA: Stanford University Press.

Swanson, M. C., Marcus, M., & Elliott, J. (2000). Rigor with support: Lessons from AVID. *Leadership, 30*, 26–27, 37–38.

Tharp, R. G. (1989). Psychological variables and constants. *American Psychologist, 44*(2), 349–59.

Tharp, R. G., Estrada, P., Dalton, S. S., & Yamauchi, L. A. (2000). *Teaching transformed: Achieving excellence, fairness, inclusion, and harmony*. Boulder, CO: Westview Press.

Timperley, H. S. & Phillips, G. (2003). Changing and sustaining teachers' expectations through professional development in literacy. *Teaching and Teacher Education, 19*, 627–41.

Tinto, V. (1993). *Leaving college: Rethinking the causes and cures of student attrition*. Chicago: University of Chicago Press.

Tobias, S. (1985). Test anxiety: Interference, defective skills, and cognitive capacity. *Educational Psychologist, 20*, 135–42.

Toliver, K. (1993). The Kay Toliver Mathematics Program. *Journal of Negro Education, 62*, 35–46.

Tollefson, N., Melvin, J., & Thippavajjala, C. (1990). Teacher's attributions for students' low achievement: A validation of Cooper and Good's attributional categories. *Psychology in the Schools, 27*, 75–83.

Tollefson, N., Tracy, D. B., Johnsen, E. P., & Chatman, J. (1986). Teaching learning disabled students goal-implementation skills. *Psychology in the Schools, 23*, 194–204.

Tollefson, N., Tracy, D. B., Johnsen, E. P., Farmer, A. W., & Buenning, M. (1984). Goal setting and personal responsibility training for LD adolescents. *Psychology in the Schools, 21*, 224–33.

Tomlinson, T. M. (1993). Education reform: The ups and downs of good intentions. In T. M. Tomlinson (Ed.), *Motivating students to learn* (pp. 3–20). Berkeley, CA: McCutchan.

Tournaki, N. & Podell, D. M. (2005). The impact of student characteristics and teacher efficacy on teachers' predictions of students' success. *Teaching and Teacher Education, 21,* 299–314.

Trawick, L. (1991). *Volitional strategy training in students with a history of academic failure.* Dissertation Abstracts International, University Microfilms No. 91–27, 987.

Tschannen-Moran, M., Woolfolk Hoy, A., & Hoy, W. K. (1998). Teacher efficacy: Its meaning and measure. *Review of Educational Research, 68*(2), 202–48.

Tucker, C. M. & Herman, K. C. (2002). Using culturally sensitive theories and research to meet the academic needs of low-income African-American children. *American Psychologist, 57*(10), 762–73.

Tucker, C. M., Porter, T., Reinke, W. M., Herman, K. C., Ivery, P. D., Mack, C. E. et al. (2005). Promoting teacher efficacy for working with culturally diverse students. *Preventing School Failure, 50*(1), 29–34.

Tucker, C. M., Zayco, R. A., Herman, K. C., Reinke, W. M., Trujillo, M., Carraway, K., et al. (2002). Teacher and child variables as predictors of academic engagement among low-income African-American children. *Psychology in the Schools, 39*(4), 477–88.

Turner, J. C. & Meyer, D. K. (1995). Motivating students to learn: Lessons from a fifth-grade classroom. *Middle School Journal, 27,* 18–25.

Turner, J. C., Midgley, C., Meyer, D. K., Gheen, M. H., Anderman, E., Kang, Y., et al. (2002). The classroom environment and students' reports of avoidance strategies in mathematics: A multimethod study. *Journal of Educational Psychology, 94*(1), 88–106.

Urdan, T. C. (1997). Achievement goal theory: Past results, future directions. In M. L. Maehr & P. R. Pintrich (Eds.), *Advances in motivation and achievement* (Vol. 10, pp. 99–141). Greenwich, CT: JAI Press.

—— (2001). Contextual influences on motivation and performance: An examination of achievement goal structures. In F. S. Salili, C. Chui, & Y. Hong (Eds.), *Student motivation: The culture and context of learning* (pp. 171–201). New York: Kluwer Academic/Plenum Publishers.

Urdan, T. C., Kneisel, L., & Mason, V. (1999). Interpreting messages about motivation in the classroom: Examining the effects of achievement goal structures. In T. C. Urdan (Ed.), *Advances in motivation and achievement* (Vol. 11, pp. 123–58). Greenwich, CT: JAI Press.

Urdan, T. C. & Midgley, C. (2003). Changes in perceived classroom goal structure and pattern of adaptive learning during early adolescence. *Contemporary Educational Psychology, 28,* 524–51.

Usher, E. L. & Pajares, F. (2006). Sources of self-efficacy and self-regulatory efficacy beliefs of entering middle school students. *Contemporary Educational Psychology, 31,* 125–41.

Usinger, J. (2005). Parent/guardian visualization of career and academic future of seventh graders enrolled in low-achieving schools. *Career Development Quarterly, 53,* 235–45.

Van Overwalle, F., Segebarth, K., & Goldchstein, M. (1989). Improving performance of freshmen through attributional testimonies from fellow students. *British Journal of Educational Psychology, 59,* 75–85.

Vansteenkiste, M., Lens, W., & Deci, E. L. (2006). Intrinsic versus extrinsic goal contents in self-determination theory: Another look at the quality of academic motivation. *Educational Psychologist, 41*(1), 19–31.

Vermeer, H. J., Boekaerts, M., & Seegers, G. (2000). Motivational and gender differences:

Sixth-grade students' mathematical problem solving behavior. *Journal of Educational Psychology, 92*(2), 308–15.

Villegas, A. M. (1991). *Culturally responsive pedagogy.* Princeton, NJ: Educational Testing Service.

Vygotsky, L. S. (1962). *Thought and language.* Cambridge, MA: MIT Press.

—— (1978). *Mind in society: The development of higher psychological processes.* Cambridge, MA: Harvard University Press.

Wade, S. (1992). How interests affect learning from text. In K. A. Renniger, S. Hidi, & A. Krapp (Eds.), *The role of interest in learning and development* (pp. 255–78). Hillsdale, NJ: Lawrence Erlbaum Associates.

Walker, E. N. (2006). Urban high school students' academic communities and their effects on mathematics success. *American Educational Research Journal, 43*(1), 43–73.

Warren, L. L. & Payne, B. D. (1997). Impact of middle grades' organization on teacher efficacy and environmental perceptions. *Journal of Educational Research, 90*(5), 301–08.

Watt, K. M., Powell, C. A., Mendiola, I. D., & Cossio, G. (2006). Schoolwide impact and AVID: How have selected Texas high schools addressed the new accountability measures? *Journal of Education for Students Placed at Risk, 11*(1), 57–73.

Wehlage, G. G., Rutter, R. A., Smith, G. A., Lesko, N., & Fernandez, R. R. (1989). *Reducing the risk: Schools as communities of support.* Philadelphia: Falmer Press.

Weiner, B. (1979). A theory of motivation for some classroom experiences. *Journal of Educational Psychology, 71*, 3–25.

—— (1985). An attributional theory of achievement motivation and emotion *Psychological Review, 92*(4), 548–73.

—— (1986). *An attributional theory of motivation and emotion.* New York: Springer-Verlag.

—— (1990). History of research in motivation. *Journal of Educational Psychology, 82*, 616–22.

—— (1992). *Human motivation: Metaphors, theories and research.* Newbury Park, CA: Sage.

—— (2000). Intrapersonal and interpersonal theories of motivation from an attributional perspective. *Educational Psychology Review, 12*(1), 1–14.

—— (2001). Intrapersonal and interpersonal theories of motivation from an attributional viewpoint. In F. S. Salili, C. Chui, & Y. Hong (Eds.), *Student motivation: The culture and context of learning* (pp. 17–30). New York: Kluwer Academic/Plenum Publishers.

Weiner, B. & Kukla, A. (1970). An achievement analysis of achievement motivation. *Journal of Personality and Social Psychology, 15*, 1–20.

Weinstein, C. E. & Mayer, R. (1986). The teaching of learning strategies. In M. C. Wittrock (Ed.), *Handbook of research on teaching* (pp. 315–27). Thomson Learning, www.thomsonrights.com.

Weinstein, R. S. (1993). Children's knowledge of differential treatment in schools: Implications for motivation. In T. M. Tomlinson (Ed.), *Motivating students to learn* (pp. 197–224). Berkeley, CA: McCutchan.

—— (2002). *Reaching higher: The power of expectations in schooling.* Cambridge, MA: Harvard University Press.

Weinstein, R. S., Gregory, A., & Strambler, M. J. (2004). Intractable self-fulfilling prophecies. *American Psychologist, 59*(6), 511–20.

Weinstein, R. S. & McKown, C. (1998). Expectancy effects in "context": Listening to the voices of students and teachers. In J. Brophy (Ed.), *Expectations in the classroom* (Vol. 7, pp. 215–42). Greenwich, CT: JAI Press.

Welch, O. M. & Hodges, C. R. (1997). *Standing outside on the inside*. Albany, NY: State University of New York Press.

Wentzel, K. R. (1989). Adolescent classroom goals, standards for performance, and academic achievement: An interactionist perspective. *Journal of Educational Psychology, 81*, 131–42.

—— (1991). Social and academic goals at school: Motivation and achievement in context. In M. L. Maehr & P. R. Pintrich (Eds.), *Advances in motivation and achievement* (Vol. 7, pp. 185–212). Greenwich, CT: JAI Press.

—— (2000). What is it that I'm trying to achieve? Classroom goals from a content perspective. *Contemporary Educational Psychology, 25*, 105–15.

Wheelock, A. (1992). *Crossing the tracks*. New York: New Press.

Whipp, J. L. & Chiarelli, S. (2004). Self-regulation in a web-based course: A case study. *Educational Technology Research and Development, 52*(4), 1042–1629.

White, K., Hohn, R., & Tollefson, N. (1997). Encouraging elementary students to set realistic goals. *Journal of Research in Childhood Education, 12*, 48–57.

Wibrowski, C. R. (1992). *Self-regulated learning processes of inner-city students*. Dissertation Abstracts International, 53 (4), AAI9224865.

Wigfield, A. & Eccles, J. (1989). *Anxiety and worries about math and English before and after junior high transition*. Paper presented at the annual meeting of the American Educational Research Association, San Francisco.

—— (2000). Expectancy-value theory of motivation. *Contemporary Educational Psychology, 25*, 68–81.

—— (2001). Introduction. In A. Wigfield & J. Eccles (Eds.), *Development of achievement motivation* (pp. 1–11). San Diego: Academic Press.

Wigfield, A. & Eccles, J. S. (1992). The development of achievement task values: A theoretical analysis. *Developmental Review, 12*, 265–310.

Wigfield, A., Galper, A., Denton, K., & Sefeldt, C. (1999). Teachers' beliefs about former head start and non-head start first-grade children's motivation, performance, and future educational prospects. *Journal of Educational Psychology, 91*(1), 98–104.

Wiggins, G. (1993). *Assessing student performance*. San Francisco: Jossey-Bass.

Wilkins, J. L. M. & Brand, B. R. (2004). Change in preservice teachers' beliefs: An evaluation of a mathematics methods course. *School Science and Mathematics, 104*(5), 226–32.

Wilson, J. D. (1996). An evaluation of the field experiences of the innovative model for the preparation of elementary teachers for science, mathematics, and technology. *Journal of Teacher Education, 47*(1), 53–59.

Winne, P. H. (2001). Self-regulated learning viewed from models of information processing. In B. J. Zimmerman & D. H. Schunk (Eds.), *Self-regulated learning and academic achievement: Theoretical perspectives* (pp. 153–90). Mahwah, NJ: Lawrence Erlbaum Associates.

Wolleat, P. L., Pedro, J. D., Becker, A. D., & Fennema, E. (1980). Sex differences in high school students' causal attributions of performance in mathematics. *Journal for Research in Mathematics Education, 11*, 356–66.

Wolters, C. A. (1998). Self-regulated learning and college students' regulation of motivation. *Journal of Educational Psychology, 90*(2), 224–35.

Wolters, C. A., Yu, S., & Pintrich, P. R. (1996). The relation between goal orientation and students' motivational beliefs and self-regulated learning. *Learning and Individual Differences, 8*, 211–38.

Wolters, C. W. (2004). Advancing achievement goal theory: Using goal structures and goal orientations to predict students' motivation, cognition, and achievement. *Journal of Educational Psychology, 96*(2), 236–50.

Wood, E., Woloshyn, V., & Willoughby, T. (1995). *Cognitive strategy instruction for middle and high schools*. Cambridge, MA: Brookline Books.

Yee, D. K. & Eccles, J. S. (1988). Parent perceptions and attributions for children's math achievement. *Sex Roles, 19*, 317–33.

Yowell, C. M. & Smylie, M. A. (1999). Self-regulation in democratic communities. *The Elementary School Journal, 99*(5), 469–90.

Zeidner, M. (1998). *Test anxiety: The state of the art*. New York: Plenum Press.

Zeidner, M. & Matthews, G. (2005). Evaluation anxiety. In A. J. Elliot & C. S. Dweck (Eds.), *Handbook of competence and motivation* (pp. 141–63). New York: Guilford Press.

Ziegler, A. & Heller, K. A. (2000). Effects of attribution retraining with female students gifted in physics. *Journal for the Education of the Gifted, 23*(2), 217–43.

Zimmerman, B. J. (1994). Dimensions of academic self-regulation: A conceptual framework for education. In B. J. Zimmerman & D. H. Schunk (Eds.), *Self-regulation of learning and performance* (pp. 3–24). Hillsdale, NJ: Lawrence Erlbaum Associates.

—— (1995). Self-monitoring during collegiate studying: An invaluable tool for academic self-regulation. In P. Pintrich (Ed.), *Understanding self-regulated learning number 63*. San Francisco: Jossey-Bass.

—— (1998). Developing self-fulfilling cycles of academic motivation: An analysis of exemplary instructional models. In D. H. Schunk & B. J. Zimmerman (Eds.), *Self-regulated learning: From teaching to self-reflection* (pp. 1–19). New York: Guilford.

—— (2000). Self-efficacy: An essential motivation to learn. *Contemporary Educational Psychology, 25*, 82–91.

—— (2001). Theories of self-regulated learning: An overview and analysis. In B. J. Zimmerman & D. H. Schunk (Eds.), *Self-regulated learning and academic achievement: Theoretical perspectives* (pp. 1–37). Mahwah, NJ: Lawrence Erlbaum Associates.

—— (2002). Becoming a self-regulated learner: An overview. *Theory into Practice, 41*(2), 64–70.

Zimmerman, B. J., Bandura, A., & Martinez-Pons, M. (1992). Self-motivation for academic attainment: The role of self-efficacy beliefs and personal goal setting. *American Educational Research Journal, 29*, 663–76.

Zimmerman, B. J., Greenberg, D., & Weinstein, C. E. (1994). Self-regulated academic study time: A strategy approach. In B. J. Zimmerman & D. H. Schunk (Eds.), *Self-regulation of learning and performance* (pp. 181–202). Hillsdale, NJ: Lawrence Erlbaum Associates.

Zimmerman, B. J. & Kitsantas, A. (1997). Developmental phases in self-regulation: Shifting from process goals to outcome goals. *Journal of Educational Psychology, 89*(1), 29–36.

Zimmerman, B. J. & Martinez-Pons, M. (1986). Development of a structured interview for assessing student use of self-regulated learning strategies. *American Educational Research Journal, 23*, 614–28.

—— (1990). Student differences in self-regulated learning: Relating grade, sex, and giftedness to self-efficacy and strategy use. *Journal of Educational Psychology, 82*(1), 51–59.

Zimmerman, B. J. & Ringle, J. (1981). Effects of model persistence and statements of confidence on children's efficacy and problem solving. *Journal of Educational Psychology, 73*, 485–93.

Author Index

Subject Index

Note: A number followed by the letter *f* indicates a figure, *t* denotes a table, and *e* indicates an exhibit.